Microsoft Press

P9-BEE-982

Enterprise Development

using Microsoft

Visual Basic 6.0

Microsoft
Mastering

PUBLISHED BY
Microsoft Press
A Division of Microsoft Corporation
One Microsoft Way
Redmond, Washington 98052-6399

Copyright © 1999 by Microsoft Corporation

All rights reserved. No part of the contents of this book may be reproduced or transmitted in any form
or by any means without the written permission of the publisher.

Library of Congress Cataloging-in-Publication Data
Microsoft Mastering : Enterprise Development Using Microsoft Visual
    Basic 6.0 / Microsoft Corporation.
        p. cm.
    ISBN 0-7356-0901-2
    1. Microsoft Visual BASIC.   2. Computer software--Development.
    3. Web site development.   I. Microsoft Corporation.
    QA76.73.B3M5445   1999
    005.26'8--dc21   99-33875
                                                              CIP

Printed and bound in the United States of America.

2 3 4 5 6 7 8 9   WCWC   4 3 2 1 0 9

Distributed in Canada by Penguin Books Canada Limited.

A CIP catalogue record for this book is available from the British Library.

Microsoft Press books are available through booksellers and distributors worldwide. For further information about international editions, contact your local Microsoft Corporation office or contact Microsoft
Press International directly at fax (425) 936-7329. Visit our Web site at mspress.microsoft.com.

Intel is a registered trademark of Intel Corporation. ActiveX, FrontPage, Microsoft, Microsoft Press,
MSDN, Visual Basic, Visual C++, Visual FoxPro, Visual InterDev, Visual J++, Visual Studio, Windows,
and Windows NT are either registered trademarks or trademarks of Microsoft Corporation in the United
States and/or other countries. Other product and company names mentioned herein may be the trademarks
of their respective owners.

The example companies, organizations, products, people, and events depicted herein are fictitious. No
association with any real company, organization, product, person, or event is intended or should be
inferred.

Acquisitions Editor: Eric Stroo
Project Editor: Wendy Zucker

Acknowledgements

Authors:
David Chesnut
Jo Berry
Shawn Lock

Program Manager: Sharon Wetherby

Lead Instructional Designer: Jo Berry

Instructional Designer: Shawn Lock

Subject Matter Expert: David Chesnut

SME Consultant: Greg Cermak (STEP Technology)

Technical Help:
Jim Lewallen and Don Willits (help with Disconnected Recordsets and ADO)
Mark Bader (help with Visual Basic Debugging)

MCS Consultant: Jim Keane

Production Manager: Miracle Davis

Production Coordinators:
Miracle Davis
Jenny Boe (S&T Onsite)

Library:
Marlene Lambert (Online Training Solutions, Inc.)
Susie Bayers (Online Training Solutions, Inc.)

Media Production: Geoff Harrison (Modern Digital)

Editor: Reid Bannecker (S&T OnSite)

Build and Testing Manager: Julie Challenger

Book Production Coordinator: Katharine Ford (ArtSource)

Book Design: Mary Rasmussen (Online Training Solutions, Inc.)

continued on next page

Book Layout:
R.J. Cadranell (Online Training Solutions, Inc.)
Jennifer Murphy (S&T Onsite)

Companion CD-ROM Design and Development: Jeff Brown

Companion CD-ROM Production: Eric Wagoner (Write Stuff)

About This Course

This course is designed to teach Microsoft Visual Basic programmers, who currently build desktop applications and access corporate databases, the basics of how to build three-tier, client/server solutions.

Course Content

The course content is organized into the following nine chapters.

Chapter 1: Microsoft's Enterprise Development Strategy

Chapter 1 describes the architecture of an enterprise solution with respect to Microsoft's Enterprise Development Strategy. The chapter also discusses the attributes of the business problem that is solved in this course, the Island Hopper News sample application, and how Microsoft technologies were used to build the technical solution. The chapter also introduces the Process and Application Models in the Microsoft Solution Framework (MSF), and uses the Application Model to divide the Island Hopper News sample application into user, business, and data services. The chapter concludes with a discussion of Visual Studio and the tools you can use to develop enterprise-wide solutions.

Chapter 2: Building COM DLLs with Visual Basic

Chapter 2 focuses on building COM DLLs that run in the MTS environment. Students learn when business services are used in an enterprise solution and the various ways that business services are implemented using Visual Basic. Students then learn to create a COM DLL that implements a business service and test it from a simple client application. Advanced component development topics, such as registration and version control, are also discussed.

Chapter 3: Introduction to Microsoft Transaction Server (MTS)

Chapter 3 discusses issues related to developing COM components that will be used by many clients and describes how Microsoft Transaction Server (MTS) provides services to address these issues. MTS is introduced as a product that provides application infrastructure, or plumbing. The chapter describes the MTS architecture and the services that it provides. Students learn to use the MTS Explorer to create a package, add an existing component to a package, and export a package to configure client computers.

Chapter 4: Using MTS Transaction Services

Chapter 4 describes the transaction services that Microsoft Transaction Server (MTS) provides to facilitate application development in a multi-user environment. Students learn to create COM DLLs that take full advantage of transactions. They also learn about the importance of object state in the MTS programming model and how just-in-time activation changes the way objects behave in the MTS environment. Then, they learn when it is appropriate to store object state for an MTS component, and how to manage object state in MTS objects. Students also learn how to trap errors and debug MTS components using Visual Basic.

Chapter 5: Accessing Data from the Middle Tier

Chapter 5 describes the issues related to database access from middle-tier components. Students learn about Microsoft's Universal Data Access platform for developing multi-tier enterprise applications, and review the ActiveX Data Object (ADO) model. Students then review how to use ADO to retrieve and update records in an SQL Server database. They expand on this skill by considering issues related to middle-tier data access, such as cursors and disconnected recordsets. Finally, students learn how to call stored procedures from components by using ADO.

Chapter 6: Building Stored Procedures with SQL

Chapter 6 describes how to implement business and data services with stored procedures. Students learn to use the Visual Database Tools to connect and view a database. Students learn to write a stored procedure that uses basic SQL programming constructs. Students also learn how to write and debug stored procedures that generate return codes. They learn about the characteristics of SQL transactions and how they work with Microsoft Transaction Server (MTS) transactions.

Chapter 7: Implementing Security

Chapter 7 describes how to implement end-to-end security in an enterprise solution. First, students learn about the security architecture in MTS and how to specify declarative security for components and packages. Students learn about the security repercussions of handling data access in the middle tier using ODBC connection pooling. Then, students learn how to implement security in SQL Server and how SQL Server security integrates with MTS security.

Chapter 8: Implementing COM with Visual Basic

Chapter 8 expands on Chapter 2 by describing how interfaces can help components adapt to changing user, business, and data requirements. Students learn how to create and implement interfaces, and how to use dual interfaces. Finally, students learn how binding defines how a client application connects to an object.

Chapter 9: Advanced Client/Server Technologies

Chapter 9 contains a review of the sample application students used in the course. It also introduces several advanced technologies that run under the Windows NT Server 4.0 operating system, such as Microsoft Message Queue Server, that can be used to extend the sample application to build more robust and scalable applications.

Labs

Most chapters in this course include a lab that gives the student hands-on experience with the skills learned in the chapter. A lab consists of one or more exercises that focus on how to use the information contained in the chapter. Lab hints, which provide code or other information that will help you complete an exercise, are included in Appendix B. You will see the following icon in the margin, indicating that a lab hint is given.

Lab Hint Icon

Lab Scenario

The scenario used for most labs in this course is the Island Hopper News sample application. Island Hopper News is a sample enterprise application that ships with Visual Studio 6. It demonstrates a complete three-tier solution to a business problem. The application allows customers to place and read classified advertisements on a Web site. There is also a Visual Basic client that employees use to maintain the classified advertisements.

The business services layer of Island Hopper consists of Microsoft Transaction Server (MTS) components that handle the business logic of all transactions. Active Server Pages (ASP) files access the components when customers place advertisements, and the Visual Basic client also accesses the components when managers are working with the advertisements.

Island Hopper News stores its data in a Microsoft SQL Server database. There are several tables and stored procedures that implement business rules and optimize data access. The MTS components use ADO to access data and call the stored procedures.

The labs focus on only a few key Island Hopper News features because Island Hopper News is too large an application to be built completely in class.

The following table lists the tasks you perform using Island Hopper News, and provides a description of the lab in which you will accomplish the task.

Task	Lab description
View classified ads, customer information, and other Island Hopper elements.	In Lab 1: Exploring Island Hopper, you learn the basics of the Island Hopper application by using the Web client and Visual Basic client to view Island Hopper information like classified ads.
Create an MTS component.	In Lab 4.1: Creating an MTS Component, you use Visual Basic 6.0 to create an Island Hopper MTS component, and implement a method to retrieve a classified ad given an ad ID.
Cache and return unique database IDs in the middle tier.	In Lab 4.2: Using the Shared Property Manager, you create an Island Hopper MTS component that uses the shared property manager to cache IDs used for entries in the database.

table continued on next page

Task	Lab description
Use ActiveX Data Objects (ADO) to retrieve and update ads.	In Lab 5: Using ADO to Implement Business Services, you create an Island Hopper MTS component that works with classified ads in the database. You implement a method that retrieves a recordset filled with classified ads. You also implement a method that calls a stored procedure to update a classified ad.
Create a Stored Procedure.	In Lab 6: Creating and Debugging Stored Procedures, you will create a stored procedure that updates a given classified ad.
Configure Application Security.	In Lab 7.1: Implementing Security in MTS, you will configure MTS to authenticate clients using the Island Hopper MTS components using Windows NT group accounts and MTS roles.
Configure Data Security.	In Lab 7.2: Implementing Security in SQL Server, you will configure SQL Server to use integrated security to authenticate Island Hopper MTS components accessing the database.

Lab Setup

To complete the exercises and view the accompanying solution code, you will need to install the lab files that are found on the accompanying CD-ROM.

Software Installation

These software installation instructions are for setting up a single-server computer to use for labs. Although other, multi-computer configurations can be used, this course is designed and tested for use on a single, large server running Windows NT Server 4.0. Software installation should be completed in the order shown below.

These instructions are for a computer that has one hard drive containing one partition formatted with DOS 6.22. If you install on a different configuration, some instructions may vary. You will need the following disk sets to follow these instructions:

◆ Windows NT Server 4.0 CD and setup disks.

◆ Microsoft Visual Studio 6.0 CD set.

◆ MSDN Library Visual Studio 6.0 release CD set.

◆ *Enterprise Development Using Visual Basic 6* CD.

1. Install Windows NT Server 4.0.

   • Configure the display for 256 colors (the Island Hopper Web client will not run properly on a system using fewer than 256 colors). An ideal screen resolution is 800x600.

   • Configure the Windows Explorer to show all files. This allows you to see DLLs when you do the labs.

2. Install Windows NT 4.0 Service Pack 3.

3. Install SQL Server 6.5.

   • It is recommended that you configure SQL Server to autostart at boot time.

   • After SQL Server is installed, reconfigure the SQL Server service to log on using the Administrator account. You can change this by going to the Services applet on the control panel, selecting the MSSQLServer service and clicking the **Startup** button. The T-SQL Debugger will not work properly if the MSSQLServer service logs on as the system account.

   • Set up the sa account with no password. Some labs use this login.

4. Install SQL Server 6.5 Service Pack 4.

5. Install the Microsoft SQL Debugging Server Setup. This setup is located on Disk 2 of Microsoft Visual Basic 6.0 Enterprise Edition in the Sqdbg_ss folder.

6. Install Internet Explorer 5. Internet Explorer 5 is included on the *Enterprise Development Using Visual Basic 6* CD-ROM in the IE5 folder.

7. Install Windows NT 4.0 Option Pack. The Windows NT 4.0 Option Pack can be downloaded from the Windows NT Server Home Page.

   a. Perform an Upgrade Plus and select the following software from the setup screen:

Software	Components
Front Page 98 Server Extensions	All subcomponents
Internet Information Server	Accept defaults.
Microsoft Data Access components	Accept defaults.
Microsoft Management Console	
Microsoft Message Queue	All subcomponents
Windows NT Option Pack common files	
Microsoft Transaction Server	All subcomponents

   b. When prompted for MTS setup information, specify the following:
      - Install in \Program Files\Mts.
      - Configure the administrative account as Local.

   c. When prompted for MSMQ setup information, specify the following:
      - Install as a PEC (Primary Enterprise Controller).
      - Enterprise is *ComputerName*Enterprise.
      - Site name is *ComputerName*Site.
      - Install directory is \Program Files\MSMQ.
      - When asked for the location and size of the Data Device and Log Device, set Data Device to C:\Program Files\MSMQ, 80 MB and Log Device to C:\Program Files\MSMQ, 20 MB.
      - Set the Connected Network name to *ComputerName*Network. Set the Protocol to IP.

8. Install Microsoft Visual Basic 6.0 Enterprise Edition.

  a. Upgrade Internet Explorer 4.01 as required, upgrading only newer items.

  b. Perform a Custom installation and select the following:

Software	Components
Microsoft Visual Basic 6.0	All subcomponents
ActiveX	
Data Access	OLEDB and all subcomponents Microsoft ODBC Drivers (verify that the SQL Server ODBC driver is selected) Remote Data Objects and Controls Data Environment
Enterprise Features and Tools	All subcomponents to all levels
Tools	All subcomponents to all levels

  c. Do a Custom install of MSDN with the following selections:

  - Full Text Search Index
  - VB Documentation
  - VS Shared Documentation
  - Platform SDK Documentation

  d. When Visual Basic 6.0 setup resumes, do not install any of the other Client Tools or the Server Components. This should finish the Visual Basic 6.0 setup.

9. Install Island Hopper. **Island Hopper components must be installed in the following order.** Read the READMEC.HTM that comes with the Island Hopper sample for uninstall instructions, if required. Run each of the following from the \SampApps\IslandHopper\SampleC directory on the *Enterprise Development Using Visual Basic 6* CD-ROM.

  a. Run Client.exe.

  - Choose setup from the WinZip startup screen.
  - The name of your IIS/MTS server is localhost.

b. Run Source.exe.

- Choose setup from the WinZip startup screen.
- The name of your IIS/MTS server is localhost.

c. Run Server.exe.

- Choose setup from the WinZip startup screen.
- The name of the machine running SQL is (local).

d. Run Database.exe.

- Choose setup from the WinZip startup screen.
- The SQL Server user is sa, no password.

10. Use the SQL Enterprise Manager query tool to run the script sp.sql against the Classifieds database. The script is in the \SampApps\IslandHopper\SQLScripts\sp.sql directory on the *Enterprise Development Using Visual Basic 6* CD-ROM.

11. Use the ODBC Data Source Administrator on the Control Panel to create a system DSN for SQL Server called Classifieds.

a. On the ODBC Data Source Administrator, click the System DSN tab.

b. Click **Add**.

c. Select SQL Server and click **Finish**.

d. Set the **Name** field to **Classifieds,** and the **Server** field to **(local)**, then click **Next**.

e. Select the option for SQL Server authentication and set the **Login ID** field to **sa** with a blank password, then click **Next**.

f. Change the default database to Classifieds and click Next.

g. Click **Next** again, then click **Finish**.

h. Click **Test Data Source** to ensure that the new DSN is working properly. If it is, click **OK.** The Classifieds DSN is now configured properly.

Self-Check Questions

This course includes a number of self-check questions at the end of each chapter. You can use these multiple-choice questions to test your understanding of the information that has been covered in the course. Answers to self-check questions are provided in Appendix A. Each answer includes a reference to the associated chapter topic, so that you can easily review the content.

CD-ROM Contents

The *Enterprise Development Using Visual Basic 6* CD-ROM that is included with this book contains multimedia, lab files, sample applications, and sample code that you may wish to view or install on your computer's hard drive. The content on the CD-ROM must be viewed by using an HTML browser that supports frames. A copy of Microsoft Internet Explorer has been included with this CD-ROM in case you do not have a browser or do not have one that supports frames, installed on your computer. Please refer to the ReadMe file on the CD-ROM for further instructions on installing Internet Explorer.

To begin browsing the content that is included on the CD-ROM, open the file, default.htm.

Lab Files

The files required to complete the lab exercises, as well as the lab solution files, are included on the accompanying CD-ROM.

Note 701 kilobytes (KB) of hard disk space is required to install the labs.

Multimedia

This course provides numerous audio/video demonstrations and animations that illustrate the concepts and techniques that are discussed in this course. The following icon will appear in the margin, indicating that a multimedia title can be found on the accompanying CD-ROM.

Multimedia Icon

In addition, at the beginning of each chapter is a list of the multimedia titles that are found in the chapter.

> **Note** You can toggle the display of the text of a demonstration or animation on and off by choosing **Closed Caption** from the **View** menu.

Sample Code

This course contains numerous code samples.

Sample code has been provided on the accompanying CD-ROM for you to copy and paste into your own projects. The following icon appears in the margin, indicating that this piece of sample code is included on the CD-ROM.

Sample Code Icon

Internet Links

The following icon appears in the margin next to an Internet link, indicating that this link is included on the accompanying CD-ROM.

Internet Link Icon

Sample Applications

A number of sample applications are included in the SampApps folder on the *Enterprise Development Using Visual Basic 6* CD-ROM. The Island Hopper Sample news application is included here as well as sample applications for some of the chapters that demonstrate the code presented in those chapters.

Island Hopper News

The scenario used for most labs in this course is the Island Hopper News Sample. Island Hopper is a sample enterprise application that ships with Visual Studio 6. It demonstrates a complete three-tier solution to a business problem. The application allows customers to place and read classified advertisements on a Web site. There is also a Visual Basic client that employees use to maintain the classified advertisements. Island Hopper is located in the \SampApps\IslandHopper directory.

Chapter Sample Applications

Some of the sample applications used in chapters are included in the SampApps folder that demonstrate the code presented in those chapters. Each sample is located in a chapter-specific folder. For example, the People sample for Chapter 2 is located in \SampApps\C02\People.

Chapter 2: Building COM DLLs with Visual Basic

◆ People

This sample contains a People COM component that exposes **Employee** and **Customer** classes. The classes add and remove customer and employee information to text files. Also a PeopleClient application is included that uses the People component to add or remove customers from a customer file. Chapter 2 explains the basics of creating and using COM objects and uses the People component for code examples.

Chapter 4: Using MTS Transaction Services

◆ MarkBank

This is the Bank of Mark sample used by Mark Bader in the Visual Basic 6 Features for MTS expert point of view.

Chapter 5: Accessing Data from the Middle Tier

◆ Furniture

This sample contains an MTS component that exposes a **Furniture** class. This sample code is shown in the Disconnected Recordset animation. The **Furniture** class will retrieve a disconnected recordset and return it to the client. It will also accept a disconnected recordset from the client and submit changes in the recordset against the database. Chapter 5 explains the basics of using disconnected recordsets.

Chapter 6: Building Stored Procedures with SQL

◆ TSQLDebug

This project contains a code sample that uses an ADO **Command** object to execute the **Customer_Remove** stored procedure. This project is used in the demonstration for the T-SQL Debugger. You can use this project to study how to step into the T-SQL debugger from Visual Basic code.

Conventions Used In This Course

The following table explains some of the typographic conventions used in this course.

Example of convention	Description
Sub, If, Case Else, Print, True, BackColor, Click, Debug, Long	In text, language-specific keywords appear in bold, with the initial letter capitalized.
File menu, **Add Project** dialog box	Most interface elements appear in bold, with the initial letter capitalized.
Setup	Words that you're instructed to type appear in bold.
Event-driven	In text, italic letters can indicate defined terms, usually the first time that they occur. Italic formatting is also used occasionally for emphasis.
Variable	In syntax and text, italic letters can indicate placeholders for information that you supply.
[expressionlist]	In syntax, items inside square brackets are optional.
{While	Until}	In syntax, braces and a vertical bar indicate a choice between two or more items. You must choose one of the items, unless all of the items are enclosed in square brackets.

`Sub HelloButton_Click()`
`Readout.Text = _`
`"Hello, world!"`
`End Sub`
	This font is used for code.

table continued on next page

Example of convention	Description
ENTER	Capital letters are used for the names of keys and key sequences, such as ENTER and CTRL+R.
ALT+F1	A plus sign (+) between key names indicates a combination of keys. For example, ALT+F1 means to hold down the ALT key while pressing the F1 key.
DOWN ARROW	Individual direction keys are referred to by the direction of the arrow on the key top (LEFT, RIGHT, UP, or DOWN). The phrase "arrow keys" is used when describing these keys collectively.
BACKSPACE, HOME	Other navigational keys are referred to by their specific names.
C:\Vb\Samples\Calldlls.vbp	Paths and file names are given in mixed case.

The following guidelines are used in writing code in this course:

◆ Keywords appear with initial letters capitalized:

```
' Sub, If, ChDir, Print, and True are keywords.
Print "Title Page"
```

◆ Line labels are used to mark position in code (instead of line numbers):

```
ErrorHandler:
Power = conFailure
End Function
```

◆ An apostrophe (') introduces comments:

```
' This is a comment; these two lines
' are ignored when the program is running.
```

◆ Control-flow blocks and statements in **Sub, Function,** and **Property** procedures
   are indented from the enclosing code:

```
Private Sub cmdRemove_Click ()
  Dim Ind As Integer
  ' Get index
  Ind = lstClient.ListIndex
  ' Make sure list item is selected
  If Ind >= 0 Then
      ' Remove it from list box
      lstClient.RemoveItem Ind
      ' Display number
      lblDisplay.Caption = lstClient.ListCount
  Else
      ' If nothing selected, beep
      Beep
  End If
End Sub
```

◆ Intrinsic constant names appear in a mixed-case format, with a two-character
   prefix indicating the object library that defines the constant. Constants from the
   Visual Basic and Visual Basic for Applications object libraries are prefaced with
   "vb"; constants from the ActiveX Data Objects (ADO) Library are prefaced with
   "ad"; constants from the Excel Object Library are prefaced with "xl". Examples
   are as follows:

```
vbTileHorizontal
adAddNew
xlDialogBorder
```

For more information about coding conventions, see "Programming Fundamen-
tals" in the MSDN Visual Basic documentation.

Table of Contents

Chapter 1:
Microsoft's Enterprise Development Strategy

In this chapter, you will learn about client/server technologies and Microsoft's Enterprise Development Strategy. Then, you will learn about the sample business application, Island Hopper News, which you will use to apply practical development skills throughout this course. You will also learn about the Process and Application Models in the Microsoft Solution Framework (MSF). Finally, you will learn about Visual Studio and the tools you can use to develop enterprise-wide solutions.

Objectives

After completing this chapter, you will be able to:

♦ Explain the general terms related to client/server architecture. p2

♦ Describe the high-level architecture of an enterprise solution using Microsoft's Enterprise Development Strategy.

♦ Describe the Component Object Model (COM) and its advantages. p6

♦ Describe the main features of the Process and Application Models in the Microsoft Solutions Framework (MSF).

♦ Describe the Island Hopper News sample used as the business problem in this course. p15

♦ List the Microsoft development tools, products, and technologies p32 that will be used to build the technical solutions to the course labs.

1

Introduction to Enterprise Development

In this section, you will learn about terms and concepts related to client/server applications. You will also learn about the architecture of Internet applications, and how traditional client/server and Internet architectures are coming together in Microsoft's Enterprise Development Strategy. You will learn how Merrill Lynch uses Microsoft technologies to develop enterprise-wide applications. Then, you will learn about the Component Object Model (COM) and the role it plays in the Enterprise Development Strategy. Finally, you will learn which elements of the Enterprise Development Strategy are covered in this course.

Client/Server Architecture and Terms

By understanding the main concepts and terms of client/server technologies, you will develop a foundation for the rest of this course. You will explore each of these concepts in more depth throughout this course.

The Client/Server Model

Client/server describes physical deployment models where the client computer makes a request to the server computer and the server computer services or re-sponds to the request.

This course uses two definitions for client/server. Client/server is a model of com-puting whereby client applications running on a desktop or personal computer access information on remote servers or host computers. The client portion of the application is typically optimized for user interaction, whereas the server portion provides the centralized functionality for multiple users.

Client/server is also used to refer to a request and service-the-request relationship. For example, if one COM object is calling another, the first COM object can be referred to as the client.

Services and Tiers

Tiers are a logical concept. The three tiers are generally described as user (first), business (second or middle), and data (third) service tiers. A service is a unit of application logic that implements operations, functions, or transformations that are applied to objects. For example, a reusable business service can be implemented as a COM component that ensures a purchase does not exceed the buyer's credit limit.

The concept of tiers emphasizes segmenting applications into the three types of services, and is not about implementing the services nor about the number of physical computers involved in deploying the solution.

For more information about services, see "The Application Model and Services" on page 19 in this chapter.

Two-Tier Client/Server Architecture

Two-tier applications represent a first step in separating database-specific access logic out of the client application and placing it on a server. Usually, this is done by implementing services as stored procedures that execute on the server against a database. This makes maintenance, upgrades, and general administration of that code easier because the code only exists on the server and not on every client. Also, the database management system (DBMS) provides the centralized functionality required when supporting many users.

The following illustration shows a simple diagram of a two-tier client/server architecture. In this example, business services could reside on the server.

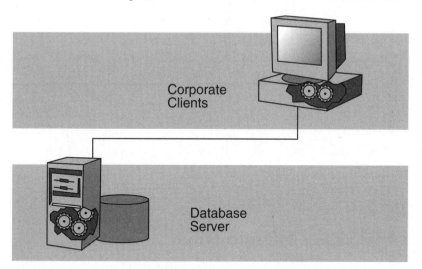

Corporate
Clients

Database
Server

Three-Tier Client/Server Architecture

A three-tier client/server architecture provides additional flexibility for building applications as they grow in complexity. It describes both the application model (user, business, and data services) and the actual deployment of services. An application model is a conceptual view of an application that establishes the definitions, rules, and relationships that structure the application. Some services reside on client computers, typically user services, while business and data services generally reside on server computers that provide centralized, multi-user functionality.

The following illustration describes a general scenario. User services run on a client computer, shared business services represent the middle tier and run on a server computer, and shared data services are the third tier, also running on a server computer.

Corporate Clients

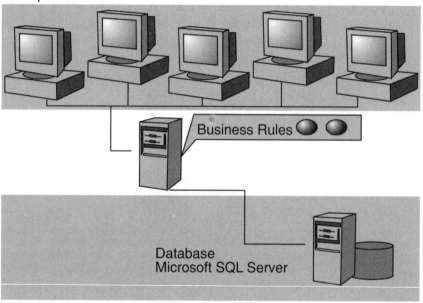

Business Rules

Database
Microsoft SQL Server

The decision to build a two-tier or three-tier application depends on the application requirements. This course focuses on three-tier systems that serve enterprise-wide applications.

Application Infrastructure

A server computer provides the centralized, multi-user functionality in a three-tier architecture. Other terms for this functionality are application infrastructure and plumbing. The application infrastructure is the software that supports concurrent access to a shared service, usually business and data services. For example, access to stored procedures and data on a database server are controlled by a Relational

Database Management System (RDBMS). This course uses Microsoft SQL Server 6.5 for the RDBMS. This is software that works with the operating system to provide the centralized, multi-user functionality for most data services. For information about manipulating data with stored procedures, see Chapter 6, "Building Stored Procedures with SQL" on page 187.

Microsoft Transaction Server (MTS) is software that works with the operating system to provide the application infrastructure for sharing business services implemented as components. Recent studies show that as much as 30-40 percent of corporate IT budgets for application development are targeted at developing that application infrastructure. MTS reduces those costs because it provides centralized, multi-user functionality. For information about using MTS to administer component-based transactions, see Chapter 3, "Introduction to Microsoft Transaction Server (MTS)" on page 69, and Chapter 4, "Using MTS Transaction Services" on page 95.

The following illustration shows the three-tier client/server architecture with the addition of MTS as the application infrastructure.

Corporate Clients

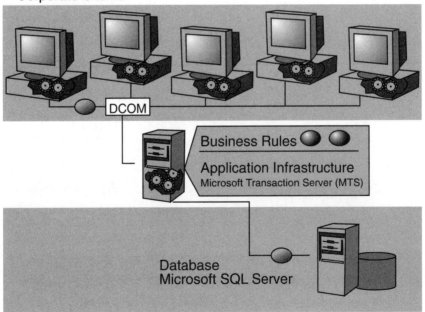

Component Object Model

In this course, most shared business services are implemented as components that are built by using Microsoft Visual Basic. Components and the Component Object Model (COM) form the core of Microsoft's Enterprise Development Strategy. For more information, see "Microsoft's Enterprise Development Strategy" on page 12 in this chapter.

The following table lists terms and definitions related to components and COM that are used in this course.

Term	Definition
Component Object Model (COM)	An industry-standard architecture for developing object-oriented components.
COM component	Physical file (for example, .exe, .dll, .ocx) that contains classes. COM component is an umbrella term for ActiveX document, ActiveX control, Automation Server, and so on. The term component may be used once a COM component context is established.
COM DLL	A COM component implemented as a DLL. COM DLL is sometimes referred to as an in-process component.
COM EXE	A COM component implemented as an EXE. COM EXE is sometimes referred to as an out-of-process component.
Class	The definition of an object, including code and data elements. Class is a template for constructing objects. A COM component may contain several classes.
Object	An instance of a class, created at run time.

For more information about working with components, see Chapter 2, "Building COM DLLs with Visual Basic" on page 39. For more information about COM, see "Introduction to COM" on page 9 and "Implementation of COM" on page 11 in this chapter, and Chapter 8, "Implementing COM with Visual Basic" on page 257.

The Internet

The Internet represents another potential form of three-tier client/server architecture. To see the animation "The Internet," see the accompanying CD-ROM.

Early Internet technologies did not take advantage of the processing power of the client computer. Client browsers simply translated the HTML files. Developers who wanted to provide enhanced features had to rely on technologies such as server-side scripting through the Common Gateway Interface (CGI).

Newer technologies can now exploit client-processing power and extend server capabilities. Dynamic HTML (DHTML), Java applets, client-side scripting, and ActiveX controls now take advantage of the client processor. Web clients can access shared business services through Active Server Pages (ASP). ASP files both pass information to the client, and take information from the client and pass it to business rules in the middle tier. The ASP files call COM components that enforce business rules. The COM components run in an MTS environment that provides the application infrastructure required by multiple users accessing the ASP files. For more information about MTS, see Chapter 3, "Introduction to Microsoft Transaction Server (MTS)" on page 69.

The following illustration shows the interaction of Web clients with three-tier client/server systems.

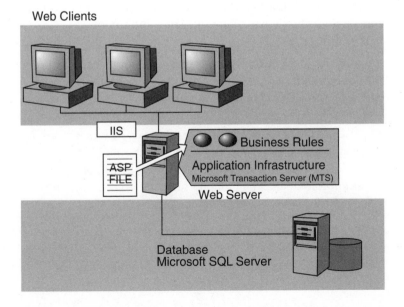

This course focuses on the implementation of services on the second and third tiers in an enterprise environment. You use MTS to manage and deploy components created with Visual Basic, and create and use SQL-Server-stored procedures.

If you want to learn more about developing client user interfaces with Visual Basic, consult the Microsoft Mastering Series course *Mastering Microsoft Visual Basic 6 Development*. To learn more about developing Internet client/server applications, including how to access MTS components from ASP files, consult *Mastering Web Application Development Using Visual InterDev 6*. For more information about these courses, go to the Microsoft Mastering Series Web site at http://msdn.microsoft.com/mastering/default.asp.

Merrill Lynch Case Study

Now that you have reviewed the basic concepts related to three-tier client/server applications, you can look at how one organization approaches enterprise development. The Client Architecture Group at Merrill Lynch develops three-tier applications for a large and dispersed audience. To see the expert point-of-view "Enterprise Development at Merrill Lynch," see the accompanying CD-ROM.

Several facets of enterprise development emerge from the developers' experience at Merrill Lynch:

◆ The scalability of an application must be planned for from the start.

◆ Data and transaction modeling is an important part of the design process and must be followed by performance testing and tuning.

◆ The user, business, and data services should be loosely coupled to adjust to scalability requirements. This reinforces the point that tiers are a logical concept and not tied to implementation of the services or the number of physical computers involved in deploying the solution.

A Merrill Lynch team has developed a three-tier Automated Trading Management System that takes advantage of the Internet, Internet Information Server (IIS), and MTS to connect to a DB2 database system on their mainframe. The team developed the application to consolidate different trading applications into a single system and provide new trading capabilities for customers.

Using Internet Explorer as the client interface, brokers can request and view information from the database. Six Windows NT servers running IIS and MTS form the middle tier and process requests utilizing 30 business logic components. The data tier consists of the DB2 database located on the host mainframe.

Twenty-five thousand Merrill Lynch brokers and their customers use the application, which processes about one million transactions per day.

The Merrill Lynch application shows the capabilities of enterprise development using Microsoft development tools. You can unite existing applications with new applications that combine user, business, and data services.

Introduction to COM

The evolution of the client/server architecture, the growth of the Internet, and constant innovation in computing hardware and software have brought powerful and sophisticated applications to users' desktops and across their networks. With such sophistication, problems have come for application developers, software vendors, and users:

♦ Many applications are large and complex, time-consuming to develop, difficult and costly to maintain, and risky to extend with additional functionality.

♦ Applications come prepackaged with a wide range of features but most features cannot be removed, upgraded independently, or replaced with alternatives.

♦ Applications are not easily integrated—data and functionality of one application are not readily available to other applications, even if the applications are written in the same programming language and running on the same computer.

♦ Traditional service architectures tend to be limited in their ability to evolve robustly as services are revised and versioned.

The solution is a system in which application developers create reusable software components. A component is a reusable piece of software that can be plugged into other components from other vendors or developers with relatively little effort. For example, a component might take a request from a client computer to search a database for a specific record and then return the result to the client.

The Component Object Model (COM) is an object-based programming model designed to promote software interoperability. It allows two or more applications or components to easily cooperate with one another, even if different vendors wrote them, at different times and in different programming languages, or if they are running on different computers running different operating systems. To support its interoperability features, COM defines and implements mechanisms that allow applications to connect to each other as software objects.

The Advantages of COM

COM offers five main advantages:

◆ Binary compatibility

Any programming language that can create structures of pointers and explicitly or implicitly call functions through pointers can create and use COM components. COM components can be implemented in a number of different programming languages and used from clients that are written using completely different programming languages. COM ensures complete binary compatibility between the client you develop in Microsoft Visual Basic and the components developed in other languages, such as Microsoft Visual C++, Microsoft Visual J++, and other third-party development tools.

◆ Cross-platform interoperability

Developers need to write COM components for a specific platform, such as Windows NT or UNIX. A COM component written for a specific platform will not run on another platform, but can communicate with COM objects running on other platforms. You can build COM components for many platforms, including Windows 95, Windows NT, Macintosh, and UNIX. To keep up to date on the availability of COM on new platforms, go to the official Microsoft COM Web site at http://www.microsoft.com/com/?RLD=59.

◆ Location transparency

Location transparency means that a component can be called by a client in one way, regardless if the component is in the same process, in a different process on the same computer, or in a process on a separate computer.

◆ Code reusability

The next major advantage of COM is an enhancement of DLL technology. COM components contain classes that expose groups of methods, known as interfaces, through which clients interact with objects. Because these interfaces are documented, code that implements those interfaces can be reused by many clients.

◆ Version control

COM components are said to be self-versioning. Interfaces implemented by classes are static and, once defined, cannot change. New functionality can be added to a COM component by adding a new interface to a class while still supporting old interfaces. You can change the implementation of an old interface without affecting clients that already use the class. Functionality is not lost when COM components are upgraded; it is always enhanced or added.

For more information, see "Interfaces" on page 258 in Chapter 8, "Implementing COM with Visual Basic."

Using COM to build an enterprise-level solution requires an organized approach to application development. For information about the software development cycle, see "The MSF Process Model" on page 15 in this chapter.

Implementation of COM

The Component Object Model (COM) by itself is a specification for how objects and their clients interact together. As a specification it defines a number of standards for interoperability. While the specification dictates a component's responsibilities, it does not specify how those responsibilities are implemented. Instead, the COM specification defines:

◆ How an object is instantiated from a class.

◆ How a client accesses features of the object.

◆ The object's responsibility for destroying itself when it is no longer in use.

The COM Libraries

In addition to being a specification, COM is also an implementation contained in what are called the COM Libraries. The implementation is provided through libraries, as DLLs, that includes:

◆ A small number of fundamental API functions that facilitate the creation of COM applications, both clients and servers. COM supplies basic object creation functions for clients, and supplies the facilities to servers to expose their objects.

◆ Implementation locator services, through which COM determines from a class identifier which server implements that class and where that server is located. This includes support for a level of indirection, usually a system registry, between the identity of an object class and the packaging of the implementation. The clients are thus independent of the packaging, which can change in the future. That is, changing locations of servers implies changing registry settings on clients, but not changing the client code.

◆ Transparent remote procedure calls when an object is running in a different process or on a different computer.

The COM Libraries are implemented for several operating systems, including Microsoft Windows 3.1, Microsoft Windows 95, Microsoft Windows NT, the Apple Macintosh, and Solaris. Microsoft is also working with other vendors to port COM to other platforms as well. For more information about how businesses are using COM in enterprise development, go to the Microsoft COM Web site by at http://www.microsoft.com/com/?RLD=59.

Microsoft's Enterprise Development Strategy

Microsoft's Enterprise Development Strategy enables organizations to build modern, scalable business solutions that improve the flow of information inside and outside the organization. Solutions built with Microsoft's Enterprise Development Strategy are dynamic and able to change with evolving business needs. They can be centrally managed and maintained, and can be integrated with existing systems and data.

The core of Microsoft's Enterprise Development Strategy is the integration of Internet and traditional client/server application development through the Component Object Model (COM). Through COM, client/server applications take advantage of features such as Dynamic HTML (DHTML); scriptlets; transactions; message queuing; security; and directory, database and data access. COM allows solutions to be assembled from a marketplace of reusable software components rather than being built from scratch. This component-based approach lets you build and test applications more efficiently.

The Distributed Component Object Model (DCOM) is a wire protocol that enables software components to communicate directly over network boundaries. DCOM enables components in distributed applications to communicate with other components and access distributed Windows platform services. A benefit of DCOM is that it makes network communication transparent to components, which communicate with other components in exactly the same way whether they are remote or running strictly on the local computer.

The following illustration shows the architecture of Microsoft's Enterprise Development Strategy, combining Internet and three-tier client/server applications.

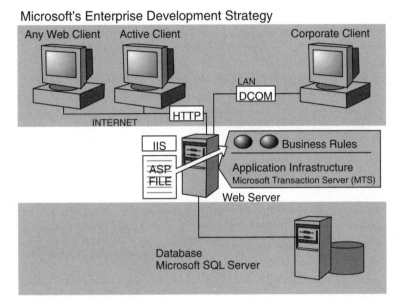

Important features of Microsoft's Enterprise Development Strategy include:

◆ Internet computing

Create enterprise solutions that exploit the communication capabilities of the Internet, while providing end users with the flexibility and control of client-computer applications and technologies. For example, ActiveX controls are COM components that you can insert into a Web page or other application to reuse packaged functionality that you or another programmer previously developed. Scriptlets are Web pages based on DHTML that you can use as a control in any application that supports controls.

◆ Interoperability

Develop new applications that work with existing applications and extend those applications with new functionality.

◆ True integration

Deploy scalable and manageable distributed applications with key capabilities such as security, management, transaction monitoring, component services, and directory services. Products and technologies such as SQL, MTS, Windows NT, and COM provide these services.

◆ Lower cost of ownership

Develop applications that are easier to deploy and manage, and easier to change and evolve over time.

◆ Faster development time

Achieve all of the above using an integrated set of development tools.

Scope of the Course

Microsoft's Enterprise Development Strategy encompasses a broad set of application technologies and a comprehensive architecture. Developing enterprise-wide solutions requires a team with a diverse set of technological and project management skills. This course will provide you with a better understanding of the technologies involved in developing three-tier applications.

Enterprise Development Using Microsoft Visual Basic 6 focuses on the second and third tiers of the three-tier client/server model and Enterprise Development Strategy. You use Visual Basic to build COM DLLs and deploy them using MTS. You utilize MTS as the application infrastructure for your COM DLLs, and invoke business and data services in a SQL Server database. You gain hands-on experience with Microsoft Windows NT Server, Visual Basic, construction and use of COM DLLs, MTS, Microsoft SQL Server, and ActiveX Data Objects.

The following illustration highlights the focus of this course.

Microsoft's Enterprise Development Strategy

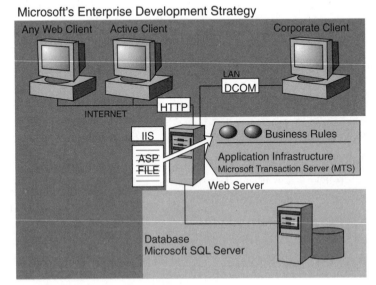

Other courses in the Mastering Series curriculum cover building traditional two-tier client/server and Internet applications, including:

◆ *Mastering Microsoft Visual Basic 6 Development*

This intermediate course addresses data access issues in a traditional two-tier client/server environment. It explains how to build and use COM components and ActiveX controls in a single-user environment.

◆ *Mastering Web Application Development Using Visual InterDev 6*

This intermediate course covers building Web front ends using technologies such as HTML, ActiveX controls, and scripting. A major area of focus is the construction and use of ASP files on the Web server. It explains how to access SQL databases through ActiveX Data Objects (ADO) and introduces how to access back-end services through MTS. Visual Basic and Visual InterDev are the development tools used in this course.

For more information about Microsoft Mastering Series courses described in this topic, go to the Microsoft Mastering Series Web site at http://msdn.microsoft.com/mastering/default.asp.

The Island Hopper News Sample Application

In this section, you will learn about the Island Hopper News sample application that you will use in many of the course labs. You will learn about the Process and Application Models from the Microsoft Solutions Framework that relate to the sample application. You will also learn about the user, business, and data services in Island Hopper News. Finally, you will see how services were mapped to components in the physical design of the sample.

The MSF Process Model

Microsoft Solutions Framework (MSF) is a guide for planning, building, and managing distributed computing systems. Like a compass, MSF guides product developers and consultants in a consistent direction without involving everyone in the details of how to get there.

This allows everyone to agree on the higher-level aspects of the project, including vision, architecture, responsibilities, and many other factors that determine the success of a distributed computing application. Once you establish a shared vision, you can use detailed methodologies to achieve your goals if necessary. MSF also serves as a useful tool for measuring progress against the original goals for the project.

MSF models help provide the foundation for effective distributed computing by addressing the areas identified as key requirements for next-generation systems throughout the planning, building, and managing life cycle. This course emphasizes the Process and Application Models. This topic describes the Process Model. For information about the Application Model, see "The Application Model and Services" on page 19 in this chapter.

The Process Model

The MSF development process consists of four distinct phases: Envisioning, Planning, Developing, and Stabilizing. These four phases are the critical planning, assessment, and coordination milestones between the customers and the project team. In this course, you will work with the Island Hopper News sample application and other lab exercises from the perspective of an application developer in the Developing phase.

Each phase of the development process culminates in an externally visible milestone (deliverables are visible to the internal and external team). These milestones are points in time when all team members synchronize their deliverables with customers and end users; with operations, support, and help desk personnel; with the distribution channel (commercial software); and with other key project stakeholders.

The following illustration shows the four phases in the MSF development process

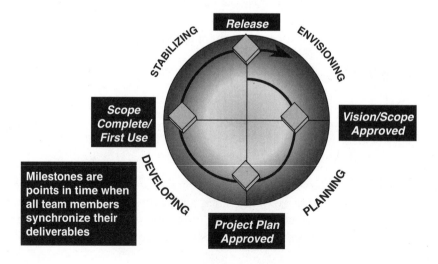

The Developing Phase: Scope Complete/First Use

The Developing Phase culminates in the Scope Complete/First Use milestone. At this milestone, all features have been completed and the product is ready for external testing and stabilization. This milestone is the opportunity for customers and end users, operations and support personnel, and key project stakeholders to evaluate the product and identify any remaining issues that need to be addressed before it ships.

The deliverables at the Scope Complete/First Use milestone include:

◆ Updated Risk Management Plan

◆ Documentation

◆ Versioned Functional Specification

◆ Updated Schedule

Introduction to Island Hopper News

To demonstrate the integration of many of the technologies in Visual Studio, Microsoft has developed a sample application named Island Hopper News. The application is designed as a teaching tool for developers and includes key technologies and products such as Visual Basic, MTS, ActiveX Data Objects (ADO), and SQL Server. You will use the Island Hopper News sample in many of the labs in this course.

The Island Hopper News sample is a fictitious, online newspaper designed to be published on the Web. It contains sections on local, national, and international news, as well as sports and local classified advertisements. Only the classified advertisement section is developed in this version of Visual Studio.

Visual Studio provides two versions of the sample, Levels A and C. Level A is a two-tier implementation suitable for a small company intranet. Level C is a three-tier implementation suitable for deployment on the Internet. This course focuses on the Level C application. It provides an example of the technologies needed to develop enterprise-wide applications.

For more information about the Island Hopper News sample, see the Samples Section in the Visual Studio Help Documentation.

Island Hopper News Sample, Level C

Customers access the Island Hopper News through a Web site where they view and place classified ads. Island Hopper News employees update customer records, invoices, and payments by using a client application developed with Visual Basic that runs in Windows 95 or Windows NT.

Both the Visual Basic client and the Web client access the same set of COM components running in MTS on Windows NT Server. The Visual Basic client accesses additional components related to tracking and billing customers. The Visual Basic application uses DCOM, and the Web application uses ASP files, to directly access the middle-tier components. All changes—including updates to ads, new ads, and billing—are securely transacted to a SQL Server database.

To see the demonstration "Island Hopper Web Client," see the accompanying CD-ROM.

To see the demonstration "Island Hopper Visual Basic Client," see the accompanying CD-ROM.

Using Island Hopper News in this Course

In many of the labs in this course you will use Visual Basic, MTS, and SQL Server to build components similar to those found in the Island Hopper News sample. You will take a close look at the sample to see one way developers can implement the technologies used in enterprise development.

The Envisioning and Planning phases of the Island Hopper News case study have been completed for you. In the lab exercises in this course, you will work within the scope of the Developing Phase of the Process Model.

An important deliverable in the Developing Phase is a product for external testing and feedback by users. In the lab exercises throughout this course, you will be developing different aspects of the Island Hopper News design. The chapters ahead provide you with opportunities to take an in-depth look at important aspects of developing enterprise applications. You will gain hands-on experience in developing several of the features in the second and third tiers of the Island Hopper News sample.

The next section discusses the application architecture of Island Hopper News and the physical design of the components. Later chapters focus your efforts on the implementation of these components.

The Application Model and Services

An application model is a conceptual view of an application that establishes the definitions, rules, and relationships that structure the application. It serves as a basis for exchanging ideas during the logical design of an application, and it determines how applications are built. An application model shows how the application is structured, not how it will be implemented. An organization may use more than one application model to accommodate the different types of applications that it is developing. Understanding the particular application model is essential for the project team to effectively develop applications that will be successful in the organization.

A simple analogy helps to explain the concept of a model. When someone mentions a house, we assume without knowing any particulars that the house has an entrance, bedrooms, bathrooms, a kitchen, and so on. Even if a particular house is very different from this model (for example, it may have a sleeping loft rather than bedrooms), the model serves as a starting point for discussing form and function.

Similarly, an application model describes in general terms what an application is or, more exactly, what people think a typical application is.

Services in the Application Model

A service is a unit of application logic that implements operations, functions, or transformations that are applied to objects. Services can enforce business rules, perform calculations or manipulations on data, and expose features for entering, retrieving, viewing, or modifying information.

The MSF Application Model introduces a new paradigm for structuring applications. In the MSF view, an application is constructed from a logical network of consumers and suppliers of services. These services can be distributed across both physical and functional boundaries to support the needs of many different applications. COM is the enabling technology when building applications with Microsoft products and technologies.

The MSF Application Model defines three categories of services: user, business, and data. These services promote a three-tiered logical model for distributed applications. The MSF Application Model is the recommended approach for designing such applications.

The Application Model offers a new perspective on creating applications. Breaking functionality into logical services rather than creating individual monolithic applications allows multiple applications to share common services.

The following illustration shows the relationship between services in an application.

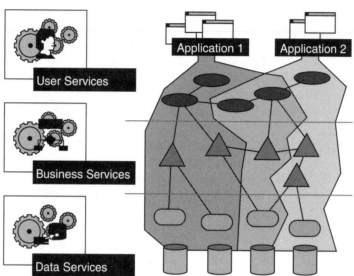

User Services

User services are the units of application logic that provide an application with its interface. The user of an application can be a person or another application. Therefore, an application's interface may be a graphical user interface and/or a programmatic interface.

For instance, Microsoft Excel has a rich graphical user interface that is implemented by using a workbook/worksheet metaphor. Along with its graphical user interface, Excel also provides a comprehensive set of programmatic interfaces offering the same features and functionality in the form of Automation. The two types of interface are semantically equivalent and are both considered user services.

An application's user services are responsible for managing all aspects of the interaction between the user and the application. Achieving this requires an understanding of the users, the activities that they will need to perform, and the interaction styles that are best suited to the different combinations of user and activity.

Business Services

Business services are the units of application logic that control the sequencing and enforcing of business rules and the transactional integrity of the operations that they perform. Business services transform raw data into information for the user through the appropriate application of rules.

The goal of a properly designed business service is to isolate business rule enforcement and data transformation logic from their consumers (user and other business services) and from the underlying data services. Isolating the business services logic from the user and data services yields the following advantages:

◆ Flexibility in deciding how and where to deploy the business services: components on an application server, or stored procedures in a database management system (DBMS) or even on the client.

◆ The ability to place different user interface logic in front of a standard set of business services. For example, a set of business services for performing operations on a customer is implemented as a single component running on an application server. The services that the component provides could be used in any of the following client scenarios: as macros running inside Microsoft Office, from a custom application developed with Microsoft Visual Basic, or from inside HTML pages running inside Microsoft Internet Explorer.

◆ Greater ease in maintaining business rules and logic by isolating changes from the application's user and data services.

◆ The ability to replace implementations of business services. For example, the set of business rules embodied within a set of business services may vary from country to country; however, the interfaces to those services remain constant.

Data Services

Data services are the units of application logic that provide the lowest visible level of abstraction used for manipulating data. Data services maintain the availability and integrity of both persistent and nonpersistent data. Data services control and provide access to data in such a way that business services need not know where the data is located, how the service is implemented, or how it is accessed.

While it is possible to identify discrete user and business services, such as services that relate to a customer, services at the data service level are more granular. For example, a system may contain service components for customers, employees, and vendors. At the business service level, each service component would have a unique set of attributes, services, and rules. However, at the data service level, the services represent examples of an entity to the organization. Therefore, a data service component named Account Information might be implemented that provides Create, Read, Update, Delete, and Rollback services for employees, vendors, and customers.

Data services implement the data storage and provide the abstraction that relates the schema within business services onto the target data store. Data services are not restricted to permanent, nonvolatile, or structured data. Data services can handle any situation where a defined interface can access and manipulate the data.

Island Hopper News Services

The implementation of the Island Hopper News sample application evolved from the following set of user, business, and data services. The problem space developed in the Envisioning Phase is separated into services in the Planning Phase. This separation should be documented by the development team in the functional specification.

Some of the services provide functionality for both customers and Island Hopper News employees. Others are used only by employees through the Visual Basic client, such as those that deal with customer payments.

User Services

User services manage interaction between the user and the application. In the Island Hopper News sample, customers use a Web client and employees use a Visual Basic client. Examples of user services include:

- ◆ View Island Hopper News sections. Only the advertisements section is developed in the version shipped with Visual Studio.

- ◆ Choose between browsing existing advertisements and placing new advertisements.

- ◆ Choose options to add, view, and modify customer information.

- ◆ View account activities and invoices, and enter payment information.

Business Services

Business services implement business logic by taking user input and passing the information to the data services for processing at the database level. Examples of business services include:

- ◆ Verifying that all information is provided when adding new customers.

- ◆ Ensuring that advertisements (ads) are billed according to the length of time the ad appears and the number of words.

- ◆ Making sure ads don't run before the next day.

- ◆ Ensuring invoices are generated when new ads are placed.

Data Services

Data services maintain the integrity of data and provide access to data. Examples of data services include:

◆ Making sure customers can't be deleted until all their invoices are deleted.

◆ Retrieving a list of customers from the customer table.

◆ Updating the ad table.

It is important to remember that the services represent a logical view that does not dictate the location or implementation of the services. For example, you can implement a business service anywhere and with whatever technology is appropriate. This could include a business rule being implemented as an event procedure on a Visual Basic client, a COM object running in an MTS environment, or a stored procedure in a relational database management system (RDBMS). The logical view is also not necessarily tightly coupled with the distribution of those services across the computers in the solution.

The services that this topic discusses are part of the overall logical design of an application. The next section discusses the move from logical design to physical implementation, and the high-level design process.

Island Hopper News Physical Design

Once the services have been identified, one of the next steps in the process is to design the physical components of Island Hopper News, based on the many requirements of the application. Requirements may include performance, security, number of users, future scalability, robustness, and so on.

The following illustration shows the COM components for Island Hopper News.

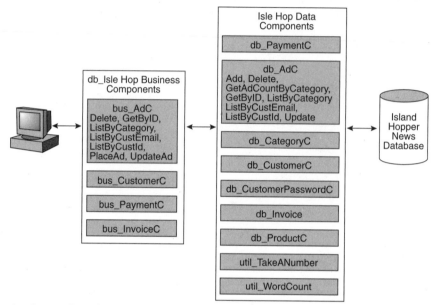

As depicted in the illustration, Island Hopper News components follow a specific naming convention. Business components are prefixed by "bus_," and all database components are prefixed by "db_." Finally, each name ends with a "C" to indicate that it is a method in the Level C version of Island Hopper News. Utility components are prefixed with "util_" and do not end with a "C."

Many of the lab exercises in this course focus on the bus_AdC and the db_AdC components.

The following table provides a description of the role of each business component in the Island Hopper News sample.

Name	Description
bus_AdC	Manages classified ads. Creates instances of db_AdC, db_CategoryC, db_ProductC, where necessary to carry out database functions. Reused from Level A with added function.
bus_CustomerC	Manages customer information.
bus_InvoiceC	Manages invoices. Written using Visual C++.
bus_PaymentC	Manages customer payments.

The following table provides a description of each data access component in the Island Hopper News sample.

Name	Description
db_AdC	Sends data to and retrieves data from the Advertisements table in the Classifieds database.
db_CategoryC	Sends data to and retrieves data from the Categories table in the Classifieds database.
db_CustomerC	Sends data to and retrieves data from the Customers table in the Classifieds database.
db_CustomerPasswordC	Sends data to and retrieves data from the CustomerPasswords table in the Classifieds database.
db_InvoiceC	Sends data to and retrieves data from the Invoices and InvoiceDetails table in the Classifieds database.
db_PaymentC	Sends data to and retrieves data from the Payments table in the Classifieds database. Written using Visual C++.
db_ProductC	Sends data to and retrieves data from the Products table in the Classifieds database.
util_TakeANumber	Utility component that assigns unique IDs to customers, invoices, and ads.
util_WordCount	Utility component that counts words in ads to calculate ad price. Written using Visual C++.

The following table provides a description of the database tables that make up the Island Hopper News sample.

Table name	Description
Advertisements	Stores classified ads.
Categories	Stores categories for classified ads.
CustomerPasswords	Stores passwords for customers.
Customers	Stores customer information.
InvoiceDetails	Stores information about each ad on an invoice (a customer can have more than one classified ad on the same invoice).
Invoices	Stores information about an invoice.
Payments	Stores information about customer payments.
Products	Stores information about classified ads.
TakeANumber	Assigns unique ID numbers for ads, categories, and customers.

Lab 1: Exploring Island Hopper News

In this lab, you will explore the Visual Basic and Web clients for the Island Hopper News sample application. You will also view the Island Hopper News project in Visual Studio.

Estimated time to complete this lab: **30 minutes**

To complete the exercises in this lab, you must have the required software. For detailed information about the labs and setup for the labs, see "Labs" in "About This Course."

Objectives

After completing this lab, you will be able to:

- Use and understand the Island Hopper clients.

- Open the Visual Basic group projects for the server components and the Visual Basic client.

- Understand the structure of the lab setup for the other labs in the course.

Prerequisites

There are no prerequisites for this lab.

Exercises

The following exercises provide practice working with the concepts and techniques covered in this chapter:

- Exercise 1: Using the Island Hopper Clients

   In this exercise, you will use the Web client and a Visual Basic client that are included with the Island Hopper News sample application. Customers view and place classified advertisements by using the Web client. Employees browse and update advertisements, maintain customer information, enter payments, and view account activity by using the Visual Basic client. You will explore the functionality of each client to familiarize yourself with the features in the sample application.

- Exercise 2: Examining the Visual Basic Projects

   In this exercise, you will examine the Visual Basic group projects for the server components and the Visual Basic client. You will examine the basic flow of execution through the client and server components that occurs when placing an ad in the Island Hopper Classified Ads.

Exercise 1: Using the Island Hopper Clients

In this exercise, you will use the Web client and a Visual Basic client that are included with the Island Hopper News sample application. Customers view and place classified advertisements by using the Web client. Employees browse and update advertisements, maintain customer information, enter payments, and view account activity by using the Visual Basic client. You will explore the functionality of each client to familiarize yourself with the features in the sample application.

▶ **Using the Web client to view and place advertisements**

You are a customer that is using the Web client to view and submit advertisements to Island Hopper News Web site.

1. Open Internet Explorer and go to http://localhost/islandhopperc.

   The only option that is operational from the Island Hopper start page is Classified Ads. Click **Classified Ads**.

2. Click **Browse an Ad** and examine some of the items for sale.

   For each category, there are several advertisements. Click any advertisement to see details about it. Note that each page on the Web site has a **View Script** button that you can use to examine the code behind the Web pages.

3. Click **Place an Ad** and then click **New User**. Enter your user information and click **Submit**. (Note the last name, e-mail name, and password that you enter because you will use it again in this exercise.) You are now returned to the logon page.

4. To place an advertisement log on by using your e-mail name and password, and then enter a new advertisement. This form uses a business rule that requires a Start Date of at least the following day.

   Click **Preview**. Examine the advertisement and make any changes that are required by clicking **Change**. Place the advertisement by clicking **Submit**. The Ad ID is displayed.

5. Click **Browse Ads** and view the advertisement you just placed.

6. Click **Place an Ad** and enter several new advertisements.

▶ **Using the Visual Basic client**

You are now an employee, using the Visual Basic client to work with billing, customer invoices, advertisement maintenance, and so on.

1. To start the Island Hopper Visual Basic client, click the Windows **Start** button, point to **/Programs/Island Hopper**, and click **Island Hopper C**.

2. Click **Browse Ads** to view the advertisement you placed earlier.

   The same COM components that implement the business and data services used to browse advertisements from the Web client are being used from the Visual Basic client. To stop browsing advertisements, click **Close**.

3. From the Visual Basic client startup screen, click **Customer Maintenance**. Click

Update in the Customer Search group. Find your customer account by typing your e-mail address and click **Retrieve**. The account information appears. Note the Customer ID. Change the billing address, and click **Save**.

4. Click **Add** in the Customer Search group. Add a new customer.

   The same COM components that implement the business and data services used to add a customer from the Web client are being used from the Visual Basic client. To finish and return to the startup screen, click **Close**.

5. Click **Ad Maintenance**. Retrieve advertisement information by typing the last name you entered as a customer and click **Search by Last Name**. The list of customers that match that last name are shown. Click the correct customer name on the list and then click **Retrieve**. The advertisements that have been entered for that customer now appear in the Ad Maintenance window.

6. Double-click an advertisement to see the details. As an employee, you can update the advertisement from the Ad Details window. Change any advertisement field, click **Save** and then click **Close**.

7. In the Ad Maintenance window, click **Close** to return to the startup window.

8. Click **Account Activity**. Enter your e-mail address and click **Retrieve**. (If you don't remember the e-mail address, you can go to the Customer Maintenance window and search by last name to find the details for a customer.) Double-click one of the advertisements to view its description. Note the invoice number of one of the advertisements. Click **Close** to return to the startup window.

9. Click **Payments**. Enter your e-mail address and click **Retrieve**. Enter the information to make a payment of $10.00 against the invoice you examined previously, and then click **Save**. Click **Close** to return to the startup window.

10. Click **Account Activity** to view the new payment and then click **Close**.

11. Click **Exit** to close the Island Hopper Visual Basic client.

Exercise 2: Examining the Visual Basic Projects

In this exercise, you will examine the Visual Basic group projects for the server components and the Visual Basic client. You will examine the basic flow of execution through the client and server components that occurs when placing an ad in the Island Hopper News Classified Ads.

▶ **Examining the Visual Basic client**

1. Open the Windows NT Explorer and view the list of files in C:\Program Files\Island Hopper\ScenarioC\Source. There are three subfolders:

   - Server_Components
   - VBClient
   - Web

   These subfolders hold their respective source files for the Island Hopper News application. The Web subfolder holds a Visual InterDev project that will not be examined in this course.

2. Open the VBClient subfolder and double-click **Classifieds.vbg**. This Visual Basic group project file contains projects for the Visual Basic client and an error log utility.

   You will see both projects, ClassifiedsEXE and ErrPlus, in the Project Group window. In the Forms folder of the ClassifiedsEXE project, you can open each of the forms that you used in the previous exercise.

3. Click **Project** and then click **References**. Note the references to the ADO, bus_*, and db_* type libraries. Click **Cancel** to close the **References** dialog box.

4. Click **View** and then click **Object Browser**. Select **bus_AdC** in **Project/Libraries** list box. Click the **Ad** class to view the members of **Ad**.

   The **bus_AdC** object is a COM component and **Ad** is a class within the COM component.

5. Click the **PlaceAd** method of **Ad** to view the function return type and parameters. An object of type **bus_AdC** is created and the **PlaceAd** method is called whenever a user places a new ad through the Web or Visual Basic client. Close the Object Browser window.

6. Bring up the code window by selecting a form in the Project Explorer and clicking **View, Code**.

7. Find the code in ClassifiedsEXE that uses **bus_AdC.Ad** to place a new ad for the Island Hopper News Classified Ads. Click **Edit** and then click **Find**. Select **Current Project** and search for **objAd.PlaceAd. objAd** is a variable of type **bus_AdC.Ad**. **PlaceAd** returns an Ad ID that eventually appears for the user.

▶ **Examining the server components**

1. While in Visual Basic, Click **File** and then click **Open Project**. In the C:\Program Files\IslandHopper\ScenarioC\Source\Server_Components\ folder, click **Server_Components.vbg**.

   Each of the server components for Island Hopper News is implemented in a separate Visual Basic project, and this group project contains all of them, except those implemented in Visual C++.

2. In the Project Group window, open the Class Modules folder of the **bus_AdC** project. **Ad** is the only class in the COM component.

3. Double-click the **Ad** class module to display the code window. View the comments at the top of the code module.

4. In the **Procedure** list box, click **PlaceAd**. View the comments and notice that the **PlaceAd** method of a **bus_AdC.Ad** object creates instances of other server components:

   - db_CategoryC.Category
   - util_TakeANumber.TakeANumber
   - util_WordCountLib.WordCount
   - db_ProductC.Product
   - bus_InvoiceCLib.bus_Invoice
   - db_AdC.Ad

   The **bus_AdC.Ad** object has to update many tables and ensure that many business rules are adhered to when an advertisement is placed. The **bus_AdC** object uses many other COM components to help it do the work it needs to get done. You will re-implement some of the code in **PlaceAd** in later labs.

5. In the **bus_AdC.Ad PlaceAd** method, find the declaration of the objAd variable that is of type **db_AdC.Ad**. Then, find the call to **objAd.Add** later in the **PlaceAd** method. The **PlaceAd** method passes many of the parameters that were passed to it from the Visual Basic client. Also examine **UpdateAd**. You will re-implement some of the **UpdateAd** code in later labs.

6. Right-click on the code that calls **objAd.Add** and then click **Definition**. This will display the **db_AdC.Ad** code window and display the **Add** method. Notice that the **db_AdC.Ad** class uses ADO to access the SQL Server database.

7. Now you have traced the flow of execution from the Visual Basic client to **bus_AdC** to **db_AdC**. Notice that **db_AdC** uses ADO to place an ad in the Island Hopper News Classified Ads database. Now trace through the Visual Basic client and server components that are used when an advertisement is updated. Understanding the basic flow of execution for placing and updating ads will assist you in the remaining labs.

Visual Studio Enterprise Edition

In this section, you will learn about the development tools available in *Microsoft Visual Studio, Enterprise Edition*, and how they are used together to build enterprise solutions. First, you will learn about the integrated features available to develop applications. Then, you will learn about the strengths that each application brings to the development process.

This course focuses on developing enterprise solutions using *Microsoft Visual Basic, Enterprise Edition*, and other Microsoft technologies such as Microsoft Transaction Server (MTS). Visual Basic is used because of its rapid application development functionality in a course environment. Depending on the enterprise solutions you are developing, you may need to choose additional development tools. This section provides a brief introduction to the strengths each programming language in Visual Studio brings to enterprise development.

Integrated Application Development

Visual Studio 6, Enterprise Edition, offers an integrated suite of powerful, proven tools that allows you to build the most cost-effective enterprise solutions by fully supporting Windows NT development, complete integrated database support, and team-based development. Using Visual Studio, you can build open, distributed Web applications, scale traditional client/server applications to multi-tier server-based solutions, and access the flexibility of component-based development.

Visual Studio offers integration by sharing common technologies across applications. You can choose a language based on your technical needs. Because Visual Basic, Visual J++, and Visual C++ all rely on the same native source code compiler, you can create distributed applications and debug the interaction between components written in these languages.

The following features help integrate development activities.

Debugging Tools

Visual Studio provides a robust set of debugging tools across the suite. Visual Studio debugging support includes breakpoints, break expressions, watch expressions, and the ability to step through code one statement or one procedure at a time and display the values of variables and properties. Many of the languages supported in Visual Studio include special debugging features, such as edit-and-continue capability, setting the next statement to execute, remote debugging of Active Server Pages, and procedure testing while the application is in Break mode.

Visual Analyzer

Distributed three-tier applications are inherently complicated. If you join a new team working on such an application, or inherit such an application from another developer, it can be a challenge to figure out what all the pieces of the application are and how they interact with each other. Visual Studio Analyzer aids you in understanding these applications. For example, a Visual Basic component (running on computer A) might invoke a DCOM object written in Visual C++ (running on computer B), which, in turn, issues SQL statements to a database server (running on computer C) via an ActiveX Data Object. Visual Studio Analyzer collects the events from the different computers and records them in a local log. Visual Studio Analyzer displays the application, the COM object, and the database server graphically as components on the application diagram. The diagram is annotated with the interactions between the application and the COM object, and the interactions between the COM object and the database server.

Database Tools

Microsoft Visual Database Tools, now integrated into all members of the Visual Studio suite, provide extensive support for building data-centric applications rapidly. With Microsoft Visual Database Tools, you can:

◆ Connect to and explore any ODBC or OLE-DB database (including Microsoft SQL Server and Oracle).

◆ Create and modify databases using database diagrams.

◆ Design, execute, and save complex queries.

◆ Add, update, and delete data stored in database tables.

◆ Design objects, such as tables, triggers, and stored procedures, in Microsoft SQL Server and Oracle databases.

◆ Drag database objects onto a design surface to bind controls to those objects.

Using Visual Studio 6, Enterprise Edition, you can interactively debug and view SQL stored procedures from each development environment. Using integrated SQL debugging, you can implement stored procedures in an SQL database and verify or debug them in the context of the application that is calling them. Using the power of distributed computing technology, you can step from Visual C++, Visual J++, Visual Basic script, or Visual Basic source code executing on a client computer to Microsoft SQL Server 6.5 source code executing on a remote server computer.

Component Management

Microsoft Repository allows component information to be shared—not only by multiple team members, but also by multiple tools. Microsoft Repository enables tool interoperability across the application life cycle by providing an open, extensible framework for storing software components and information about them (such as their methods, data types, and relationships to other components). There are other benefits of component-based development that you can realize, including more effective component management and higher levels of automation. *Visual Studio 6.0* provides access to repository components through Visual Component Manager, Visual Modeler, Visual InterDev, Visual J++, and Visual Basic. Numerous third-party products also provide access to the repository.

Microsoft Development Tools

Visual Studio is a suite of tools specifically designed for building enterprise applications. You can choose the proper tool based on your technical needs. This topic lists the strengths each tool brings to enterprise development. For more information about the development tools and server technologies in Visual Studio, go to Microsoft's Visual Studio Web site by at http://msdn.microsoft.com/vstudio/default.asp.

Microsoft Visual Basic

Visual Basic 6.0 provides the most productive development through Rapid Application Development (RAD) functionality and enhanced data connectivity. You can create applications by assembling components such as ActiveX controls, non-visual COM components and Active Documents. These components are meant to encapsulate business functions, allowing you to re-use components in many different applications.

For more information about using Visual Basic to build components, see Chapter 2, "Building COM DLLs with Visual Basic" on page 39, and Chapter 4, "Using MTS Transaction Services" on page 95.

Microsoft Visual C++

Visual C++ is the most productive C++ tool for optimized, highest-performance, enterprise-wide development. Enhancements to the product include IntelliSense Technology with statement completion, edit-and-continue debugging functionality, and updates to Microsoft Foundation Classes (MFC). The latest C++ compiler technology in Visual C++ is finely tuned for performance, producing significantly faster and smaller 32-bit applications for the Windows 95 and Windows NT Workstation operating systems. The Active Template Library (ATL) is a set of template-based C++ classes with which you can easily create small, fast COM objects.

Microsoft Visual InterDev

Visual InterDev is a comprehensive development tool for data-driven Web applications. It includes end-to-end RAD features to help you design, build, debug, and deploy your applications fast. You can use drag-and-drop functionality to integrate client- and server-side components built with Visual Basic, Visual J++, Visual C++, and Visual FoxPro. Visual InterDev provides features to allow the automatic deployment of Web components (HTML and ASP pages, server-side COM Components and client-side ActiveX Controls and Applets) to Web sites for testing.

Microsoft Visual J++

Visual J++ allows Java developers access to the full capabilities of the Windows platform. The entire Win32 API is accessible from within Java applications. If you are looking for a faster graphical user interface, the entire Win32 User Interface library can be used inside Java applications. Windows applications written in Java can be easily deployed and maintained, lowering the cost of supporting Windows components.

Microsoft Visual FoxPro

Visual FoxPro 6.0 is a critical tool for building components that can be deployed and scaled in client/server, Internet, and intranet environments. These components are typically three-tier business rules servers and other components that work with data, whether local or remote. Visual FoxPro gives you the necessary tools to manage data—whether organizing tables of information and running queries, creating an integrated relational database management system (RDBMS), or programming a fully developed data management application for end users.

Self-Check Questions

To see the answers to the Self-Check Questions, see Appendix A.

1. **True or False: Application infrastructure is software that supports concurrent access to a shared service, usually business and data services.**

   A. True

   B. False

2. **Which item is not defined in the COM specification?**

   A. How an object is created from a component

   B. How a client accesses features of the object

   C. The object's responsibility for destroying itself when it is no longer in use

   D. The suite of interfaces each component should support

3. **Choose the correct statement related to enterprise development.**

   A. Microsoft's Enterprise Development Strategy is only concerned with intranets and LANs.

   B. Components that execute in the middle tier can be accessed by ASP files and other COM clients such as applications built by using Visual Basic.

   C. Stored Procedures can only be used to implement data services and never business services.

   D. Visual Basic should always be used to build COM components which run in the middle tier.

4. **Select the statement that incorrectly describes a Microsoft development tool.**

   A. Visual Basic is a Rapid Application Development (RAD) tool.

   B. Visual C++ is designed to help programmers build optimized, high-performing, enterprise solutions.

   C. Visual InterDev is a RAD tool used to build Web applications.

   D. Visual Basic can always be used without support of the other development tools to build Enterprise solutions.

5. What is the correct description of the development phase in the MSF Process Model?

A. You define a vision statement that articulates the ultimate goals for the product or service and provides clear direction.

B. The development phase provides the opportunity for customers and end users, operations and support personnel, and key project stakeholders to evaluate all features of the product.

C. Testing activities, bug finding, and fixing are the primary foci, and the product is formally turned over to the operations and support groups.

D. Customers and team agree on what is to be delivered, and how it will be built, reassess risk, establish priorities, and finalize estimates for schedule and resources.

6. Which of the following is not a characteristic of services in the Application Model?

A. Services can be distributed across both physical and functional boundaries to support the needs of many different applications.

B. According to MSF, a service is always implemented as an API.

C. COM components can be used to implement many services.

D. Stored procedures can be used to implement many services.

Student Notes:

Chapter 2:
Building COM DLLs with Visual Basic

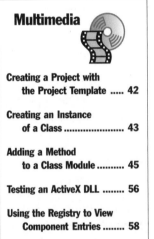

Multimedia

In this chapter, you will learn how to implement business services in Component Object Model (COM) dynamic-link libraries (DLLs) by using Visual Basic. First, you will learn how to build COM DLLs in Visual Basic through the use of ActiveX DLL projects. Then, you will learn how to control the version of your component. Finally, you'll learn how to test and register your COM DLLs.

Objectives

After completing this chapter, you will be able to:

♦ List the ways that you can implement business services in an enterprise solution that you develop in Visual Basic.

♦ Use class modules to define an object in a Visual Basic project.

♦ Create a COM DLL that exposes methods.

♦ Set compile properties for a COM DLL.

♦ Test a COM DLL.

♦ Register a COM DLL.

Implementing Business Services Using Visual Basic

Business services are the units of application logic that control the sequencing and enforcing of business rules and the transactional integrity of the operations they perform. Business services transform data into usable information through the appropriate application of rules. In this course, you will implement business services as COM DLLs (also called components) that run under Microsoft Transaction Server (MTS).

For information about the differences between user, business, and data services, see "The Application Model and Services" on page 19 in Chapter 1, "Microsoft's Enterprise Development Strategy."

Using COM Components

COM components are units of code that provide a specific functionality. Using COM, you can build different components that work together as a single application. By breaking up your code into components, you can make decisions later about how to most effectively distribute your application.

Visual Basic can build COM components as executable files (EXEs) or DLLs. However, to be usable in MTS, COM components must be built as DLLs.

In this course, you will implement business services as COM DLLs built with Visual Basic. Each component implements specific services in the Island Hopper solution. For example, the **bus_AdC** component implements methods that create, update, and delete advertisements.

This chapter teaches you how to use Visual Basic to build COM components that implement business services. In the next chapter, you will learn how to use these components with MTS.

Creating COM DLLs in Visual Basic

In this section, you will learn how to create a new DLL project in Visual Basic.

You will learn how to add class modules to a Visual Basic project. You will also learn how to add methods to a class module and use the built-in events for classes. Finally, you'll learn how to raise errors from your DLL to the client application.

Choosing the Type of COM Component

With Visual Basic, you can build and run in-process or out-of-process COM components. In-process components are COM DLLs. Out-of-process components are COM EXEs.

The following table shows the advantages and disadvantages of using in-process and out-of-process components.

Type of COM component	Advantages	Disadvantages
In-process DLL	Provides faster access to objects.	Is less fault-tolerant. If the DLL fails, the entire host process fails.
Out-of-process EXE	Faults are limited to just the out-of-process EXE. If the EXE fails, other processes in the system will not fail.	Is slower because method calls must be marshalled between processes.

Note Visual Basic refers to COM DLLs as ActiveX DLLs and COM EXEs as ActiveX EXEs. This course uses the terms COM DLL and COM EXE, except when explicitly referring to Visual Basic project options.

MTS Constraints

MTS places constraints on the COM components that will run under it. Components:

◆ Must be compiled as a COM DLL.

◆ Must provide a type library that describes their interfaces.

◆ Must be self-registering.

Visual Basic satisfies the last two requirements automatically when building COM components. For more information about COM DLLs in MTS, see Chapter 3, "Introduction to Microsoft Transaction Server (MTS)" on page 69.

Creating a Visual Basic Project

When you create a new project in Visual Basic, you choose a template on which to base the new project. To create a COM component, you choose either the ActiveX EXE or the ActiveX DLL template in the **New Project** dialog box. Selecting either type of template sets a number of default values that are important for creating components.

Tip You can change the project type later by changing the project properties.

To see the demonstration "Creating a Project with the Project Template," see the accompanying CD-ROM.

The following illustration shows the standard Visual Basic templates.

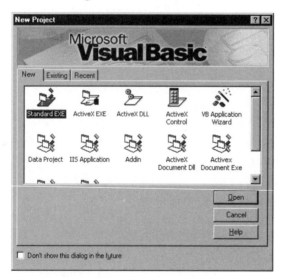

Using Class Modules

A class module is a type of Visual Basic code module. It is similar to a form module with no user interface. Each class module defines one type of object.

A class is a template that defines the methods and properties for an object. Class modules in Visual Basic contain the code that implements the methods for a class. A single COM component can contain multiple class modules. At run time, you create an object by creating an instance of a class.

For example, you can create a **Customer** class that has methods such as **AddCustomer** and **RemoveCustomer**.

Adding a Class Module to a Project

When you create a new DLL project in Visual Basic, Visual Basic creates a project with one class module.

You can add a new class module by clicking **Add Class Module** on the **Project** menu in Visual Basic. You can then add methods, properties, and events to the class.

Creating an Instance of a Class

From a client, there are two ways to create an instance of a class. You can use the **CreateObject** function or the **New** operator. In either case, you must assign the instance to an object variable. The **New** operator is the fastest way to create an object. For more information about how **CreateObject** and **New** create objects, see "Activating a COM Object" on page 60 in this chapter.

To see the animation "Creating an Instance of a Class," see the accompanying CD-ROM.

The following example code creates an instance of the **Customer** class by using the **CreateObject** function:

```
Dim objCustomer As Customer
Set objCustomer = CreateObject("People.Customer")
```

You can also create an instance of a class by using the **New** operator. For example:

```
Dim objCustomer As Customer
Set objCustomer = New Customer
```

Note Avoid using the more compact syntax, **Dim objCustomer As New Customer**, to create an object. Although this saves a line of code, Visual Basic will not create the object until it is used. This syntax causes Visual Basic to insert checks inside your code to determine if the object is created yet, and to create it when it is first used. The overall result is less efficient code.

Both of the previous code examples declare **objCustomer** as type **Customer**. Because the **Customer** type is defined in the component that provides the **Customer** class, you must add a reference to that component by clicking **References** on the **Project** menu in Visual Basic.

Note When creating MTS objects from classes within the same Visual Basic project, use the **CreateObject** function. The **New** operator does not use COM to create classes in the same project. MTS cannot manage classes that are not created through COM.

Once you have created an object, you can use methods and properties of the object. The following example code invokes the **AddCustomer** method of the **Customer** object:

```
objCustomer.AddCustomer "Joe", "Programmer", 31
```

Using the Initialize and Terminate Events

Class modules have two built-in events: **Initialize** and **Terminate**.

To add code to a class module event, open a Visual Basic code window for the class, and click **Class** in the **Object** drop-down list box.

Initialize Event

The **Initialize** event occurs when an instance of a class is created, but before any properties have been set. You can use the **Initialize** event to initialize any data used by the class, as shown in the following example code:

```
Private Sub Class_Initialize()
  'Store current date in gdtmToday variable.
  gdtmToday = Now
End Sub
```

Terminate Event

The **Terminate** event occurs when an object is destroyed. Objects are destroyed implicitly when they go out of scope or explicitly when they are set to **Nothing**. Use the **Terminate** event to save information, or to perform actions that you want to occur only when the object terminates. For example:

```
Private Sub Class_Terminate()
  'Delete temporary file created by this object
  Kill gstrTempFileName
End Sub
```

Creating Methods for Classes

To add methods to a class, you create public **Sub** or **Function** procedures within the class module. The public **Sub** and **Function** procedures will be exposed as methods for objects that you create from the class.

To create a method for an object, you can either type the procedure heading directly in the code window or click **Add Procedure** on the **Tools** menu and complete the dialog box.

To see the demonstration "Adding a Method to a Class Module," see the accompanying CD-ROM.

The following example code defines an **AddCustomer** method that adds a new customer to a file:

```
Public Sub AddCustomer (ByVal strFirst as String, ByVal strLast as
String, ByVal intAge As Integer)
  Open mstrDataFilename For Append Lock Write as #1
  Write #1, strFirst, strLast, intAge
  Close #1
End Sub
```

To view the properties and methods you have defined for an object, you can use the Object Browser. For information about using the Object Browser, see "Object Browser" in Visual Basic Help.

Note You can also create properties and events for class modules, but this is not recommended for a component that will be used in MTS. For more information, see "MTS Programming Best Practices" on page 132 in Chapter 4, "Using MTS Transaction Services."

Raising Errors

Robust error handling is essential when developing COM components for use with MTS.

In Visual Basic, a procedure passes unhandled errors to the calling procedure. If the error is passed all the way to the topmost calling procedure, the program terminates. A component returns unhandled errors to the client. If the client doesn't handle the error, then the client will terminate.

It is especially important to know whether errors have occurred when using components with MTS. A component must report to MTS whether its work was completed successfully. By trapping the error, you can notify MTS of the status of the component's work.

Using the Raise Method

Visual Basic uses the internal **Err** object to store information about any error that occurs. When you create a COM component, you can provide error messages to the client application through the **Err** object. To pass an error back to a client application, you call the **Raise** method of the **Err** object.

The **Raise** method has the following syntax:

Err.Raise (*Number, Source, Description, HelpFile, HelpContext*)

The error number can be either an error that you've trapped or a custom error number that you define. To create a custom error number, add the intrinsic constant **vbObjectError** to your error number. The resulting number is returned to the client application. This ensures that the error numbers do not conflict with the built-in Visual Basic error numbers.

The following example code uses the **Raise** method to identify the source of the error as the module in which the error occurred:

```
Public Sub AddCustomer(ByVal strFirst As String, ByVal strLast As
String, ByVal intAge As Integer)
  On Error GoTo ErrorHandler
  Open mstrDataFilename For Append Lock Write As #1
  Write #1, strFirst, strLast, intAge
  Close #1
  Exit Sub
```

code continued on next page

code continued from previous page

```
ErrorHandler:
    'Clean up our mess
    Close
    'Report error to client
    Err.Raise Err.Number, "People Customer Module", Err.Description

End Sub
```

Working with COM DLL Projects

In this section, you will learn about the project settings and compile options for DLLs in Visual Basic.

You will learn about the properties that you can set for DLL projects, such as the project type, name, and description. You'll also learn how to make a DLL available to multiple users through the **Instancing** property and how to use other property settings for class modules. Then, you'll learn how to preserve the compatibility of your components with client applications through compile options. Finally, you will learn how to test a DLL.

Setting Properties for Projects

When you create a new project with Visual Basic, you set a number of properties that affect how your COM component will run.

In Visual Basic, you set properties for a project by clicking **Project** *ProjectName* **Properties** on the **Project** menu. You can then click the **General** tab of the **Project Properties** dialog box to select the options you want.

Project Type

The Project Type field provides the four template options: Standard EXE, ActiveX EXE, ActiveX DLL, and ActiveX Control. When you create a new ActiveX DLL or ActiveX EXE project, Visual Basic automatically sets the **Project Type** property.

The project type determines how some other project options can be set. For example, options on the **Component** tab are not available when the project type is set to **Standard EXE**.

Startup Object

For most DLLs, set the Startup Object field to (**None**). If you want initialization code to run when the DLL is loaded, set the **Startup Object** property to **Sub Main**. If you want initialization code to run when an instance of a class is created, use the **Class_Initialize** event as explained in "Using the Initialize and Terminate Events" on page 44 in this chapter.

Project Name

The Project Name field specifies the first part of the programmatic identifier for the component. This, combined with the class name, forms a complete programmatic identifier. For example, if the project name is **bus_AdC**, and the class name is Ad, then the programmatic identifier is **bus_AdC.Ad**. This is the name used by a client when it calls the **CreateObject** function.

Project Description

The **Project Description** field enables you to enter a brief description of the component.

The contents of this field will appear in the **References** dialog box when you select references for other Visual Basic projects. The text also appears in the Description pane at the bottom of the Object Browser.

Upgrade ActiveX Controls

Selecting the **Upgrade ActiveX Controls** check box ensures that any ActiveX controls referenced by your project are the most up-to-date. If this check box is selected, and new ActiveX controls are loaded onto the computer, Visual Basic will automatically reference the new controls when you reload the project.

Unattended Execution

The **Unattended Execution** check box specifies whether the component will be run without user interaction. Unattended components do not have a user interface. Any run-time functions, such as messages that normally result in user interaction, are written to an event log.

Retained In Memory

Normally when all references to objects in a Visual Basic COM DLL are released, Visual Basic frees data structures associated with the project. If the objects are recreated, those data structures must be recreated as well. This situation occurs often in the MTS environment, which results in slower performance.

If you select the **Retained In Memory** option, Visual Basic will not unload internal data structures when the DLL is no longer referenced. This works much more efficiently in the MTS environment.

> **Note** Microsoft Transaction Server Service Pack 1 automatically enables this feature at run time even if you have not selected it at design time.

Threading Model

The **Threading Model** list box allows you to choose whether your component is single-threaded or apartment-threaded. When creating components for MTS, you should make them apartment-threaded because MTS works best with this model.

Setting Properties for Class Modules

To determine how a class module is identified and created by client applications, set properties for each class module in the COM component.

Name Property

To create a name for the class, set the **Name** property in the **Properties** dialog box. This name will be used by the client application to create an instance of a class.

The following example code creates an instance of a class named **Customer** that is defined in the component named People:

```
Dim ObjCustomer As Customer
Set ObjCustomer = CreateObject ("People.Customer")
```

Instancing Property

The **Instancing** property determines whether applications outside the Visual Basic project that defines the class can create new instances of the class, and if so, how those instances are created.

The following illustration shows the **Instancing** property settings available for a DLL.

When you create a business object, set the **Instancing** property to **MultiUse**.

The following table defines each of the **Instancing** property settings for a DLL.

Setting	Description
Private	Other applications are not allowed access to type library information about the class and cannot create instances of it. **Private** objects are used only within the project that defines the class.
PublicNotCreatable	Other applications can use objects of this class only if the component creates the objects first. Other applications cannot use the **CreateObject** method or the **New** operator to create objects of this class. Set the **Instancing** property to this value when you want to create dependent objects.
MultiUse	Allows other applications to create objects from the class. One instance of your component can provide any number of objects created in this fashion.
GlobalMultiUse	Similar to MultiUse, except properties and methods of the class can be invoked as though they were global functions. It is not necessary to create an explicit instance of a class, because one will automatically be created.

Class Modules and COM

When developing and debugging Visual Basic COM DLLs, it is important to understand how class modules in your Visual Basic project relate to COM. Each class module in your project compiles into a COM class in the COM DLL. When you compile your COM DLL, it contains identifiers that client applications, including Visual Basic clients, use to create and utilize your classes.

The following illustration shows how a Visual Basic project maps to a COM DLL and what identifiers are created automatically by Visual Basic during compilation.

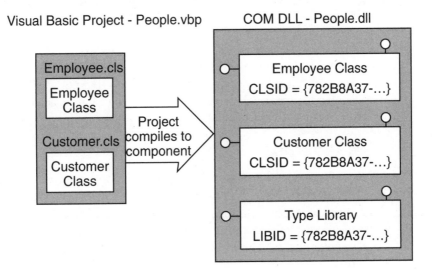

Globally Unique Identifiers

Globally Unique Identifiers (GUIDs) are 128-bit values used to identify elements in the system. GUIDs are generated using an algorithm developed by the Open Software Foundation. It generates a random GUID that is guaranteed to be statistically unique. That is, no two generated GUIDs will be the same on any given computer, at any given time.

COM uses GUIDs to identify classes and other elements used in clients and components. When Visual Basic compiles a COM DLL, it automatically generates GUIDs to identify any COM elements that the DLL contains.

COM Classes

Every class module in your Visual Basic project compiles into a COM class in the DLL. To identify this new class in the system, Visual Basic generates a class identifier (CLSID). The CLSID is a GUID that is used by client applications to create the class.

When you write clients that create COM classes, don't use CLSIDs, but do use programmatic identifiers (ProgIDs). ProgIDs are a human readable string that identifies a specific COM class. The following example code shows how the ProgID **People.Customer** is used to instantiate the Customer COM class:

```
Set objCustomer = CreateObject("People.Customer")
```

ProgIDs are more readable to programmers and end users and therefore easier to use. However, Visual Basic must convert the ProgID to a CLSID before creating the COM object. For more information about how Visual Basic creates COM objects, see "Activating a COM Object" on page 60 in this chapter.

COM Interfaces

In Visual Basic, class modules expose properties and methods to a client. When Visual Basic compiles a class module, it creates a COM interface to expose the properties and methods in the class module. A COM interface is a collection of semantically related functions that are grouped together. Because interfaces only contain functions, properties in the class module are exposed through **Get** and **Set** functions.

An interface identifier (IID) identifies COM interfaces. IIDs are also GUIDs. Visual Basic generates an IID for each interface it creates in your COM DLL. Client applications use the IID to access the properties and methods in your class module. When you write Visual Basic clients, Visual Basic hides the details of using the IID so that you don't need to use it in your code.

It is possible to implement interfaces from other components and class modules in your own class modules. For more information on implementing interfaces, see "Creating and Implementing Interfaces" on page 261 in Chapter 8, "Implementing COM with Visual Basic."

Type Libraries

A type library is a collection of descriptive information about a component's classes, its interfaces, methods on those interfaces, and the types for the parameters for those methods. Type libraries are used by Visual Basic to check method calls on objects and ensure that the correct number of parameters and types are being passed. You can view information in type libraries by using the Object Browser.

MTS uses type libraries to determine the classes, interfaces, and parameter types for methods in a COM DLL. Once MTS has this information, it can manage the component when clients call it.

Library Identifiers (LIBIDs) identify type libraries. LIBIDs are GUIDs that uniquely identify type libraries. When you compile a project that contains one or more class modules, Visual Basic generates a type library for the component that describes all of the classes and their properties and methods. The type library is placed inside the COM DLL that can then be used by clients to use the classes.

Type libraries are also used to enable early binding in Visual Basic. For more information about early binding, see "Introduction to Binding" on page 273 in Chapter 8, "Implementing COM with Visual Basic."

Version Compatibility

To compile a project in Visual Basic click **Make** on the **File** menu. ActiveX DLL projects in Visual Basic will always compile as DLLs. When updating DLLs and compiling new versions, you must determine what kind of compatibility you want to maintain with clients that were compiled to use the previous version of your DLL.

Version compatibility is very important when building components for use in multi-tier client/server environments. When you compile an ActiveX EXE or ActiveX DLL project in Visual Basic, its classes expose methods that clients will use. If at some point you change a class in a component by deleting a property or method, that component will no longer work with old clients.

In COM a unique identifier, called a class identifier (CLSID), identifies each Visual Basic class. Also, a unique interface identifier (IID) identifies the Visual Basic interface for each class. A unique type library ID identifies the type library for your component. These identifiers are all created by Visual Basic when you compile your project. Applications that use your component use these identifiers to create and use objects. If these identifiers change in a new version of a component, existing applications will not be able to use the new version.

To help control this, Visual Basic provides several options for version compatibility.

▶ **To set the version compatibility for a project**

1. Click **Project Properties** on the **Project** menu.

2. Click the **Component** tab and then select the desired **Version Compatibility** option.

The following illustration shows the **Component** tab of the **Project Properties** dialog box.

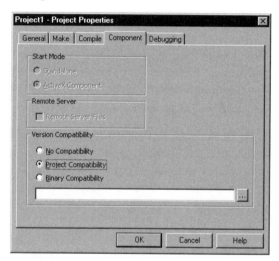

There are three options for version compatibility:

◆ **No Compatibility**

Each time you compile the component, the type library ID, CLSIDs, and IIDs are recreated. Because none of these identifiers match the ones existing clients are using, backward compatibility is not possible.

◆ **Project Compatibility**

Each time you compile the component, the CLSIDs and IIDs are recreated, but the type library remains constant. This is useful for test projects so you can maintain references to the component project. However, each compilation is not backward compatible with existing clients.

This is the default setting for a component.

◆ Binary Compatibility

Each time you compile the component, Visual Basic keeps the type library ID, CLSIDs, and IIDs the same. This maintains backward compatibility with existing clients. However, if you attempt to delete a method from a class, or change a method's name or parameter types, Visual Basic warns you that your changes will make the new version incompatible with previously compiled applications.

If you ignore the warning, Visual Basic creates new CLSIDs and IIDs for the component, breaking its backward compatibility.

Tip Choosing **No Compatibility** or **Project Compatibility** causes Visual Basic to generate new identifiers with each compile of the project. Because the old identifiers are never removed from the registry, the registry soon becomes filled with useless identifiers. Choosing **Binary Compatibility** avoids creating useless identifiers. Also, the RegClean utility provided with Visual Basic can search for and remove these old registry entries.

Many problems that occur during object creation are due to incorrect CLSIDs and other identifiers. You can avoid these problems by selecting **Binary Compatibility** for your version compatibility. You then avoid regenerating new identifiers for each component build and keep them consistent for the clients that are using them.

Testing a COM DLL

You can use Visual Basic to build an application for testing a DLL in an isolated environment before putting it into production.

In Visual Basic, create a project group. A project group is a collection of projects. When you create a project group, you can use one project in the group to test another.

▶ **To test a DLL in Visual Basic**

1. Open the Visual Basic DLL project you want to test.
2. On the **File** menu, click **Add Project**, and then click **New Standard EXE**.

   This adds a new project with its own template to the Project Group window.
3. To make the new project the start-up project, right-click the new project, and then click **Set as Start Up**.

   Whenever you run the group project, this project will start first.

4. In the new project, add a reference to the ActiveX DLL project by clicking **References** on the **Project** menu, and then selecting the ActiveX DLL project.

5. In the project, add a command button to the form.

6. In the **Click** event for the command button, add code that creates an instance of a class that is defined in the DLL, and then call any methods you want to use for testing the component, as shown in the following example code:

```
Dim objCustomer as Customer
Set objCustomer = New Customer
ObjCustomer.Remove "Joe", "Programmer"
```

You can trace the source code of the DLL by setting a breakpoint on the line that invokes the method. When execution stops at the breakpoint, you can step into the source code for that method in the DLL.

To see the demonstration "Testing an ActiveX DLL," see the accompanying CD-ROM.

For information about debugging and testing COM components, see "Testing and Debugging ActiveX Components" in the Component Tools Guide in Visual Basic Help.

COM DLL Registration

In this section, you will learn about the registry. You will first learn how to register and remove a COM DLL from the registry. Then, you will learn about the entries that are placed in the registry that enable clients and the COM libraries to locate, create, and use classes in a COM DLL. Finally, you will learn how Visual Basic uses the entries in the registry to create objects.

Registering a COM DLL

Before you can use a COM DLL, it must be registered. Clients use entries in the registry to locate, create, and use classes in the COM DLL.

Registering a COM DLL

There are several ways to register a COM DLL:

◆ Create a Setup program.

When you run the Setup program, the component is registered.

◆ Compile the DLL in Visual Basic.

When you compile the DLL, it is automatically registered on the computer where it is compiled.

◆ Run Regsvr32.exe.

Regsvr32 is a utility that will register a DLL. It is installed in your Windows NT \System32 folder. Pass the DLL file name as an argument to the Regsvr32 utility, as shown in the following example code:

```
Regsvr32.exe bus_AdC.dll
```

Note When you add a COM component to MTS, MTS will register the component automatically on the server where it is installed. For more information, see "Configuring a Client to Use MTS Components" on page 88 in Chapter 3, "Introduction to Microsoft Transaction Server (MTS)."

Unregistering a COM DLL

When a component is no longer needed, it can be unregistered.

Depending on how the Setup program was written, some DLLs that are installed as part of a Setup program can be unregistered through the Control Panel. You can unregister these DLLs by using the Add/Remove Programs icon in the Control Panel.

To remove a DLL entry from the registry manually, run Regsvr32.exe, including the /u option and the name of the DLL file, as shown in the following example code:

```
Regsvr32.exe /u bus_AdC.dll
```

Registry Keys

When a COM DLL is registered, entries are placed in the registry to allow clients and the COM libraries to locate, create, and use classes in the COM DLL. The registry entries for COM classes are located in HKEY_CLASSES_ROOT in the system registry. Visual Basic generates three registry keys when you compile a COM DLL: ProgID key; CLSID key; and TypeLib key. If you understand these registry keys, you are better able to debug a component when it doesn't work properly.

To see the demonstration "Using the Registry to View Component Entries," see the accompanying CD-ROM.

ProgID Key

The ProgID keys are located at:

\HKEY_CLASSES_ROOT\<progid>

For example, the ProgID key for a class identified as **People.Employee** is \HKEY_CLASSES_ROOT\People.Employee. The ProgID has one subkey called CLSID. This contains the CLSID for the class, and this is how a ProgID can be mapped to the CLSID that is then used to instantiate a COM class.

The following registry example shows the ProgID key for **People.Employee** and its subkeys:

```
\People.Employee = "People.Employee"
    Clsid = "{782B8A37-BCF9-11D1-AF7C-00AA006C3567}"
```

CLSID Key

The CLSID keys are located at:

\HKEY_CLASSES_ROOT\CLSID\<clsid>

For example, if the CLSID for **People.Employee** is {782B8A37-BCF9-11D1-AF7C-00AA006C3567}, the CLSID entry is \HKEY_CLASSES_ROOT\CLSID\ {782B8A37-BCF9-11D1-AF7C-00AA006C3567}. Knowing the CLSID for a class, you can locate the DLL that contains the class by looking for the InprocServer32 key. This will contain the complete file location of the DLL, and is how the COM libraries locate DLLs when they are given just a CLSID.

Visual Basic also generates additional subkeys for a CLSID key. The following table explains some of the more common keys generated.

Key	Description
InprocServer32	Specifies the location of the in-process server (DLL) for this class.
LocalServer32	Specifies the location of the out-of-process server (EXE) for this class.
ProgID	Specifies the programmatic identifier for this class. This string can be used to locate the ProgID key.
Programmable	Specifies that this class supports automation. There is no value associated with this key.
TypeLib	Specifies the type library identifier that can be used to locate the type library.
Version	Specifies the version of this class. This is in a *major.minor* format.

The following registry example shows the CLSID key for **People.Employee** and its subkeys:

```
\CLSID
    {782B8A37-BCF9-11D1-AF7C-00AA006C3567} = "People.Employee"
        InprocServer32 = <path to People.dll>
        ProgID = "People.Employee"
        Programmable
        TypeLib = "{782B8A33-BCF9-11D1-AF7C-00AA006C3567}"
        VERSION = "1.0"
```

TypeLib Key

The TypeLib keys are located at:

HKEY_CLASSES_ROOT\TypeLib\<libid>

You can find the LIBID from the TypeLib subkey in the CLSID key. The type library key is merely used to locate a type library. There are three subkeys that do this:

Key	Description
Version	Specifies the version of the type library. It is listed in a *major.minor* format.
Language Identifier	Specifies, as a number, what language the type library supports. For example, the language ID for American English is 409. Generally this will be 0, which specifies that the type library is language neutral.
Operating System Version	Specifies the operating system version, which is generally Win32. This subkey will contain the file location of the type library. For Visual Basic type libraries, this will always be in the COM DLL that was compiled from the Visual Basic project.

The following registry example shows the LIBID key for **People.Employee** and its subkeys:

```
\TypeLib
    {782B8A33-BCF9-11D1-AF7C-00AA006C3567}
        1.0
            0
                win32 = <path to People.dll>
```

Activating a COM Object

When you create a COM object using the **CreateObject** function, or **New** keyword, Visual Basic performs a number of steps to create the object. These steps are transparent to you, but understanding how an object is actually created by Visual Basic will help when problems occur while creating an object.

When you call the **CreateObject** function, you provide the ProgID of the class to be created. Because COM classes can only be created from CLSIDs, Visual Basic must first convert the ProgID into its associated CLSID. In order to do this, Visual Basic follows these steps:

◆ Step 1: Call **CLSIDFromProgID**

To convert the ProgID into a CLSID, Visual Basic calls the **CLSIDFromProgID** function from the COM Library. This COM API searches the registry for the ProgID key. Recall that the ProgID key has a subkey that contains the associated CLSID. COM retrieves this and returns it to Visual Basic.

Note that when you use the **New** operator, Visual Basic will skip this step by obtaining the CLSID at design time. This makes the **New** operator slightly faster than the **CreateObject** function.

◆ Step 2: Call **CoCreateInstance**

Next, Visual Basic calls the **CoCreateInstance** API passing the CLSID. This is another COM API that will search the registry for the given CLSID. Once found, COM searches for the subkey InprocServer32 or LocalServer32. Whichever one is present has the location of the DLL or EXE that contains the desired class. If both are present, Visual Basic always selects the InprocServer32 entry.

◆ Step 3: Launch the server

Once COM has the location of the component server, it launches the server. If the server is a DLL, it is loaded into the Visual Basic application's address space. If the server is an EXE, it is launched with a call to the Windows API **CreateProcess**. After the server is loaded, COM requests an instance of the desired object and returns a pointer to the requested interface.

The specific interface that Visual Basic requests is **IUnknown**. **IUnknown** is supported by all COM classes, so it is a safe interface to request. For more information about the **IUnknown** interface, see "The IUnknown Interface" on page 260 in Chapter 8, "Implementing COM with Visual Basic."

◆ Step 4: Get the programmatic interface

Now that Visual Basic has the **IUnknown** interface, it generally queries for the default programmatic interface on the object. This interface, which is generally a dual interface, will expose all of the properties and methods for the object. For more information, see "Dual Interfaces" on page 272 in Chapter 8, "Implementing COM with Visual Basic."

♦ Step 5: Assign the interface

Finally, Visual Basic assigns the programmatic interface pointer to the object variable in the **Set** statement. In the following example code, **objEmployee** is the object variable that is set to the returned interface pointer:

```
Set objEmployee = CreateObject("People.Employee")
```

Once the interface is assigned, you can begin using it by calling methods and properties on the object variable.

Lab 2: Building a Component

In this lab, you will create a component called Math. The Math component has one class called **Root**, which has one function called **SquareRoot**. **SquareRoot** calculates the square root of a number and returns the result.

You will implement the **SquareRoot** method. Then you will test the component by creating a test project for it.

To see the demonstration "Lab 2 Solution," see the accompanying CD-ROM.

Estimated time to complete this lab: **30 minutes**

To complete the exercises in this lab, you must have the required software. For detailed information about the labs and setup for the labs, see "Labs" in "About This Course."

Objectives

After completing this lab, you will be able to:

♦ Create a Visual Basic ActiveX DLL project.

♦ Trap and raise errors.

♦ Create a test project.

Prerequisites

There are no prerequisites for this lab.

Exercises

The following exercises provide practice working with the concepts and techniques covered in this chapter:

- ◆ Exercise 1: Creating a Visual Basic Component

  In this exercise, you will create the Math component. First you will create the ActiveX DLL project in Visual Basic, set its properties, and create the **Root** class. Then you will implement the **SquareRoot** function on the **Root** class to calculate and return the square root of the number passed in. Finally, you will implement an error handler in **SquareRoot** so that if a negative value is passed in, an error is raised to the client.

- ◆ Exercise 2: Testing the Component

  In this exercise, you will test the **Root** class you created in Exercise 1. First you will create a test project and add it to the existing Math project. Then you will use the test project to create an instance of the **Root** object and call the **SquareRoot** method to verify that it works correctly.

Exercise 1: Creating a Visual Basic Component

In this exercise, you will create the Math component. First you will create the ActiveX DLL project in Visual Basic, set its properties, and create the **Root** class. Then you will implement the **SquareRoot** function on the **Root** class to calculate and return the square root of the number passed in. Finally, you will implement an error handler in **SquareRoot** so that if a negative value is passed in, an error is raised to the client.

▶ **Create the project**

1. Start Visual Basic 6.0 and create a new ActiveX DLL project.

2. On the **Tools** menu, click **Options**. On the **Environment** tab, click **Prompt To Save Changes**, and click **OK**.

3. On the **Project** menu, click **Project1 Properties**. Set the following properties:

   - Set the **Project Name** to **Math**.

   - Select **Unattended Execution**.

   - On the **Component** tab, set the project to be binary compatible with Math.dll by clicking **Binary Compatibility**, and click **OK**. Math.dll is located in the \Labs\Lab02\Solution folder.

> **Note** If you do not see Math.dll in the **Compatible ActiveX Component** open dialog box, configure Windows Explorer to show all files and list file extensions.

4. Change the name of the class module from **Class1** to **Root**.

5. Save the project and class module as Math.vbp and Root.cls.

▶ **Declare the SquareRoot function**

1. Edit the **Root** module and add the following line of code at the beginning of the module:

   ```
   Option Explicit
   ```

2. Declare the following function in the **Root** module:

   ```
   Function SquareRoot (ByVal dblNumber As Double) As Double
   End Function
   ```

▶ **Implement the SquareRoot function**

1. Edit the **SquareRoot** function and turn on error handling, using the following code:

   ```
   On Error GoTo ErrorHandler
   ```

2. Call the Visual Basic **Sqr** function to find the square root of **dblNumber** and assign the result to the return value of the **SquareRoot** function.

3. Create an error handler that traps any errors that may occur.

4. Inside the error handler, raise the error to the client using the following code:

   ```
   Err.Raise Err.Number, "Math Module: SquareRoot", Err.Description
   ```

To see an example of how your code should look, see Lab Hint 2.1 in Appendix B.

5. Save the project.

6. On the **File** menu, click **Make Math.dll** and click **OK** to create the Math.dll component.

Exercise 2: Testing the Component

In this exercise, you will test the **Root** class you created in Exercise 1. First you will create a test project and add it to the existing Math project. Then you will use the test project to create an instance of the **Root** object and call the **SquareRoot** method to verify that it works correctly.

▶ **Create the test project**

1. Open the Math project you created in Exercise 1.

2. On the **File** menu, click **Add Project** and add a Standard EXE project to the Math project.

3. Change the name of the project to TestMath.

4. Place controls on the form and set their properties as follows.

Control	Property	Value
Command button	**Caption**	SquareRoot
	Name	cmdSquareRoot
Text box	**Name**	txtNumber
	Text	
Text box	**Name**	txtAnswer
	Text	
Label	**Caption**	Number:
Label	**Caption**	Answer:

The following illustration shows how your form should look.

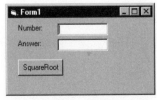

5. On the **Project** menu, click **References** and add a reference to the Math project.

6. Save the new project and form as TestMath.vbp and TestMath.frm.

7. Save the group project as Math.vbg.

▶ **Call the Math component**

1. Edit the form module and declare a global variable called **objRoot** of type **Math.Root**.

2. In the **Form_Load** event, create a new instance of the **Math.Root** object and assign it to **objRoot**.

3. In the **cmdSquareRoot_Click** event, turn on error handling using the following code:

```
On Error GoTo ErrorHandler
```

4. Call **objRoot.SquareRoot**, passing the value from the **txtNumber** text box as the argument.

5. Assign the result to the **txtAnswer** text box.

6. In the error handler, display a message box that shows the error source and error description.

   To see an example of how your code should look, see Lab Hint 2.2 in Appendix B.

7. Right-click **TestMath** in the Project Group window and select **Set as Start Up**.

8. Save the project.

9. On the **Tools** menu, select **Options**.

10. On the **General** tab, select **Break on Unhandled Errors**.

11. Run the TestMath project and test the **Root** module. Try entering a value of 9 and clicking the **SquareRoot** button. You should get an answer of 3. Try entering a value of −9 and clicking **SquareRoot**. This should display an error message.

Self-Check Questions

To see the answers to the Self-Check Questions, see Appendix A.

1. Which Visual Basic project template would you use to build an in-process COM component?

A. ActiveX Control

B. ActiveX DLL

C. ActiveX EXE

D. Standard EXE

2. How do you export a method from a class module in Visual Basic?

A. Mark the Visual Basic project for unattended execution.

B. Set the **Instancing** property to **MultiUse**.

C. Add the **Public** keyword before the method.

D. Set the Visual Basic project type to **ActiveX DLL**.

3. What are all of the ways in which an in-process component can be registered?

A. When you run Setup for the component, when you run RegSvr32.exe, and when you compile the component with Visual Basic

B. When you run Setup for the component, and when you compile the component with Visual Basic

C. When you run RegSvr32.exe, and when you compile the component with Visual Basic

D. When you run Setup for the component, and when you run RegSvr32.exe

4. How can you test an in-process component in Visual Basic so that you can trace into each method call as it runs?

A. Create a project group by adding a test project to the original component's project. Then add a reference to the component. Write code to call methods in the component and use the debugger to step into each method.

B. Create a separate test project and add a reference to the component project. Write code to call methods in the component and use the debugger to step into each method.

C. In the component project, set breakpoints on the methods you want to step through. Run the component in the Visual Basic debugger, and then run a separate test project that calls the component.

D. In the component project, add a reference to a test project. Set breakpoints on the methods you want to step through, and run the component in the Visual Basic debugger. Then run the test project and call the methods.

5. To avoid generating new CLSIDs and other identifiers each time your component is built in Visual Basic, set the Version Compatibility option for the project to:

A. No Compatibility

B. Project Compatibility

C. Binary Compatibility

D. None of the above

6. True or False: When creating COM objects in code, the CreateObject function offers a slight performance improvement over using the New operator.

A. True

B. False

Chapter 3:
Introduction to Microsoft Transaction Server (MTS)

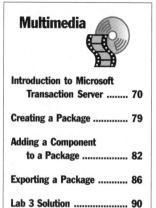
In this chapter, you will learn about the services that Microsoft Transaction Server (MTS) provides to facilitate application development in a multi-user environment. First, you will learn about the architecture of MTS and the requirements for Component Object Model (COM) dynamic-link libraries (DLLs) that are developed for this environment. Then, you will learn how to create a package, which is what MTS uses to define a set of components. Finally, you will learn how to deploy a package on an MTS server and how to configure a client application to use it.

Objectives

After completing this chapter, you will be able to:

♦ List the issues related to developing multi-user, three-tier applications.

♦ Explain how MTS addresses these issues.

♦ Describe the MTS architecture.

♦ Create a package with the MTS Explorer.

♦ Add an existing component to the MTS package.

♦ Configure a client computer to use MTS components.

Overview of MTS

The application infrastructure in a multi-user environment is composed of the services that enable many users to access the application and underlying data at the same time, while the services maintain the integrity of the data and processes that keep the business in working order. The application infrastructure includes services that manage resources, such as threads and database connections, security, and transactions.

While a three-tier model has been available for some time, developers were forced to spend a large portion of development time creating the application infrastructure under which these applications can run.

MTS eases the transition from single-user to multi-user development by providing the application infrastructure for building scalable, robust enterprise applications. MTS is a component-based transaction processing system for building, deploying, and administering server applications. MTS is part of the Windows NT 4.0 Option Pack.

To see the expert point-of-view "Introduction to Microsoft Transaction Server," see the accompanying CD-ROM.

MTS Concurrency Model

When a distributed application provides services to multiple users, it can receive simultaneous calls from clients. Also, it can have its business logic running in more than one process on more than one computer. The synchronization issues involved with managing multiple threads on multiple computers are very complex to program. Using a simple concurrency model to develop distributed applications enables you to focus on writing the business logic for your application rather than the synchronization code.

MTS provides this simple concurrency model through activities. An activity is the path of execution that occurs from the time a client creates an MTS object until the client releases that object. During the activity, the client makes calls to the MTS object. To service those calls, the MTS object may create additional MTS objects that are part of the same activity. The activity ensures that all MTS objects created on behalf of the original client do not run in parallel. You can think of an activity as a single logical thread of execution. Using activities enables you to write your MTS components from the point of view of a single user.

Resource Management

As an application scales to a larger number of clients, objects in the application must share resources such as network connections, database connections, memory, and disk space, and use them only when necessary. Effective resource management improves scalability. Two MTS resource managers are:

◆ Just-in-Time Activation

MTS helps conserve server memory by keeping an instance of an object alive only when a client is calling the object. This practice is known as just-in-time activation, and it allows the server to handle more clients than is possible when the object remains active.

When a client calls a method on an object, MTS activates the object by creating it and allowing the client call to proceed. When the call returns and the object is finished with its work, MTS deactivates the object by removing it from memory. Later, when the client calls the object again, MTS reactivates the object.

You can take advantage of just-in-time activation by building the component to indicate to MTS when its work is complete. For more information, see "Just-in-Time Activation" on page 113 in Chapter 4, "Using MTS Transaction Services."

◆ Connection Pooling

MTS also allows the use of resource dispensers, which can pool resources for more efficient use. For example, the ODBC 3.0 Driver Manager is an ODBC resource dispenser. When an ODBC database connection is released, the ODBC resource dispenser returns the connection to a pool, rather than releasing it immediately. If another MTS object requests the same connection, the connection will be assigned from the pool, saving unnecessary network trips to re-create the connection. For more information, see "Connection Pooling" on page 123 in Chapter 4, "Using MTS Transaction Services."

Security

Because more than one client can use an application, a method of authentication and authorization must be used to ensure that only those users authorized to do so access business logic.

MTS provides security by allowing you to define roles. A role defines which users (Windows NT user accounts and groups) are allowed to invoke interfaces on a class. You map each role to specific classes or interfaces on those classes. Then you add Windows NT users and groups to their appropriate roles. MTS ensures that those Windows NT users and groups can only access the classes and interfaces to which their roles are mapped. You don't have to write any special code in your components to handle this. It's automatically provided by MTS.

For more information about setting security for components that run under MTS, see "Implementing Security in MTS Applications" on page 223 in Chapter 7, "Implementing Security."

All-or-Nothing Work Management

Work done in a distributed multi-user application can involve changes to database tables and even nondatabase entities such as message queues. Often more than one object in an activity is initiating changes. Because the work in any single object can fail, the application must be able to handle situations where some objects fail, but others succeed. Work cannot be left in an inconsistent state where some of the work is done, but other parts are not.

Transactions provide an all-or-nothing simple model of managing work. Either all the objects succeed and all the work is committed, or one or more of the objects fail and none of the work is committed. Based on the outcome, any database tables or files affected by the work will either all be changed, or not changed at all. They will not be left in an inconsistent state.

The programming required to manage transactions across multiple databases and nondatabase entities is very difficult to implement in an application. MTS provides this transaction management service as part of its application infrastructure. MTS automatically creates transactions for components when they are activated. MTS also automatically handles cleanup and rollback of a failed transaction. When you use MTS, you don't have to write any transactional code in your components.

MTS Architecture

In this section, you will learn how COM components run under the MTS architecture. The MTS architecture consists of the MTS environment and supporting services. First you will learn about the MTS environment, which consists of components, packages, and server processes. You will also learn about some of the services and technologies that work in conjunction with MTS to help manage system resources and transactions.

MTS Environment

The MTS environment consists of components and packages.

Components

An MTS application provides business services to clients. MTS applications are implemented as a collection of COM DLLs, with each DLL implementing different business services in the application. The components are registered for use in the MTS run-time environment. Such components are often referred to as MTS components, and objects created from them are often called MTS objects.

A client accesses the application by creating objects from the components and calling methods in those objects. Those objects may in turn create additional objects to complete the client's request.

To use a component with MTS, it must be a COM DLL. Components that are implemented as executable (.exe) files cannot run in the MTS run-time environment. Other requirements, such as self-registration and type library support, are met automatically when you create the component with Visual Basic. For more information about component requirements, search for "Transaction Server Component Requirements" in Microsoft Transaction Server Help.

Packages

Each component that runs under MTS must belong to a package. A package contains a group of related component classes and their associated type libraries. You create a package and add components to it by using the MTS Explorer. You can then deploy and administer the components in the package as a group.

The following illustration shows the architecture of the IsleHop_Classifieds package in the Island Hopper application.

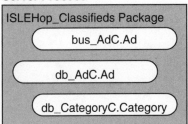

Server Process

ISLEHop_Classifieds Package

bus_AdC.Ad

db_AdC.Ad

db_CategoryC.Category

Packages define security boundaries for your application. MTS will not check security when one component calls another inside the same package. However, MTS does check security when a method is called from outside the package. Therefore, when you decide in which packages to place your components, you must deploy them to match the security needs of your application.

Packages also define fault isolation boundaries for your application. Unless otherwise specified, the components in a package all run in the same server process. If one component fails, it will cause all the components in the process to fail. It will not cause components in other packages to fail because those components will be running in separate processes. This is an additional factor to consider when determining in which packages to put your components.

Tip Resource pooling is on a per-process basis. By grouping components that share expensive resources, such as database connections, in the same package, you can improve the scalability of your application. For more information, see "Connection Pooling" on page 123 in Chapter 4, "Using MTS Transaction Services."

You can specify that a package load in the client's process, in which case all objects created from that package will exist in the client's address space. For more information, see "Creating a Package" on page 79 in this chapter.

For more information about how to make components available to client applications, see "Deploying an MTS Component" on page 85 in this chapter. For more information about setting security for a package, see "Implementing Security in MTS Applications" on page 223 in Chapter 7, "Implementing Security."

Supporting Services

MTS uses several system resources that are not part of the MTS environment to provide important resource and data management capabilities to MTS components. With the exception of the Shared Property Manager, MTS uses all of the following services automatically on your component's behalf.

Resource Managers

A resource manager is a system service that manages durable data. Resource managers ensure that data will not be lost or corrupted in the event of a system failure. Examples of resource managers include:

◆ Databases, such as Microsoft SQL Server 6.5 and Oracle versions 7.3.3 and 8.0

◆ Durable message queues, such as Microsoft Message Queue Server (MSMQ)

◆ Transactional file systems

MTS automatically works with resource managers on your component's behalf. For example, if your component uses a transaction that performs database updates on a Microsoft SQL Server database, MTS will create and manage the transaction in the SQL Server database automatically. You don't have to write any transactional code in your components.

MTS supports resource managers that implement either the OLE Transactions protocol or the X/Open XA protocol. The MTS Software Development Kit (SDK) provides a toolkit for developing resource managers. For more information about downloading the MTS SDK, go to the Transaction Server Support Resources Web site at http://support.microsoft.com/support/transaction/default.asp.

For more information about resource manager protocols, search for "Enlisting Resources for Transactions" in Microsoft Transaction Server Help.

Resource Dispensers

A resource dispenser is a service that manages nondurable, shared-state data on behalf of the components within a process. Resource dispensers are similar to resource managers, but resource dispensers do not guarantee durability. They are useful for managing shared state data that does not need the overhead of being protected from a system failure. MTS provides two resource dispensers:

◆ ODBC resource dispenser
◆ Shared Property Manager

The MTS SDK provides a toolkit for developing resource dispensers.

ODBC Resource Dispenser

The ODBC resource dispenser manages pools of database connections for MTS components that use the standard ODBC interfaces. The resource dispenser automatically reclaims and reuses database connections. This reduces the memory and network connections that the database connections consume on the MTS server and increases scalability. The ODBC 3.0 Driver Manager is the ODBC resource dispenser. The Driver Manager DLL is installed with MTS.

Shared Property Manager

The Shared Property Manager provides synchronized access to application-defined, process-wide properties (or variables). You can use it for a variety of tasks, such as maintaining a Web page hit counter, caching static data, or providing smart caching to avoid database hotspots. For more information, see "The Shared Property Manager" on page 118 in Chapter 4, "Using MTS Transaction Services."

Microsoft Distributed Transaction Coordinator

Microsoft Distributed Transaction Coordinator (DTC) is a system service that coordinates transactions that span multiple resource managers. Work can be committed as one transaction even if the transaction spans multiple resource managers on separate computers.

The DTC was first released as part of Microsoft SQL Server 6.5 and is included in MTS. The DTC ensures that transactional work is all committed, or none is committed.

Using the MTS Explorer

In this section, you will first learn about the MTS Explorer, which helps you manage COM components that run under MTS. Then, you will learn how to use the MTS Explorer to create packages and add components to packages. Finally, you will see what happens to the registry when components are added to and removed from a package.

MTS Explorer Overview

The MTS Explorer runs as a Microsoft Management Console (MMC) snap-in. It is the administrative tool that you use to manage components and packages. Using the MTS Explorer, you can:

◆ Create a package.

◆ Add and delete components from a package.

◆ Set package properties, such as security, identity, and activation.

◆ Set component class properties, such as transaction and security.

◆ Distribute packages.

◆ Install and maintain packages.

◆ Monitor transactions.

The following illustration shows the MTS Explorer interface.

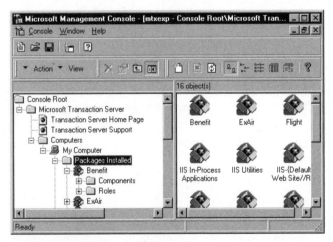

MTS Explorer Views

The MTS Explorer has several views that change the information that is displayed in the right pane of the Explorer window, such as the List and Property views. You can change the view type by clicking the **View** menu.

To display all of the properties for the items in the selected folder, click **Property** on the **View** menu. The following table shows what properties are displayed for each folder type.

Folder	Properties
Computers	Name, Timeout
Packages Installed	Name, Security, Authentication, Shutdown, Run Always, Account, and Package ID, Activation
Components	Prog ID, Transaction, DLL, CLSID, Threading, and Security
Roles	Name, Role ID
Interfaces	Name, InterfaceID, Proxy DLL, TypeLib File
Methods	Name
Role Membership	Name, Role ID

For more information about the properties in Property view, search for "Property View" in Microsoft Transaction Server Help.

To display the status of computers or components, click **Status** on the **View** menu. The following table shows what status properties are displayed for each folder type.

Folder	Properties
Computers	Name, DTC
Components	Prog ID, Objects, Activated, In Call

For more information about the properties in Status view, search for "Status View" in Microsoft Transaction Server Help.

You will next learn how to use the MTS Explorer to create and deploy packages. To learn how to set security for MTS applications by using the MTS Explorer, see "Implementing Security in MTS Applications" on page 223 in Chapter 7, "Implementing Security."

Creating a Package

An MTS application is implemented as a group of COM DLLs. The components in an application must reside in one or more packages.

To summarize, a package is:

◆ A group of components that performs related tasks for an application.

◆ A process that hosts its components.

◆ A trust boundary that enables you to control security for a group of components.

For more information about packages, see "MTS Environment" on page 73 in this chapter.

To see the demonstration "Creating a Package," see the accompanying CD-ROM.

▶ **To create a new package**

1. In the left pane of the MTS Explorer, double-click the computer in which you want to create a new package.

2. Click the Packages Installed folder.

3. On the **Action** menu, click **New**, and then click **Package**.

   – or –

   Right-click the Packages Installed folder, click **New**, and then click **Package**.

4. In the Package Wizard, click **Create an Empty Package**.

   You can click **Install pre-built packages** to add an existing package that is created with the package export function. For more information, see "Exporting a Package" on page 86 in this chapter.

5. Enter a name for the new package, and then click **Next**.

6. In the **Set Package Identity** dialog box, select the appropriate **Account** option. This setting specifies which Windows NT user account the package will use when it runs as a server process. The **Interactive user** option sets the user identity to the user currently logged on to the Windows NT server. To specify a particular user, select the **This user** option and specify a Windows NT server account name and password. For more information, see "Setting Package Identity" on page 231 in Chapter 7, "Implementing Security."

Setting Package Properties

Once you have created a package, you can set package properties, such as how the package is accessed, how security is enabled, and whether the package runs in a server process or the client's process.

 Tip If you need to force package processes to shut down, you can do so by right-clicking **My Computer** and choosing **Shutdown Server Processes**.

To set properties for a package, right-click the package in the MTS Explorer, and then click **Properties**.

The following illustration shows the **Properties** dialog box.

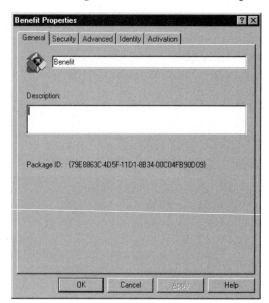

The following table describes some of the package properties and where you can set them.

Tab	Property	Description
General	Name	Displays the name of the package.
	Description	Displays a user-defined description of the package.
Security	Authorization	Enables MTS to check the security credentials of any client that calls the package.
Advanced	Server process shutdown	Determines whether the server process associated with a package always runs, or whether it shuts down after a specified period of time.
	Permission	Allows you to disable deletion or changes on the package to prevent you or someone else from making accidental changes.
Identity	Account	Specifies what Windows NT user account the package uses when it runs as a server process. The default value, **Interactive User**, specifies the user account of the currently logged-on user.
Activation	Package activation type	Determines how components in the package are activated. You can select a package to run in the process of the client that called it (library package), or in a dedicated local process (server package). Selecting **Library Package** allows the package to run faster since it will be run in-process. However, it won't have process isolation, component tracking, and role checking. For this reason, it is recommended that you select **Server Package** for most scenarios.

For more information about package properties, search for "Properties, packages" in Microsoft Transaction Server Help.

Adding Components to a Package

Once you have created a new package, you can add components that implement related business services.

A component can be included only in one package on a single computer. You should keep this in mind when organizing your components into packages. For example, if you have a general-purpose component that will be used by many MTS applications, you should put this component and others like it into a single package. You can then install this package as a unit where needed.

When you add a component to a package, MTS modifies the component's registry entries on the server so it will run in the MTS run-time environment. This ensures that the package's server process can load the component. For more information about component registry entries, see "Registry Keys" on page 58 in Chapter 2, "Building COM DLLs with Visual Basic."

To see the demonstration "Adding a Component to a Package," see the accompanying CD-ROM.

▶ **To add a component to a package**

1. Double-click the Packages Installed folder, and then double-click the package in which you want to install a component.

2. Click the Components folder.

3. On the **Action** menu, click **New**, then select **Component**.

   – or –

   Right-click the Components folder, click **New**, and then select **Component**.

4. Click **Install New Component(s)**.

5. In the **Install Components** dialog box, click **Add Files** to select the component.

6. In the **Select Files to Install** dialog box, select the files you want to add, and then click **Open**.

7. In the **Install Components** dialog box, click **Finish**.

Tip If a component is moved to a new file location, or if its CLSID changes, you must update MTS with the new information. An easy way to ensure that MTS is using the latest information is to select the My Computer icon in the MTS Explorer and then click **Refresh All Components** on the **Action** menu.

Note You can also add components to the Components folder of a package by dragging DLLs that contain the classes you want from the Windows NT Explorer to the package.

Setting Class Properties

Once you have added a component to a package, you can set properties for each class in the component. The properties determine how the class participates in transactions, and whether MTS checks the security credentials of any client that calls the class.

To set the properties of a class, right-click the class in the MTS Explorer, and then click **Properties**.

The following illustration shows the **Class Properties** dialog box.

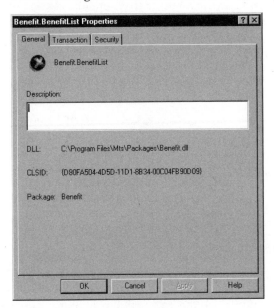

The following table describes the class properties and where you can set them.

Tab	Property	Description
General	Description	Displays general information about the class description, CLSID, and DLL file location.
Transaction	Transaction support	Determines how a class supports transactions.
Security	Authorization	Enables MTS to check the security credentials of any client that calls the class.

Tip You can automate most administrative tasks in MTS by using the MTS Administration Objects. Using a language that supports Automation, such as VBScript or Visual Basic, you can automate the MTS Administration Objects to create packages, add components, set properties, and perform other tasks. For more information about using the MTS Administration Objects, see Microsoft Transaction Server Help.

For more information about class properties, search for "Properties, components" in Microsoft Transaction Server Help.

MTS Components and the Registry

When a component is added to a package in MTS, MTS makes a number of changes to the system registry for each class in the component:

◆ A LocalServer32 key is created.

In the CLSID key for the component class, a new sub key is created called LocalServer32. It contains the path of the MTS executable, Mtx.exe. When the class is activated through COM, this executable will launch in place of the component DLL. This ensures that the MTS executable will host your DLL and that MTS services will be available to your DLL.

◆ A /p parameter is added to the Mtx.exe path.

The /p parameter specifies the identity of the package that contains the class. The MTS executable uses this parameter to determine which package to run when the class is called. (Note that when the package loads and runs inside the MTS executable, it loads all DLLs that are registered in it.)

♦ The InprocServer32 key is modified.

The InprocServer32 key is cleared so that it has an empty value and no longer points to the location of the DLL. This value is no longer necessary since the MTS executable will load the DLL.

For more information about the registry, see "COM DLL Registration" on page 56 in Chapter 2, "Building COM DLLs with Visual Basic."

Microsoft Transaction Server Add-In

Visual Basic reregisters projects when you recompile them in Visual Basic. If those projects are components registered in MTS, recompiling undoes the MTS registry entries for those components. You then have to refresh all components in MTS.

To make working with MTS easier, Visual Basic provides the Microsoft Transaction Server Add-In. When this add-in is enabled, you can recompile projects and it ensures that they remain correctly registered in MTS.

▶ **To enable the Microsoft Transaction Server Add-In**

1. Start Visual Basic.

2. Click **Add-Ins** and then click **Add-In Manager**.

3. Select the **Microsoft Transaction Server Add-In**.

4. Select the **Loaded/Unloaded** and **Load on Startup** check boxes, and then click **OK**.

5. To enable the feature that automatically refreshes MTS after you compile a project, click **Add-Ins**, click **MS Transaction Server**, and then point to **AutoRefresh after compile of active project**.

Deploying an MTS Component

In this section, you will learn how to use the MTS Explorer to export transaction server packages. You will learn how to use the resulting files to install MTS components onto MTS servers in a production environment and configure client computers to use those components.

Exporting a Package

After you have developed and tested your MTS application in a development environment, you will deploy the application to production servers and clients. You can deploy packages so that some packages reside on one computer, while other packages reside on another. In this scenario, both computers must run MTS. The components on one computer can access the components on the other.

A package and its components constitute a single unit of distribution. A package's components cannot be split across computers. However, a package can be duplicated so that copies of the package and its components reside on multiple computers.

For more information about working with multiple MTS computers, search for "Remote computer" in Microsoft Transaction Server Help.

To see the demonstration "Exporting a Package," see the accompanying CD-ROM.

▶ To export a package from a server

1. Double-click the computer that contains the package you want to export, then double-click the Packages Installed folder.

2. Select the package you want to export.

3. On the **Action** menu, click **Export**.

   – or –

   Right-click on the package and select **Export**.

4. In the **Export Package** dialog box, enter the path or browse for the folder where you want to create the package file. Type a name for the file. The component files will be copied to the same folder as the package file.

5. If you want to include any Windows NT user ids that have been mapped to roles for the package, click the **Save Windows NT user ids associated with roles** checkbox.

6. Click **Export**.

MTS creates a package file (with the .pak extension) in the folder you specified, containing information about the components and roles included in the source package, and copies the associated component files to the same directory in which the package file was created. The component files that are copied include the COM DLLs, associated type libraries, and necessary proxy stub DLLs. A Clients folder is created within the Package folder. The Clients folder contains the client application executable used to configure a client computer to access the package components.

Adhere to the following requirements while building and deploying MTS packages:

◆ Re-export a package if GUIDs change.

If any of the GUIDs that are both in the package (including class, interface, or type-library identifiers) and used by clients change, you need to re-export the package and update the client application executable.

Clients are not able to access the package's components until they run the new client application executable. Visual Basic component GUIDs change depending on how version compatibility is set up. For more information about setting version compatibility, see "Version Compatibility" on page 53 in Chapter 2, "Building COM DLLs with Visual Basic."

◆ Set the remote server name.

The generated client application executable always directs clients to the server computer from which the package was exported. If you are exporting the package from a development server for deployment on a production server, manually set the remote server name to the name of the production server. This can be done in the MTS Explorer by selecting the computer icon from which the package is being exported. Then click **Action, Properties,** and on the **Options** tab, type in the remote server name.

Once you have exported a package, you can install it on another server running MTS by using the Package Wizard to import it. Before running the Package Wizard, access the exported files either through the network, or by copying them to that server. For more information about using the Package Wizard, see "Creating a Package" on page 79 in this chapter.

MTS provides scriptable administration objects that you can use to automate deployment of your MTS packages. You can use the scriptable administrative objects to automate administration tasks, such as program configuration and deployment to server and client computers. For information about automating MTS deployment, search for "Deploying, Transaction Server applications" in Microsoft Transaction Server Help.

Configuring a Client to Use MTS Components

When you export a package, MTS creates a client application executable in the Clients folder where the package file is exported. You can run this executable from a client machine to configure it to access the components in the package remotely.

Using the MTS Explorer, you can generate a client application executable that configures a client computer to access a remote package. The client computer must have Distributed Component Object Model (DCOM) support, but does not require any MTS server files other than the client application executable to access a remote MTS server application. (Windows NT clients, version 3.x and greater, have DCOM support. Windows 95 clients must install DCOM support.) To download DCOM for Windows 95, go to the Microsoft COM Web site at http://www.microsoft.com/com/?RLD=59.

▶ **To install a client application executable on a client system**

1. Export the package that is to be used by client computers. For information about exporting packages, see "Exporting a Package" on page 86 in this chapter.

2. Locate the folder into which you exported your package. You will see a Clients subfolder that contains a single executable with the file name specified during package export.

3. Run the executable on the client computer. For example, you can copy the executable and run it on client computers, provide a shared folder for users to copy and run on their computers, or incorporate an executable into an HTML document using the <OBJECT> tag.

Tip If you want to customize the client application executable to install additional files on the client, you can create a clients.ini file that lists additional files to install. If the clients.ini file is present in the same folder where the package is being exported, the export process uses the clients.ini file to add the additional files to the client application executable. For more information about customizing the client application executable, search for "Generating MTS Executables" in Microsoft Transaction Server Help.

The client application executable performs the following steps:

◆ Copies the client application executable to a temporary folder named Clients and extracts the necessary client-side files, including type libraries and custom proxy-stub DLLs.

◆ Transfers type libraries and proxy-stub DLLs for the server package to the Remote Applications folder in the Program Files folder.

All remote applications are stored in the Remote Applications folder. Each remote application has an individual folder named by the package GUID.

Tip Visual Basic components include type-library information in the compiled DLL. Because of this, the entire component is installed on client computers in order to install the type library. You can avoid this by creating a separate .tlb file and adding it to the package.

To create a separate .tlb file

1. On the **Project** menu, choose **Project Properties**.

2. Select the **Component** tab.

3. Select the **Remote Server Files** option and click **OK**.

4. Compile the project.

For more information about type libraries generated by Visual Basic, see "Class Modules and COM" on page 51 in Chapter 2, "Creating COM DLLs with Visual Basic."

◆ Updates the system registry with the required entries for clients to use the server package remotely through DCOM, including information related to application, class, programmatic, interface, and library identifiers.

◆ Registers the application in the Add/Remove Programs option in the Control Panel so that the application can be uninstalled at a later date. All remote applications are prefaced with "Remote Application" so that you can easily find your application in the Add/Remove Programs list of installed components.

◆ Removes the Clients subfolder and files generated during installation.

The components are created remotely on the MTS server when the client uses them.

Note Do not run the client executable file on your server computer. Running the client executable on the server computer removes the registry entries required to run the server package. If you make this mistake, you must remove the application using the Add/Remove Programs option in the Control Panel (remote applications begin with "Remote Application" in the Install/Uninstall list). Then delete and re-install the package using the MTS Explorer.

Lab 3: Adding a Component to MTS

In this lab, you will create a package called Math. You will add the Math component you created in Lab 2 to this package.

To see the demonstration "Lab 3 Solution," see the accompanying CD-ROM.

Estimated time to complete this lab: **20 minutes**

To complete the exercises in this lab, you must have the required software. For detailed information about the labs and setup for the labs, see "Labs" in "About This Course."

Objectives

After completing this lab, you will be able to:

◆ Create a package.

◆ Add classes to a package.

◆ Set properties for Microsoft Transaction Server classes.

Prerequisites

Before working on this lab, you should be familiar with the following:

◆ Creating a COM DLL by using Visual Basic.

Exercises

The following exercises provide practice working with the concepts and techniques covered in this chapter:

◆ Exercise 1: Creating a Package

In this exercise, you will create a new package called Math. You will add the Math DLL you created in Lab 2 to the Math package. Finally, you will set the properties for the **Math.Root** class to require transactions.

Exercise 1: Creating a Package

In this exercise, you will create a new package called Math. You will add the Math DLL you created in Lab 2 to the Math package. Finally, you will set the properties for the **Math.Root** class to require transactions.

▶ **Create the package**

1. Start MTS Explorer, and click the Packages Installed folder.

2. Create a new package. Name the package Math and set the package identity to **Interactive user**.

▶ **Add components to the package**

1. Click the Components folder under the Math package.

2. On the **Action** menu, click **New** and then point to **Component**.

3. In the Component Wizard, click **Install new component(s)**.

4. Add the Math.dll component to the **Files to install** list and click **Finish**.

Note If you have not completed Lab 2, the Math.Root component will not exist. In this case you can drag the Math.dll file from the Labs\Lab03 directory into the **Components** folder of the Math package.

▶ **Set class properties**

1. Right-click the **Math.Root** class and click **Properties**.

2. Set the **Transaction** property to **Requires a transaction** and click **OK**.

3. Use the TestMath.exe client you created in Lab 2 to verify that the **Math.Root** class still works correctly. If you don't have the TestMath.exe client, one is provided in the Labs\Lab03 folder. While the TestMath.exe client is running, you should see the X icon for **Math.Root** spinning in MTS Explorer.

Self-Check Questions

To see the answers to the Self-Check Questions, see Appendix A.

1. One difficulty in developing scalable distributed applications is programming your applications to handle simultaneous calls from multiple clients. How does MTS help you with this problem?

A. MTS provides a single-user concurrency model in which an activity defines the logical flow of work through components. You write components as if a single user will call them.

B. Each component can be written as apartment-threaded or free-threaded. You write free-threaded components and MTS dispatches multiple client calls simultaneously through the components.

C. MTS contains a thread pool that dispatches a new thread for each client that calls. You write synchronization code in the components to handle the possibility of multiple client calls.

D. MTS uses a single thread to process all client calls. Additional client calls are queued until the thread is free to process them. This allows you to write single-user components.

2. Which of the following is a characteristic of MTS packages?

A. MTS packages can contain any type of COM component.

B. MTS components can run outside their MTS package, as long as the Unattended Execution option is set for those components.

C. An MTS package can define a fault isolation boundary so that if a component fails in the package, it does not cause other packages to fail.

D. You must design packages carefully because it is not possible to call a component in one package from another package.

3. What is the effect of setting a package's activation property to Server Package?

A. It runs as a server process and provides security for its components and fault isolation from other packages.

B. It runs as a server process and provides security for its components.

C. It runs in the client's process and provides security for its components and fault isolation from other packages.

D. It runs in a server process and provides fault isolation from other packages.

4. Which of the following statements about the client application executable is false?

A. It extracts necessary type libraries and proxy stub DLLs from the client computer so the remote components can be accessed.

B. It updates the system registry with the required entries for clients to use the server components remotely.

C. It registers the package application in the Add/Remove Programs option in the Control Panel so that the application can be uninstalled at a later date.

D. It copies all of the components in the package over to the client computer so they can be accessed locally.

5. True or False: A resource dispenser is a service that manages nondurable, shared-state data on behalf of the components in a process. A resource manager is a system service that manages durable data.

A. True

B. False

6. Which of the following modifications are made to the registry for each class in a component when it is added to an MTS package?

A. The InprocServer32 key for the component is modified to point to MTX.exe, which runs in place of the component when it is called from a client application.

B. A /p parameter is added to the path of the component listed in the InprocServer32 key, which specifies the identity of the package to run when the component is called.

C. The LocalServer32 key for the component is modified to point to MTX.exe, which runs in place of the component.

D. None of the above.

Student Notes:

Chapter 4:
Using MTS Transaction Services

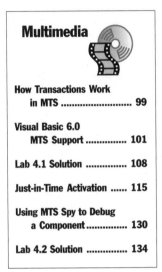

In Chapter 3, you learned how to add a COM DLL to an MTS package. In this chapter, you will learn how to build COM DLLs that take advantage of the transaction services that MTS provides. You will learn about MTS transaction services and how transactions work. You will see how MTS uses context to track information about objects and the role of context in transaction processing.

Then, you will learn about the importance of object state in the MTS programming model and how just-in-time activation changes the way objects behave in the MTS environment. You will also learn when it is appropriate to store object state for an MTS component and the different methods you can use, including the Shared Property Manager. Then, you will learn how to use connection pooling to manage database connections efficiently.

Finally, you will learn how to trap errors that can occur in MTS and how to debug MTS components using Visual Basic.

Objectives

After completing this chapter, you will be able to:

◆ Describe what a transaction is and how it conforms to the ACID properties.

◆ Describe how MTS manages context for objects.

◆ Participate in transactions by calling the **SetComplete, SetAbort, EnableCommit,** or **DisableCommit** methods of the MTS **ObjectContext** object.

◆ Describe four ways to manage state for an MTS object.

◆ Use the Shared Property Manager to store shared state for MTS objects.

◆ Manage database connections efficiently through connection pooling.

◆ Debug an MTS object at run time.

Overview

In this section, you will learn about the role of transactions in MTS. You will also learn how MTS uses context to manage objects and transactions. Finally, you will learn what steps you must take to build MTS components that take advantage of transactions and all of the other services that MTS provides.

Introduction to Transactions

As you learned in the previous chapter, transactions and transaction management are important parts of MTS. A transaction is a collection of changes to data. When a transaction occurs either all of the changes are made (committed) or none of them are made (rolled back). MTS can automatically enlist objects and their associated resources into transactions, and manage those transactions to ensure that changes to data are made correctly.

In the following illustration, three business objects work together to transfer money from one account to another. The **Debit** object debits an account and the **Credit** object credits an account. The **Transfer** object calls the **Debit** and **Credit** objects to transfer money between accounts. Both the **Debit** and the **Credit** objects must complete their work in order for a transaction to succeed. If either object fails to complete its task, the transaction is not successful and any work that was done must be rolled back in order to maintain the integrity of the accounts.

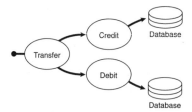

ACID Properties

A transaction changes a set of data from one state to another. For a transaction to work correctly, it must have the following properties, commonly known as the ACID (Atomicity, Consistency, Isolation, and Durability) properties:

◆ Atomicity

Atomicity ensures that all changes from all of the objects involved in the transaction are committed as one unit. Either all changes are committed, or all changes are rolled back to their original state. There is no other possible outcome. For example, if the **Debit** object fails during a transfer of money, the **Credit** object should not be allowed to succeed, since this would cause an incorrect balance in the account. All objects should succeed or fail as one unit.

◆ Consistency

Consistency ensures that durable data matches the state expected by the business rules that modified the data. For example, after the **Transfer** object successfully transfers money from one account to another, the accounts must truly have new balances.

◆ Isolation

Isolation ensures that concurrent transactions are unaware of each other's partial and uncommitted results. Work that is completed by concurrent transactions can be thought of occurring in a serial manner. Otherwise, they might create inconsistencies in the system state.

For example, consider two transfers that happen at the same time. The first transfer debits the account leaving it with an empty balance. The second transfer sees the empty balance, flags the account as having insufficient funds, and then fails gracefully. Meanwhile, the first transfer also fails for other reasons, and rolls back to restore the account to its original balance. When the changes are not isolated from each other, the two transfers resulted in an incorrect flag on the customer's account. Isolation helps ensure that these kinds of unexpected results do not occur.

◆ Durability

Durability ensures that committed updates to managed resources (such as database records) survive communication, process, and server system failures. Transactional logging enables you to recover the durable state after failures.

All of these properties ensure that a transaction does not create problematic changes to data between the time the transaction begins and the time the transaction must commit. Also, these properties make cleanup and error handling much easier when updating databases and other resources.

Two-Phase Commit

When transactions are processed on more than one server, a two-phase commit ensures that the transactions are processed and completed on all of the servers or on none of the servers.

There are two phases to this process: prepare and commit. You can use the analogy of a business contract to illustrate the two-phase commit process.

In the prepare phase, each party involved in the contract commits by reading and agreeing to sign the contract. In the commit phase, each party signs the contract.

The contract is not official until both parties have made a commitment. If one party does not commit, the contract is invalid.

MTS coordinates and supports the two-phase commit process, making sure that all objects of the transaction can commit and that the transaction commits correctly.

The Context Object

When an object is created, by the client or by another object, it must be aware of the context in which it is being used. The object may need to ensure that certain security requirements are met, or that it is running inside a transaction. It also needs a way to participate in transactions spanning multiple objects. This is contextual information that every object needs.

MTS provides context by creating an associated context object for each MTS object instance. The context object provides information about the object's execution environment, such as the identity of the object's creator, and if the object is in a transaction. The context object also holds security credentials for the object that can be checked when it creates other MTS objects. Furthermore, the context object collaborates with other context objects in the same transaction to either commit or abort the transaction. The context object makes programming your objects simpler because you don't have to manage this information yourself.

Context and Transactions

When multiple objects participate in the same transaction, MTS uses the associated context objects to track the transaction. If an object completes its work in the transaction successfully, it indicates to its context object that it is complete. If an object fails to complete its work successfully, it indicates to its context object that it has to abort the transaction. When all the objects in the transaction are finished running, MTS uses the information recorded in each context object to determine whether or not the transaction should commit. If all objects reported successful completion, then MTS commits the transaction. If one or more objects reported an abort, then MTS rolls back the transaction, undoing all changes made by all objects involved in the transaction.

To see the animation "How Transactions Work in MTS," see the accompanying CD-ROM.

Transaction Attribute

The transaction attribute for a class determines how an object of that class participates in transactions when it is created. To set the transaction attribute of a class, right-click the class name in the MTS Explorer, click **Properties**, and then click the **Transaction** tab. For more information about setting class properties, see "Adding Components to a Package" on page 82 in Chapter 3, "Introduction to Microsoft Transaction Server (MTS)."

The following table lists and describes the transaction attributes.

Transaction attribute	Description
Requires a transaction	This object must have a transaction. It enlists in the calling object's transaction or, if the caller does not have a transaction, it creates a new one.
Requires a new transaction	This object must have a new transaction created for it that is separate from any other transactions.
Supports transactions	If the calling object has a transaction, this object participates in it. If not, no transaction is created.
Does not support transactions	This object does not create a transaction.

Developing Components for MTS

In the previous chapter, you learned how to add a COM DLL to an MTS package. However, simply adding existing components to MTS does not make them scalable, or transaction aware. Components must be carefully designed and programmed for the MTS environment.

Guidelines for Developing MTS Components

To use transactions and to work most efficiently in MTS, you must follow four rules:

◆ Obtain a reference to the **ObjectContext** object.

Context information for an object is stored in the **ObjectContext** object. The **ObjectContext** object tracks the work done by the MTS object as well as its security information. Objects can get a reference to their context object by calling the **GetObjectContext** function, which is provided by MTS. MTS objects can use the context object to report whether or not they were able to complete their work successfully, or to obtain transactional or security information.

◆ Call **SetComplete**, if work succeeds.

When an object completes its work successfully while participating in a transaction, it must call the **SetComplete** method on the **ObjectContext** object. This notifies MTS that the work performed by the object can be committed when all objects involved in the transaction finish their work. Calling **SetComplete** also notifies MTS that any resources held by the object, including the object itself, can be recycled.

◆ Call **SetAbort**, if work fails.

When an object fails to complete its work while participating in a transaction, it must call the **SetAbort** method on the **ObjectContext** object. This notifies MTS that all changes made by this object and other objects in the same transaction must be rolled back. Calling **SetAbort** also notifies MTS that any resources held by the object, including the object itself, can be recycled.

◆ Manage state carefully.

State is object data that is kept over more than one method call to the object. Local or global variables are ways to keep object state. When participating in transactions, you should not store state in this manner. MTS recycles the object when the transaction completes in order to free resources, which causes any information in local and global variables to be lost. For more information about when and how to store state, see "Managing Object State" on page 113 in this chapter.

The rest of this chapter explains in detail how to write and debug efficient MTS components that take full advantage of the transaction services provided by MTS.

Visual Basic 6.0 Support for MTS Component Development

Visual Basic 6.0 provides a number of built-in features and add-ins that help make MTS component development easier:

◆ Microsoft Transaction Server Add-In

To make working with MTS easier, Visual Basic provides the Microsoft Transaction Server Add-In. When this add-in is enabled, you can recompile projects and the add-in ensures that they remain correctly registered in MTS. For more information, see "MTS Components and the Registry" on page 84 in Chapter 3, "Introduction to Microsoft Transaction Server (MTS)."

◆ **MTSTransactionMode** property

To make it easier to set the transaction attribute for a class, Visual Basic 6.0 provides a property named **MTSTransactionMode** on each class module you create. You can set this to any of the four values listed in the previous transaction attribute table. When you compile the project, Visual Basic stores this property in the type library for the component. When the component is added to an MTS package, MTS reads the **MTSTransactionMode** property value and automatically sets the transaction attribute to that value. This helps simplify the administration of Visual Basic components.

◆ MTS component debugging

Visual Basic 6.0 supports debugging MTS components within the Visual Basic IDE. This allows you to take advantage of the Visual Basic debugging environment for setting breakpoints and watches. For more information, see "Debugging a Component" on page 128 in this chapter.

To see the expert point-of-view "Visual Basic 6.0 MTS Support," see the accompanying CD-ROM.

Building MTS Components

In this section, you will learn how to build MTS components that participate in transactions. First, you will learn how to get a reference to an **ObjectContext** object, which enables you to obtain information about your object and control how MTS processes the transaction. Then, you will learn how to enlist other objects in your transaction by calling the **CreateInstance** method. You will also learn how to use the **SetAbort, SetComplete, EnableCommit,** and **DisableCommit** methods of the **ObjectContext** object to notify MTS of the completion status of your object's work. Finally, you will learn how to determine the outcome of a transaction that involves multiple objects.

Getting a Context Object

To get a reference to a context object, call **GetObjectContext**. This function returns a reference to the **ObjectContext** instance for your object.

To call the **GetObjectContext** function in Visual Basic, you must first set a reference to Microsoft Transaction Server Type Library (mtxas.dll) by clicking **References** on the **Project** menu.

The following example code calls **GetObjectContext** to return an **ObjectContext** object:

```
Dim ctxObject As ObjectContext
Set ctxObject = GetObjectContext()
```

The following example code shows how you can use **GetObjectContext** to call methods on the **ObjectContext** object without maintaining a separate object variable:

```
GetObjectContext.SetComplete
```

You can use the **ObjectContext** object in your code to:

◆ Declare that the object's work is complete.

◆ Prevent a transaction from being committed, either temporarily or permanently.

◆ Instantiate other MTS objects and include their work within the scope of your object's transaction.

◆ Find out if a caller is in a particular role.

◆ Find out if security is enabled.

◆ Find out if the object is executing within a transaction.

◆ Retrieve Microsoft Internet Information Server (IIS) built-in objects.

For information about all **ObjectContext** methods, search for "ObjectContext" in Microsoft Transaction Server Help.

Calling CreateInstance

An object often creates and uses other objects to complete its work. If the new object must participate in the same transaction, it must inherit its context from the creating object. Use the **CreateInstance** method on the **ObjectContext** object to create a new MTS object and pass context information to that new object.

CreateInstance Method

To create a new object and enlist it in the existing transaction, call the **CreateInstance** method of the **ObjectContext** object. Also, the object being created must have its transaction attribute set to **Requires a transaction** or **Supports transactions**. Any other transaction attribute does not include the object in the existing transaction.

When **CreateInstance** is called, it creates the new object. If the object is an MTS object, a new context object is created for it since all MTS objects always have an associated context object. Then, the context object inherits information such as the current activity, security information, and current transaction. At this point, the new object participates in the same transaction as the calling object.

If **CreateInstance** is used to create a non-MTS object, the object is created, but it does not have a context object, nor does it participate in the existing transaction.

The **CreateInstance** method takes one parameter: the progID of the object being created. It uses the following syntax:

objectContext.*CreateInstance* progID

The following example code creates a new **Account** object that credits a checking account with $500:

```
Set objCheckAccount = _
  GetObjectContext.CreateInstance("Checking.Account")
objCheckAccount.Credit 500
```

In this example code, if the code that creates the **Account** object later aborts the transaction, the $500 credit by the **Account** object rolls back because it was created as part of the same transaction.

CreateInstance versus CreateObject and New

You have seen three different ways to create and use objects in Visual Basic. You can:

◆ Call **CreateObject**.

◆ Use the **New** keyword.

◆ Call the **CreateInstance** method of the **ObjectContext** object.

Each of these has implications in terms of how objects are created and used in the MTS environment.

The **New** keyword offers a slight performance increase over **CreateObject,** and is therefore the fastest way to create objects. However, if the object being created is in the same project from which **New** is being called, the object is created internally in Visual Basic, instead of using COM services to create it. If the object being created is an MTS object, this has undesirable results. MTS hosts objects by intercepting creation calls through COM. If COM is not used to create an object, MTS is not able to host the object. Therefore, use **CreateObject** to create objects that are MTS objects in the same Visual Basic project from which they are being created.

Both **New** and **CreateObject** create an MTS object, but that object does not inherit its context from the caller. Therefore, it cannot participate in the existing transaction, even if its transaction attribute is set to **Requires a transaction** or **Supports transactions.** Also, it is not part of the same activity, and it does not have access to security information, such as who the original caller or creator is.

If **CreateInstance** is used to create an MTS object, then that object can participate in the existing transaction and it inherits its context from the caller. This includes the current activity, security information, and current transaction.

Calling SetComplete and SetAbort

Once you have a reference to the context object for your object, use the **SetComplete** and **SetAbort** methods to notify MTS of the completion status of the work performed by your object.

SetComplete Method

In general, each method on your MTS object should indicate whether it has completed work successfully or unsuccessfully. If the method has completed successfully, it calls the **SetComplete** method on the **ObjectContext** object before returning from the method call.

The **SetComplete** method informs the context object that it can commit transaction updates and can release the state of the object along with any resources that are being held. If all other objects involved in the transaction also call **SetComplete,** MTS commits the transaction updates of all objects.

SetAbort Method

If an MTS object's method that completes a transaction is unsuccessful, it must call the **SetAbort** method of the **ObjectContext** object before returning. **SetAbort** informs the context object that the transaction updates of this object and all other objects in the transaction must be rolled back to their original state. If an object involved in a transaction calls **SetAbort**, the updates roll back even if other objects have called the **SetComplete** method.

The following sample code calls **SetAbort** and **SetComplete**. To copy this code for use in your own project, see "Calling SetAbort and SetComplete" on the accompanying CD-ROM.

```
Public Sub Credit (ByVal lngAccount, ByVal lngAmount)

Dim strSQL as String
Dim conn as ADODB.Connection

On Error GoTo ErrorHandler

' Create SQL UPDATE statement.
strSQL = "UPDATE accounts SET amount = amount + " & _
         lngAmount & "WHERE account = " & lngAccount

' Open the connection object and execute the SQL command.
Set conn = New ADODB.connection
conn.Open "FILEDSN=" & gFileDSN
conn.Execute strSQL

' Allow MTS transaction set to proceed.
GetObjectContext.SetComplete
Exit Sub

ErrorHandler:

' Abort transaction and report error to caller
GetObjectContext.SetAbort
Err.Raise Err.Number, "Credit Module", Err.Description
End Sub
```

The sample code credits an account in the database with the amount passed by the lgnAmount parameter and calls **SetComplete** to indicate it has completed work successfully. If a failure occurs, the error handler traps the error and calls **SetAbort** to indicate that it has failed:

The previous sample code uses ActiveX Data Objects (ADO) with an SQL string to update the database. For more information about ADO and SQL, see Chapter 5, "Accessing Data from the Middle Tier" on page 141.

Calling EnableCommit and DisableCommit

The context object has **EnableCommit** and **DisableCommit** methods to enable an object to remain active in a transaction while performing work over multiple method calls. This is useful in cases where an object requires several method calls to it before its work is finished in the transaction.

For example, a furniture company has an **Orders** object that creates orders to ship furniture to customers. A customer can create an order over the Internet and request that the items be sent to a specific address. Or the customer can request to pick up the items at one of the company's stores. An IIS ASP file creates the order by calling a **CreateNewOrder** method on the **Orders** object. The **Orders** object calls **DisableCommit** since it does not yet know where to send the order. Then the ASP file either calls **ShipToAddress** (passing the address), or **SendToStore** (passing the store location), to tell the **Orders** object where to send the furniture. Each of these methods calls **SetComplete**.

EnableCommit Method

EnableCommit declares that an object's work is not necessarily finished, but that its transaction updates are consistent and could be committed in their present form. The object maintains its internal state across calls from the client until it calls **SetComplete** or **SetAbort,** or until the transaction ends. **EnableCommit** is the default for an object if it does not call any other context object methods.

EnableCommit takes no parameters. The following code example shows how to call the **EnableCommit** method:

```
GetObjectContext.EnableCommit
```

DisableCommit Method

DisableCommit declares that an object's work is not finished, and that its transaction updates are inconsistent and cannot be committed in their present form. The object maintains its internal state across calls from the client until it calls **SetComplete,** or **SetAbort,** or until the transaction ends.

DisableCommit takes no parameters. The following code example shows how to call the **DisableCommit** method:

```
GetObjectContext.DisableCommit
```

Determining Transaction Outcome

Since there are typically many MTS objects involved in a transaction, MTS must eventually determine when the transaction ends. Also, MTS must determine the transaction outcome. If all objects in the transaction called **SetComplete,** MTS commits the transaction. If any object called **SetAbort** or **DisableCommit,** MTS aborts the transaction.

Transaction Lifetime

A transaction begins when a client calls an MTS object with its transaction attribute set to **Requires a transaction** or **Requires a new transaction.** This object is considered the root of the transaction because it was the first object created in the transaction. When the transaction ends, MTS determines the outcome of the transaction and either commits or aborts the transaction.

There are three ways a transaction can end:

◆ Root object calls **SetComplete** or **SetAbort.**

◆ Transaction times out.

◆ Client releases root object.

The root object can end a transaction by calling either **SetComplete** or **SetAbort.** This is the only object that can end a transaction this way. Any other objects that are created as part of the same transaction have no effect on the transaction lifetime, even if they call **SetComplete** or **SetAbort.**

If the root object calls **EnableCommit** or **DisableCommit,** then the transaction does not end. In this way, a root object can keep a transaction alive until it acquires the information it needs from the client to end the transaction.

A transaction also ends if it times out. The default timeout for a transaction is 60 seconds. To change the timeout value, right-click the computer icon in the MTS

Explorer and then click **Properties**. Set the **Transaction Timeout** property on the **Options** tab.

Finally, a transaction ends if the client releases the root object. This happens if the root object calls **EnableCommit** or **DisableCommit** and returns to the client. Then the client releases the object.

Transaction Outcome

When a transaction ends, MTS must determine the transaction outcome, and if the transaction should commit or abort. Determining transaction outcome is analogous to group decision-making in which the group must reach a unanimous decision. If any member of the group dissents, the decision cannot be reached.

Similarly, each object in a transaction has a vote. It casts its vote by calling **SetComplete, SetAbort, EnableCommit**, or **DisableCommit**. MTS tallies each object's vote and determines the outcome. If all objects called **SetComplete** or **EnableCommit**, the transaction commits. If any object called **SetAbort** or **DisableCommit**, the transaction aborts.

Note If an object does not call **SetComplete, SetAbort, EnableCommit**, or **DisableCommit**, MTS treats the object as if it called **EnableCommit**. **EnableCommit** is the default status for an object unless it specifies otherwise.

Lab 4.1: Creating an MTS Component

In this lab, you will implement the bus_AdC component. This component contains one class called **Ad**. You will open an existing Visual Basic project in which all methods have been implemented except for **GetByID**.

Then, you will implement the **GetByID** method. **GetByID** is passed an ad ID. It uses the ad ID to retrieve an ad from the Classifieds database. Then it returns the ad to the caller.

You will use the **CreateInstance** method of the **ObjectContext** object to create Island Hopper News objects to help retrieve the ad. Also, you will call **SetComplete** if the ad is retrieved successfully, and **SetAbort** if **GetByID** fails.

To see the demonstration "Lab 4.1 Solution," see the accompanying CD-ROM.

Estimated time to complete this lab: **60 minutes**

To complete the exercises in this lab, you must have the required software. For detailed information about the labs and setup for the labs, see "Labs" in the "About This Course."

Objectives

After completing this lab, you will be able to:

◆ Use the **CreateInstance** method of the **ObjectContext** object to create objects as part of the same transaction.

◆ Use the **SetComplete** and **SetAbort** methods of the **ObjectContext** object to participate in transactions.

Prerequisites

Before working on this lab, you should be familiar with the following:

◆ Adding and deleting components in MTS packages.

◆ Creating a COM DLL by using Microsoft Visual Basic.

Exercises

The following exercises provide practice working with the concepts and techniques covered in this chapter:

◆ Exercise 1: Implementing the Bus_AdC Component

In this exercise, you will implement the **GetByID** method of the **bus_AdC.Ad** class. This method uses an instance of the **db_AdC.Ad** class to locate and retrieve an ad from the Island Hopper News database. You will locate the ad using the advertisement ID that is passed to the **GetByID** method from the client.

You do not need to write code to access the database because you will create the **db_AdC.Ad** object using the context object **CreateInstance** method. The **db_AdC.Ad** object encapsulates the database code to retrieve the ad. If the ad is retrieved successfully, you will call **SetComplete**, and if the method fails, you will call **SetAbort**.

◆ Exercise 2: Testing the Bus_AdC Component

In this exercise, you will test the bus_AdC component and the **GetByID** method that you implemented in Exercise 1. First you will add the bus_AdC.dll to the

IsleHop_Classifieds package. Then you will create a test client and test the bus_AdC component by retrieving ads.

Exercise 1: Implementing the Bus_AdC Component

In this exercise, you will implement the **GetByID** method of the **bus_AdC.Ad** class. This method uses an instance of the **db_AdC.Ad** class to locate and retrieve an ad from the Island Hopper News database. You will locate the ad using the advertisement ID that is passed to the **GetByID** method from the client.

You do not need to write code to access the database, because you will create the **db_AdC.Ad** object using the **CreateInstance** method. The **db_AdC.Ad** object encapsulates the database code to retrieve the ad. If the ad is retrieved successfully, you will call **SetComplete**, and if the method fails, you will call **SetAbort**.

▶ **Implement the GetByID method**

1. Start Visual Basic and open the Bus_AdC project located in the \Labs\Lab04.1 folder.

2. Set the **MTSTransactionMode** property for the **Ad** class module to **2 - RequiresTransaction**.

3. Find the **GetByID** method, and declare two variables at the beginning of the method. Declare **objAd** of type **db_AdC.Ad**, and declare **rs** of type **ADODB.Recordset**. **ObjAd** will reference the **db_AdC** object, and **rs** will hold a returned recordset.

4. Enter the following code to turn on error handling:

```
On Error GoTo ErrorHandler
```

5. Create an **If** block to check if **lngAdvertisementID** is greater than or equal to zero. If it is, then the advertisement ID is valid and the **If** block should run. The following steps are entered inside the **If** block:

   a. Use the **CreateInstance** method of the **ObjectContext** object to create an instance of **db_AdC.Ad** and assign it to **objAd**.

   b. Call **objAd.GetByID** and pass **lngAdvertisementID** as the parameter. Assign the returned recordset to **rs**.

6. Call **SetComplete**.

7. Assign **rs** to **GetByID** to return the recordset back to the client.

To see an example of how your code should look, see Lab Hint 4.1 in Appendix B.

▶ **Implement the GetByID error handler**

1. Create the error handler at the end of the **GetByID** method.

2. Call **Exit Function** before the error handler so the handler does not run by mistake.

3. In the error handler, call **SetAbort**.

4. Raise the error to the caller by using the following code:

```
Err.Raise Err.Number, SetErrSource(modName, "GetByID"),
Err.Description
```

5. Build Bus_AdC.dll.

Exercise 2: Testing the Bus_AdC Component

In this exercise, you will test the bus_AdC component and the **GetByID** method that you implemented in Exercise 1. First you will add bus_AdC.dll to the IsleHop_Classifieds package. Then you will create a test client and test the bus_AdC component by retrieving ads.

▶ **Register bus_AdC.dll with MTS**

1. Start the MTS Explorer and remove the current bus_AdC.dll by deleting it from the **IsleHop_Classifieds** package.

2. Add the bus_AdC.dll you just created to the **IsleHop_Classifieds** package and set its transaction attribute to **Requires a transaction**. For more information on adding components, see "Adding Components to a Package" on page 82 in Chapter 3, "Introduction to Microsoft Transaction Server (MTS)."

▶ **Test with a custom client**

1. Start Visual Basic and create a new Standard EXE project.

2. Place controls on the form and set their properties as follows.

Control	Property	Value
Command button	Caption	Retrieve Ad
	Name	cmdRetrieve
Text box	Text	None
	Name	txtAdID
Label	Caption	Advertisement ID:

This illustration shows how your form should look.

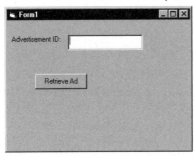

3. On the **Project** menu, click **References** and add a reference to the bus_AdC project. Also add a reference to the Microsoft ActiveX Data Objects 2.0 Library.

4. Save the new project and form as the files AdTest.vbp and AdTest.frm.

5. In the **cmdRetrieve_Click** event, turn on error handling by using the following code:

```
On Error GoTo ErrorHandler
```

6. Declare two variables. Declare **objAd** of type **bus_AdC.Ad**, and **rs** of type **ADODB.Recordset**.

7. Set **objAd** equal to a new instance of **bus_AdC.Ad**.

8. Call the **GetByID** method on **objAd**, passing txtAdID as the parameter. Set **rs** equal to the return value.

9. Use the following code to display the title of the returned **Ad**:

```
MsgBox rs(1)
```

10. In the error handler, display a message box indicating that an error occurred.

    To see an example of how your code should look, see Lab Hint 4.2 in Appendix B.

11. Save the form as AdTest.frm and the project as AdTest.vbp. Run the project and test the **GetByID** method by typing the advertisement IDs (such as 5201) and clicking **Retrieve Ad**. You can monitor the transaction outcome in the Transaction Statistics window in the MTS Explorer. Valid advertisement IDs will cause commits. Invalid advertisement IDs will cause aborts.

▶ **Test with the Island Hopper Visual Basic client (optional)**

1. Start the Island Hopper News Visual Basic client application.

2. Go to the Ad Maintenance section and retrieve any customer (such as 11901) that has placed ads.

3. Double click an ad to display the **Ad Details** form. The Visual Basic code that displays this form calls the **GetByID** method. Also, the **Previous** and **Next** buttons call the **GetByID** method.

   Each time you successfully bring up an ad in the **Ad Details** form, the transaction statistics in the MTS Explorer will show an increase in the number of committed transactions.

Managing Object State

In this section, you will learn about the importance of object state in the MTS programming model and how just-in-time activation changes the way objects behave in the MTS environment. You will also learn when it is appropriate to store object state for an MTS component and the different methods you can use. Finally, you will learn how to use the Shared Property Manager, a resource dispenser that runs in the MTS environment.

Just-in-Time Activation

One of the most important design considerations in developing MTS components is how to manage state. State management directly impacts the scalability of your MTS components. Also, MTS components must manage state differently than traditional COM components.

State and Scalability

State is object data that is kept over more than one method call to the object. State can be stored in any of the three tiers: the client, MTS objects, or the database. This course examines specifically how state is managed in the middle tier, in MTS objects, and how that impacts MTS and the design of your objects.

State stored in MTS objects is also called local state. Properties are a good example of state. An object can have properties that store a customer's name, address, and phone number. It can also have methods that use the values of these properties. One method adds the customer information to a database, and later, another method credits the customer's account. The object exists and keeps that customer information until the client releases it. An object that maintains state internally over multiple method calls like this is called a stateful object.

However, if the object doesn't expose properties, and instead the customer's name, address, and phone number are passed each time a method call is made, it is a stateless object. Stateless objects do not remember anything from previous method calls.

It is common programming practice in a single-user environment to think of an object as being active as long as you need it. Method calls are simple because the object remembers information from one call to the next. However, stateful objects can impact the scalability of an application. State can consume server resources such as memory, disk space, and database connections. And because state is often client specific, it holds the resources until the client releases the object. The decision to hold resources (either locally in a stateful object or not) has to be balanced against other application requirements.

In general, try to avoid maintaining state that consumes scarce or expensive resources. For example, storing database connections consumes scarce resources. This can reduce your scalability since there are a limited number of database connections that can be allocated, and used connections cannot be pooled.

However, other kinds of state can increase your scalability. For example, storing customer information, such as name and address, consumes relatively little memory but reduces the amount of data being passed over the network on each method call to the object.

Even following these guidelines, there are exceptions. Ultimately, extensive analysis is required to determine if a solution is scalable under normal use of the application.

State and Just-in-Time Activation

Just-in-time activation helps reduce consumption of system resources by recycling objects when they are finished with their work. It also helps ensure the isolation of transactions, so that information from one transaction is not carried into the next transaction.

When a client calls a method on an object, MTS activates the object by creating it and allowing the method call to go through to the object. When the object is finished and it calls **SetComplete** or **SetAbort,** and it returns from the method call, MTS deactivates the object to free its resources for use by other objects. Later, when the client calls another method, the object is activated again.

MTS deactivates an object by releasing all references to it, which effectively destroys the object. Because the object is destroyed, it loses all of its local state, such as local variables, and properties. However, MTS manages the client pointer so that it remains valid. When the client calls a method on the deactivated object, MTS activates it by recreating it and allowing the method call to go through. MTS manages the client's pointer to the object in such a way that the client is unaware that the object has been destroyed and recreated. However, the object's local state is reset, and it does not remember anything from the previous activation.

An object is not deactivated when it calls **EnableCommit** or **DisableCommit,** or neglects to call any context object methods. Also, an object is not deactivated when the transaction ends, for example, if the transaction times out. An object is only deactivated when it calls **SetComplete** or **SetAbort** and returns from the method call.

Just-in-time activation has a substantial effect on object state. When an object calls **SetComplete** or **SetAbort,** it loses its local state as soon as the method returns. Therefore, objects that participate in transactions must be stateless. They cannot maintain any instance data since it is lost when they are deactivated. However, this does not mean that you must design your application towards a stateless programming model. You can store and maintain state outside the object. Recommended ways to store state are discussed in the next topic.

To see the expert point-of-view "Just-in-Time Activation," see the accompanying CD-ROM.

For more information about just-in-time activation, see "Calling SetComplete and SetAbort" on page 104 in this chapter and "Overview of MTS" on page 70 in Chapter 3, "Introduction to Microsoft Transaction Server (MTS)."

Initialize and Terminate Event Limitations

Components built with Visual Basic have **Initialize** and **Terminate** events that you can use to implement startup and shutdown code for each class. However, the context object is not available in the **Initialize** and **Terminate** events. For example, if you need to read security credentials in the **Initialize** event, you cannot get that information. Also, because of just-in-time activation, the **Initialize** and **Terminate** events get called many times during a user session even though the client is not releasing its pointer to the object. This can be confusing to programmers who implement these events.

To utilize the context object during initialization or shutdown, implement the **IObjectControl** interface in your class. **IObjectControl** has three methods: **Activate**, **Deactivate**, and **CanBePooled**. MTS calls the **Activate** and **Deactivate** methods when your object is activated and deactivated respectively. You can add startup and shutdown code to these methods to handle activation and deactivation more appropriately, plus you have access to the context object within these methods.

Note If you implement the **IObjectControl** interface, you must also implement the **CanBePooled** method. Since object pooling is not currently supported in MTS, the easiest way to implement this method is to return **True**.

For more information about the **Initialize** and **Terminate** events, see "Using the Initialize and Terminate Events" on page 44 in Chapter 2, "Building COM DLLs with Visual Basic."

For more information about implementing interfaces, see "Interfaces" on page 258 in Chapter 8, "Implementing COM with Visual Basic."

Storing Object State

Just-in-time activation forces objects to be stateless. That is, if your object calls **SetComplete** or **SetAbort**, it must not keep local state in variables inside the object. However, there is a practical side to component development that must be examined.

There are times when you need to store state for MTS objects. For example, an application may need to determine a city name based on a given postal code. It can look this information up in a database, but repeatedly using a database to do lookups on this type of static data can be inefficient. It may be more efficient to store this information in an object for quick lookup.

There are a number of locations to store state. It can be stored in the client. This is useful for tasks in which a variety of information must be gathered from the user. For example, a virtual shopping basket must store items until the user decides to place an order. If a client stores the items on the client side, server resources are conserved while multiple users are shopping.

State can also be stored in a database if your state needs the protection of transactions and is likely to be accessed by other applications.

Storing State for MTS Objects

Storing state for the middle tier is more involved. This is because an object instance is only active until its transaction completes. When the object is activated again, it does not have any instance data from its previous transaction.

Instance Data

Within a transaction, it is possible to store instance data. An object does not have to call **SetComplete** or **SetAbort** when it returns from a method call. More complicated transactions may require several calls from the client, each performing part of the work, until the last method calls **SetComplete** or **SetAbort**. In these circumstances, state can be maintained as instance data in local variables over each call. When the final method calls **SetComplete** or **SetAbort**, the object is finally deactivated, releasing the instance data.

File

You can also store state in a file. Files can be located on the same computer as the objects that use them to avoid network trips. Files can also protect from concurrent access and keep state across multiple transactions. However, files do not offer record-level locking; only the entire file can be locked. Therefore, they are not useful for storing state shared with many objects because any one object can effectively lock out all other objects.

Windows NT Service

If you need faster access to state, you can store it in a Windows NT service. You can create a Windows NT service that exposes a COM object to store and retrieve data. Any object accessing state would do so through the COM object. The advantage is that the state is available to all packages on the same computer, and it is relatively fast. The disadvantage is that you must write the service and implement locking mechanisms if multiple objects can access the state.

Shared Property Manager

The Shared Property Manager (SPM) is an MTS resource dispenser that comes with MTS. It enables you to store properties programmatically and share that data with all objects in the same package. The SPM is fast because access to its properties is in the same process as the package, and it provides locking mechanisms to guard against concurrent access.

The SPM is probably the best solution for the example of the postal code lookup table. The table could be initially loaded from the database and stored in the SPM. Then all future lookups from all objects in the same package would do the lookups in the SPM. The SPM is discussed in more detail in the next topic.

The Shared Property Manager

The SPM enables you to create properties programmatically that are available to all objects in the same server process. Objects that have access to the properties must be contained within the same package. The value of the property can be any data type that can be represented by a variant.

The SPM is an object hierarchy containing three objects, as described in the following table.

Object	Use this object to:
SharedPropertyGroupManager	Create shared property groups and obtain access to existing shared property groups.
SharedPropertyGroup	Create and access the shared properties in a shared property group.
SharedProperty	Set or retrieve the value of a shared property.

You use the objects provided by the SPM to organize and access data that is shared between objects and object instances within the same server process.

Shared properties are organized by groups within the process. For example, the Island Hopper Web site can generate more interest among end users by maintaining a count of how many ads have been placed. When end users enter the Web site, the Web page returned to them has the current count of how many ads have been placed that day. As new ads are placed, the bus_AdC.Ad component increments the ad count. Another component retrieves the current count when Web pages are requested.

The following illustration shows how the current ad count can be stored in a property named **AdCount** in a property group named **AdStatistics**.

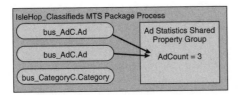

Creating a Shared Property Group

To create a shared property group like **AdStatistics**, use the **SharedPropertyGroupManager** object. To use the **SharedPropertyGroupManager** object in Visual Basic, you must first set a reference to the Shared Property Manager Type Library (mtxspm.dll). Once this reference has been set, you can create the object using the **CreateObject** function, as shown in the following example code:

```
Dim spmMgr As SharedPropertyGroupManager
Set spmMgr = New SharedPropertyGroupManager
```

Alternately, you can use the **CreateInstance** method of the **ObjectContext**. (It makes no difference which method you use.) MTS ensures that only one instance of the **SharedPropertyGroupManager** object exists per server process. If the **Shared PropertyGroupManager** object already exists, MTS creates a reference to the existing instance.

The **SharedPropertyGroupManager** object provides the following methods.

Method	Description
CreatePropertyGroup	Creates a new **SharedPropertyGroup** with a string name as an identifier. If a group with the specified name already exists, **CreatePropertyGroup** returns a reference to the existing group.
Group	Returns a reference to an existing shared property group, given a string name by which it can be identified.

Use the **CreatePropertyGroup** method to create a shared property group. It accepts four parameters: the name of the new property group, the isolation mode, the release mode, and an out parameter that returns whether or not the group already exists.

The name parameter defines the name of the shared property group. Other objects can call the **Group** method and pass this name to get a reference to the shared property group.

The isolation-mode parameter controls how locking works for the group. Because the properties in the group are shared, multiple objects can access and update properties at the same time. The SPM provides locking to protect against simultaneous access to shared properties. There are two values you can specify for locking as shown in the following table.

Constant	Value	Description
LockSetGet	0	Default. Locks a property during a Value call, assuring that every get or set operation on a shared property is atomic. This ensures that two clients can't read or write to the same property at the same time, but it doesn't prevent other clients from concurrently accessing other properties in the same group.
LockMethod	1	Locks all of the properties in the shared property group for exclusive use by the caller as long as the caller's current method is executing. This is the appropriate mode to use when there are interdependencies among properties, or in cases where a client may have to update a property immediately after reading it before it can be accessed again.

The release-mode parameter controls how the shared property group is deleted. There are two values you can specify for release as shown in the table below.

Constant	Value	Description
Standard	0	When all MTS objects have released their references on the property group, the property group is automatically destroyed.
Process	1	The property group isn't destroyed until the process in which it was created has terminated. You must still release all **SharedPropertyGroup** objects by setting them to **Nothing**.

The last parameter is a Boolean value that returns whether or not the group already exists. If it does exist, **CreatePropertyGroup** returns a reference to the existing group.

The following example code uses the **CreatePropertyGroup** method to create a new property group called **AdStatistics**:

```
Dim spmGroup As SharedPropertyGroup
Dim bExists As Boolean
Set spmGroup = _
  spmMgr.CreatePropertyGroup("AdStatistics", _
  LockMethod, Process, bExists)
```

Property groups must be created and initialized. The best time to do this is when the server creates the process. However, there is no way for the MTS objects in a process to detect process creation. Therefore, the first MTS object to access the property group must be the one to initialize it. If several MTS objects can potentially access the property group first, they must each be prepared to initialize it. Use the last parameter of **CreatePropertyGroup** to determine if the properties must be initialized. If it returns **False**, then you must create and initialize the properties.

Creating a Shared Property

Once you have created a new shared property group, you can use it to create a new property that is identified by either a numeric value or a string expression.

The **SharedPropertyGroup** object has the following methods and properties.

Method/Property	Description
CreateProperty	Creates a new shared property identified by a string expression that's unique within its property group.
CreatePropertyByPosition	Creates a new shared property identified by a numeric index within its property group.
Property	Returns a reference to a shared property, given the string name by which the property is identified.
PropertyByPosition	Returns a reference to a shared property, given its numeric index in the shared property group.

Again, the first MTS object to access a shared property group must initialize all of its properties. The MTS object should call **CreateProperty** by passing the name of the property. **CreateProperty** returns a Boolean value indicating if the property already exists. If it doesn't, the MTS object should initialize it.

This example code creates a new property called **AdCount** and initializes it to 0 if it hasn't already been created:

```
Dim spmPropAdCount As SharedProperty

Set spmPropAdCount = _
  spmGroup.CreateProperty("AdCount", bExists)

' Set the initial value of AdCount to
' 0 if AdCount didn't already exist.
If bExists = False Then
  spmPropAdCount.Value = 0
End If
```

SharedProperty Object

Once you have created or obtained a shared property such as **AdCount,** you can work with it through the **SharedProperty** object. It has one property, **Value,** which is used to set or return the value of the property.

This example code shows how to increment the **AdCount** shared property when a new ad is placed:

```
Set spmPropAdCount = spmGroup.Property("AdCount")
spmPropAdCount.Value = spmPropAdCount.Value + 1
```

Connection Pooling

As you write code to access databases from your MTS objects, you use database connections, which are scarce and expensive resources. Creating a connection and destroying a connection consumes precious time and network resources. In a three-tier environment where database connections are repeatedly created and destroyed, this can lead to performance loss.

An efficient way to handle database connections is to use the connection pooling feature of ODBC 3.0. Connection pooling maintains open database connections and manages connection sharing across different user requests to maintain high performance and to reduce the number of idle connections. Instead of actually closing the connection, the ODBC driver manager pools it for later use.

When connection pooling is enabled, and an MTS object requests a connection, the ODBC driver manager handles the request through one of three avenues:

◆ If there are no available connections in the pool, a new connection is created and returned to the object.

◆ If there are available connections in the pool and the connection properties (User Id, Password, and so forth) requested by the object match the connection properties of the pooled connection, the object is given the open connection in the pool.

◆ If there are connections available but the connection properties do not match, a new connection is created for the object with the appropriate properties.

Note If a connection is already allocated to one object, and another object requests the same connection, ODBC creates a new connection because connections in use cannot be pooled. Thus, you should try to acquire connections as late as possible and release them as soon as possible to facilitate connection pooling.

Connection pooling is a standard feature of the ODBC 3.0 and 3.5 Driver Managers. It can be used with any 32-bit ODBC driver that is thread-safe.

How to Take Advantage of Connection Pooling

Keep in mind the following issues when working with connection pooling:

◆ When using connection pooling with SQL Server or any database system that limits user log ons to a specified number, keep in mind that each user connection uses one of the licensed log ons.

◆ To ensure the use of connection pooling, always specify the connection string in a variable; use this variable to establish the connection. Do not change connection attributes with ADO parameters.

◆ Use a consistent user name and password for multiple connections, and have the server do client validation. Connection pooling does not work if each connection uses a different user name and password. For more information about how to make MTS packages use a consistent user name and password, see Chapter 7, "Implementing Security" on page 219.

◆ Avoid creating temporary objects, such as temporary stored procedures, which are deleted when the connection is freed since a connection may not be freed if it is pooled.

◆ Avoid using SQL statements to change database context. For example, setting the connection to another database can affect the next user when using a recycled connection.

◆ Currently, there is no way to limit connections in the pool. The pool grows until the DBMS runs out of connections or until memory is exhausted. In order to keep from running out of SQL Server connections, estimate your highest connection rate and control for this by setting the connection pooling timeout value.

Connection Pooling and State

A stateless component with connection pooling achieves less throughput than a stateful component that holds its database connection between method calls. However, the stateless component can be safely deactivated by MTS. As a result, the stateless component is a more scalable component.

For example, a 2,000-user stateful system with a think time of one minute would require 2,000 active component instances (and database connections). The resource overhead would consume considerable system resources, which would reduce the scalability of the application. In contrast, a 2,000-user stateless system with a think time of one minute would require (on average) fewer than 40 database connections. As the number of clients rise into the hundreds and thousands, it is important to build stateless components to conserve server resources.

Configuring the ODBC Driver to Support Connection Pooling

For the ODBC 3.5 Driver Manager, connection pooling is controlled on a driver-by-driver basis through the **CPTimeout** registry setting. If this registry entry is not present, connection pooling is disabled. The **CPTimeout** property determines the length of time that a connection remains in the connection pool. If the connection remains in the pool longer than the duration set by **CPTimeout**, the connection is closed and removed from the pool. The default value for **CPTimeout** is 60 seconds.

You can selectively set the **CPTimeout** property to enable connection pooling for a specific ODBC database driver by creating a registry key with the following settings:

\HKEY_LOCAL_MACHINE\SOFTWARE\ODBC\ODBCINST.INI\driver-name\
CPTimeout = timeout (REG_SZ)

The **CPTimeout** property units are in seconds.

For example, the following key sets the connection pool timeout to 180 seconds (3 minutes) for the SQL Server driver:

```
\HKEY_LOCAL_MACHINE\SOFTWARE\ODBC\ODBCINST.INI\SQL Server\
CPTimeout = 180
```

Note By default, your Web server activates connection pooling for SQL Server by setting **CPTimeout** to 60 seconds.

Debugging and Error Handling

In this section, you will learn about the types of errors that can occur in MTS. You will learn how to debug your MTS components using the tools provided by Visual Basic. You will also learn how to use other tools to debug your MTS components and monitor how they run under MTS.

Handling Errors in MTS

When errors occur both within and outside your MTS object, your MTS object must be capable of handling them, reporting them to MTS, and optionally, reporting them to the client.

Type of Errors

There are three types of errors that can occur in an MTS application:

◆ Business rule errors

◆ Internal errors

◆ Windows exceptions

Business Rule Errors

When an object performs an operation that violates business rules, the object causes a business rule error. An example of such an error is a client attempting to withdraw money from an empty account. You should write MTS objects that detect these types of errors. They enforce the business rules by checking client actions against business rules. For example, a **Debit** object should check an account balance before withdrawing money from it.

Business rules can also be enforced in the database itself. For example, if a client withdraws money from an empty account, it may be the database that catches this error (for example, through a stored procedure), and raises the error to the **Debit** object. For more information about using ActiveX Data Objects to handle errors, see "Error Handling" on page 156 in Chapter 5, "Accessing Data from the Middle Tier."

In either case, you should do two things: abort the current transaction and report the error to the client. The user, upon seeing the error, can then act upon that information and attempt to correct the situation. For example, the user can transfer funds from another account.

To abort the transaction, call **SetAbort** and MTS rolls back the transaction. To report the error back to the client, raise the error using the **Err.Raise** method with a custom error that you have defined. The client application (for example, an ASP file, a Visual Basic application, or another client) must be able to interpret the error that is raised to display the proper message to the user.

For more information about raising errors with Visual Basic, see "Raising Errors" on page 46 in Chapter 2, "Building COM DLLs with Visual Basic."

Internal Errors

Internal errors are unexpected errors that occur while objects are working on behalf of a client. For example, a file is missing, or network problems prevent connecting to a database.

In Visual Basic, these errors are detected and raised by Visual Basic itself. You must write code to trap these errors and attempt to correct them, or abort the transaction. If you must abort the transaction, call **SetAbort**.

Optionally you may want to raise the error to the client using the **Err.Raise** method. This informs the client that an error occurred, and the client must display an appropriate error message. The client does not usually display the actual error message since it likely is not informative to the end user. For example, you don't expect to see "File Not Found" messages on an Automated Teller Machine.

Note If the transaction aborts and you do not raise an error to the client, MTS forces an error to be raised. For more information about MTS Error codes, search for "Error Handling" in the Microsoft Transaction Server Help.

Windows Exceptions

If for some reason your MTS object causes a Windows exception (a crash), MTS shuts down the process that hosts the object and logs an error event in the Windows NT event log. For more information about packages and processes, see "MTS Environment" on page 73 in Chapter 3, "Introduction to Microsoft Transaction Server (MTS)."

MTS performs extensive internal integrity and consistency checks. If MTS encounters an unexpected internal error condition, it immediately terminates the process and aborts all transactions associated with the process. This policy, named failfast, facilitates fault containment and results in more reliable and robust systems.

When failfast occurs, the process hosting the object is terminated and an error is returned to the client.

Error Handling in Multiple Objects

Typically there are many objects created to process a client request. To report an error to the client when an object is several object calls deep from the original root object, write error-trapping code in each object using the **On Error GoTo** syntax. When an error occurs that cannot be corrected, call **SetAbort** and raise the same error to the caller using the **Err.Raise** method. Each calling object handles the error in the same way, calling **SetAbort** and raising the error to the caller. Eventually the root object returns the error to the client and the transaction is aborted. This is the simplest way to handle errors when multiple objects are working together.

Debugging a Component

When you begin testing your components, or encountering problems with them, you need to debug them. Visual Basic 6.0 supports debugging MTS components within the Visual Basic IDE. This allows you to take advantage of the Visual Basic debugging environment for setting breakpoints and watches.

Visual Basic 6.0 requires that you install Windows NT Service Pack 4 in order to debug MTS components.

▶ To debug a Visual Basic component

1. Open the component project in Visual Basic.

2. Set the **MTSTransactionMode** property to a value other than 0 - **NotAnMTSObject**.

   For more information about the **MTSTransactionMode** property, see "Developing Components for MTS" on page 99 in this chapter.

3. From the **Project** menu, click **Properties**, and then enter the start program on the **Debugging** tab. The start program is the client application that calls this component.

4. Press **F5** to begin debugging the component.

Note It is recommended that you set binary compatibility for components that are debugged by using Visual Basic. The best way to do this is to make a copy of the component DLL after it is compiled. Then set binary compatibility to the copy of the DLL. This ensures that future builds do not change any CLSIDs or interface IDs, which MTS may not detect.

After you press **F5**, Visual Basic launches the client application and runs the component in debug mode. You can place breakpoints in the component's code and set watches on variables.

You can also debug components that are not inside an MTS package. For these components, Visual Basic automatically attaches to MTS and requests a context object for the component. This allows you to test components before placing them in MTS.

Issues and Limitations

There are a number of issues and limitations when debugging MTS components in Visual Basic:

- Do not add the component to an MTS package while it is being debugged. This can cause unexpected results.
- MTS components running in the debugger always run in-process as a library package even if they are inside a server package. As a result, the component icons in the MTS Explorer do not spin as the components are debugged and component tracking and security are disabled.
- Multiple clients cannot access the component at the same time while the component is being debugged. This can cause unexpected results.
- Debugging multi-threaded issues is not supported.
- Do not export a package while one of the components is being debugged. This can cause unexpected results in the exported files.

To debug components with security enabled, or for multiple-client access, or any of the other issues listed previously, use the Visual Studio IDE debugger. For more information about using the Visual Studio IDE debugger to debug MTS components, search for "Debugging Visual Basic MTS Components" in the Microsoft Transaction Server Help.

For more information about issues and limitations of debugging in Visual Basic 6.0, see the Visual Basic 6.0 Readme file.

Debugging and Monitoring Tools

When problems occur, there are additional tools you can use to debug MTS applications.

MTS Spy

The Microsoft Transaction Server Spy (MTS Spy) attaches to MTS processes and captures information such as transaction events, thread events, resource events, object, method, and user events. This is a useful tool for diagnosing problems and monitoring components as they work.

To see the demonstration "Using MTS Spy to Debug a Component," see the accompanying CD-ROM.

Windows NT Event Log

Whenever MTS encounters an unexpected internal error condition, it immediately terminates the process, using a policy named failfast. When failfast occurs, the process hosting the object is terminated and the Windows NT event log is updated with information about the problem.

You can use the Windows NT Event Viewer to find errors logged by MTS. The error information includes what component caused the error, which can help diagnose the problem.

▶ **To find MTS events with the Windows NT Event Viewer**

1. On the **Log** menu, choose **Application**.

2. On the **View** menu, choose **Filter**.

3. Set the Source to Transaction Server and click **OK**.

For more information about events logged by MTS in the Windows NT event log, search for "MTS Error Diagnosis" in the Microsoft Transaction Server Help.

DTC Monitoring

Because MTS uses the Microsoft Distributed Transaction Coordinator (DTC) to manage transactions, you can use the MTS Explorer to monitor DTC action. Specifically, you can view trace messages, the transaction list, and transaction statistics that are all generated by the DTC. All of these views are available in the MTS Explorer under the Computer folder.

Trace Messages

The Trace Messages window lists current trace messages issued by the DTC. Tracing allows you to view the current status of various DTC activities, such as startup and shutdown, and to trace potential problems by viewing additional debugging information.

Transaction List

Use the Transaction List window to view the current transactions in which the computer participates. This also displays any transactions whose status is in doubt.

The following illustration shows the Transaction List window.

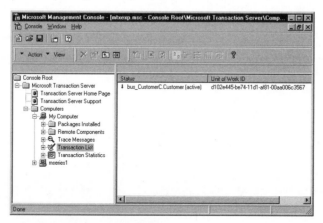

Transaction Statistics

Use the Transaction Statistics window to view information about all transactions that have occurred since the DTC was started. There is information about current transactions, how many transactions have aborted, how many have committed, and so on.

The following illustration shows the Transaction Statistics window.

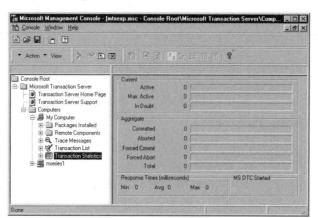

MTS Programming Best Practices

There are a number of ways in which you can improve the efficiency of the objects you manage using MTS:

♦ Minimize the number of hits required to use your objects.

If an object exposes properties, at least one roundtrip across the network occurs each time a client application accesses a property remotely. If a client has to set several properties, creating a single method to accept those values can minimize network roundtrips.

♦ Use the ADO **Recordset** object to return large amounts of data.

ADO provides a disconnected recordset that can be marshalled by value to the client. The disconnected recordset moves state to the client, freeing up server resources.

For more information, see "Disconnected Recordsets Defined" on page 163 in Chapter 5, "Accessing Data from the Middle Tier."

♦ Avoid passing or returning objects.

By default, objects are passed by reference. Extra work is required to develop an object that can be passed by value. For example, the ADO recordset described previously was built with custom marshalling to support passing the **Recordset** object by value. The objects you develop with Visual Basic don't use custom marshalling and are always passed by reference. All method calls on remote instances of your object are across the network, which consumes network resources.

♦ Avoid generating events.

If you create a component that generates events, that component must remain alive and active on the server, monitoring for the conditions to trigger events. Often this can involve consuming resources that may decrease the scalability of the server. For example, a component monitoring stock prices that generates events based on certain prices may need a constant network connection, which is a scarce resource. In general, you should avoid creating such components. For example, the stock component can be downloaded to the client computer to avoid running on the server.

♦ In general, obtain resources late and release them early.

Keeping resources such as database connections and network connections alive maximizes the possibility that another client is locked from those resources.

♦ Make objects apartment-threaded.

Enable MTS to run simultaneous client requests through objects by making them apartment-threaded. In Visual Basic, you make objects apartment-threaded by selecting the Apartment Threaded option for your project properties.

♦ In general, call **SetComplete**, even if you're not participating in a transaction.

SetComplete deactivates your object instance and frees server resources associated with the instance.

♦ Pass arguments by value (**ByVal**) whenever possible.

By default, Visual Basic passes arguments by reference. The **ByVal** keyword minimizes trips across networks because the data does not need to be returned back to the client.

Lab 4.2: Using the Shared Property Manager

In this lab, you will use the SPM to cache identifiers for Island Hopper News objects. You will implement the **GetANumber** method on the **util_TakeANumber.TakeANumber** class to return unique identifiers to Island Hopper News objects.

When new items are created in the Island Hopper News database, such as ads, customers, or invoices, new numbers must be generated to identify each item. A separate database table called TakeANumber contains the next number to be used for each item type. When a number is used from the table, the table is updated with the next number so that the next item created will have a unique ID.

Rather than access this table every time an item is created, Island Hopper News caches the numbers in a shared property group where they are controlled by the **util_TakeANumber.TakeANumber** and **util_TakeANumber.TakeANumberUpdate** classes. Both of these classes are in the IsleHop_Utilities package.

TakeANumber exposes one method called **GetANumber**. When any Island Hopper News object wants a new number for an item, it calls **GetANumber**, indicating the item type for which it needs a number. **GetANumber** gets the next number from the shared property group and returns it to the caller. This avoids repeated trips to the database for new numbers.

To keep the TakeANumber table in synch with the shared property group, **GetANumber** updates the table when every 100th number is requested. When that happens, it calls the **TakeANumber** object's **Update** method to update the database table. The TakeANumber table is always at least 100 numbers ahead of the shared property group. This ensures that when the IsleHop_Utilities package restarts, it doesn't initialize the shared property group with old numbers from the TakeANumber table.

To see the demonstration "Lab 4.2 Solution," see the accompanying CD-ROM.

Estimated time to complete this lab: **60 minutes**

To complete the exercises in this lab, you must have the required software. For detailed information about the labs and setup for the labs, see "Labs" in "About This Course."

Objectives

After completing this lab, you will be able to:

◆ Create a shared property group.

◆ Create and use shared properties.

Prerequisites

Before working on this lab, you should be familiar with the following:

◆ Adding and deleting components in MTS packages.

◆ Creating a COM DLL by using Visual Basic.

Exercises

The following exercises provide practice working with the concepts and techniques covered in this chapter:

◆ Exercise 1: Creating Shared Properties

In this exercise, you will use the Shared Property Manager to cache identification numbers, such as customer IDs and Ad IDs, that are requested by Island Hopper News objects. You will implement the **GetANumber** method on the **util_TakeANumber.TakeANumber** class, which generates and returns a number for the property group passed in.

◆ Exercise 2: Testing the Util_TakeANumber Component

In this exercise, you will test the **util_TakeANumber** component and the **GetANumber** method you created. You will create a custom standard EXE client in Visual Basic and call the **GetANumber** method to retrieve an Advertisement ID. Optionally, you can test the **util_TakeANumber** component with either the Island Hopper News Visual Basic or Web clients.

Exercise 1: Creating Shared Properties

In this exercise, you will use the Shared Property Manager to cache identification numbers, such as customer IDs and Ad IDs, that are requested by Island Hopper News objects. You will implement the **GetANumber** method on the **util_TakeANumber.TakeANumber** class, which generates and returns a number for the property group passed in.

▶ **Implement the GetANumber method**

1. Start Visual Basic and open the util_TakeANumber project located in the \Labs\Lab04.2 folder.

2. Open the **TakeANumber** class module and locate the **GetANumber** method. Insert code for the following steps after the **Dim** statements.

3. Call **spmMgr.CreatePropertyGroup** to create a property group with the name provided in the strPropGroupIn parameter. The property group will use the **LockSetGet** option and shut down when the process shuts down. Assign the return value to **spmGroup**.

> **Note** LockSetGet, Process, and other shared property constants are pre-defined in the Shared Property Manager Type Library.

To see an example of how your code should look, see Lab Hint 4.3 in Appendix B.

4. Use **spmGroup** to create a shared property called **MaxNumber**. Assign the return value to **spmPropMaxNum**.

5. Use **spmGroup** to create a second shared property called **NextNumber**. Use bResult as the second parameter, and assign the return value to **spmPropNextNum**.

6. Use bResult to determine if the **NextNumber** shared property did not exist before creation. If not, initialize the **NextNumber** property with a value of 1.

To see an example of how your code should look, see Lab Hint 4.4 in Appendix B.

7. Create an **If** block that runs if the **NextNumber** shared property is greater than the **MaxNumber** shared property. Include the following steps in the **If** block.

   a. Use **ObjectContext.CreateInstance** to create **util_TakeANumber.TakeA NumberUpdate** and assign the return value to **objTakeUpdate**.

   b. Call **objTakeUpdate.Update,** passing incQty and strPropGroupIn as parameters. Assign the result to the **NextNumber** shared property.

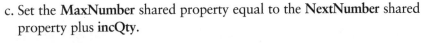

c. Set the **MaxNumber** shared property equal to the **NextNumber** shared property plus **incQty**.

d. End the **If** block.

To see an example of how your code should look, see Lab Hint 4.5 in Appendix B.

8. Increment the **NextNumber** shared property by 1.

9. Call **SetComplete**.

10. Return the **NextNumber** shared property as the function result.

11. Build util_TakeANumber.dll.

Exercise 2: Testing the Util_TakeANumber Component

In this exercise you will test the util_TakeANumber component and the **GetANumber** method you created. You will create a custom standard EXE client in Visual Basic and call the **GetANumber** method to retrieve an Advertisement ID. Optionally, you can test the **util_TakeANumber** component with either the Island Hopper News Visual Basic or Web clients.

▶ **Register bus_AdC.dll with MTS**

1. Start the MTS Explorer and remove the current util_TakeANumber.dll by deleting the util_TakeANumber.TakeANumber and util_TakeANumber.TakeANumberUpdate classes from the **IsleHop_Utilities** package.

2. Add the util_TakeANumber.dll that you just created to the IsleHop_Utilities package and set its transaction attribute to **Requires a transaction**. For more information on adding components, see "Adding Components to a Package" on page 82 in Chapter 3, "Introduction to Microsoft Transaction Server (MTS)."

▶ **Test with a custom client**

1. Start Visual Basic and create a new Standard EXE project.

2. Place controls on the form and set their properties as follows.

Control	Property	Value
Command button	Caption	Get Number
	Name	cmdGetNumber
Text box	Text	None
	Name	txtAdID
Label	Caption	Advertisement ID

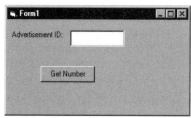

3. On the **Project** menu, click **References** and add a reference to the util_TakeANumber project.

4. Save the new project and form as the files UtilTest.vbp and UtilTest.frm.

5. Declare a global variable for the form called **objNumber** of type **util_TakeANumber.TakeANumber**.

6. In the **Form_Load** event, set **objNumber** equal to a new instance of **util_TakeANumber.TakeANumber**.

7. In the **cmdGetNumber_Click** event, call the **objNumber.GetANumber** method, passing AdvertismentID as the string parameter. Assign the result to the **txtAdID** control's **Text** property.

8. Save the project and run it. When you click **Get Number** , a new Advertisement ID is generated and displayed in the text box. Each number generated will increment by one. If you stop the UtilTest project, and shut down the IsleHop_Utilities package, the Advertisement IDs will start at the next increment of 100 the next time you run the UtilTest project. You can also start several instances of the UtilTest project to see how the shared properties work with multiple clients.

▶ **Test with the Island Hopper Visual Basic client (optional)**

1. Start the Island Hopper Visual Basic client application.

2. Place an ad, or create a customer, and verify that the ID used for the new ad or customer is successfully returned. The IDs will increment by one for each new ad or customer you create. If you stop the Visual Basic client, and shut down the IsleHop_Utilities package, the IDs will start at the next increment of 100 the next time you create an ad or customer.

▶ **Test with the Island Hopper Web client (optional)**

1. Start the Island Hopper Web client.

2. Place an ad, or create a customer, and verify that the ID used for the new ad or customer is successfully returned. The IDs will increment by one for each new ad or customer you create. If you shut down the IsleHop_Utilities package, the IDs will start at the next increment of 100 the next time you create an ad or customer.

Self-Check Questions

To see the answers to the Self-Check Questions, see Appendix A.

1. How is an object deactivated with just-in-time activation?

A. When the transaction completes or when the object returns from a method call after calling **SetComplete** or **SetAbort**, MTS releases all references to the object by destroying it and making its resources available to other objects.

B. When the object returns from a method call after calling **SetComplete** or **SetAbort,** the client releases all references to the object, destroying it and making its resources available to other objects.

C. Each time the object returns from a method call, MTS releases all references to the object, destroying it and making its resources available to other objects.

D. The object calls the **DeActivate** method on the **ObjectContext** object. Then MTS releases all references to the object, destroying it and making its resources available to other objects.

2. If an object does not explicitly call SetComplete, SetAbort, EnableCommit, or DisableCommit, what is the default status of the object?

A. SetComplete

B. SetAbort

C. EnableCommit

D. DisableCommit

3. How do you programmatically enable an object to participate in transactions on Microsoft Transaction Server?

A. Call the transaction functions **BeginTrans**, **CommitTrans**, and **Rollback**.

B. Modify the component to call the methods **SetComplete** and **SetAbort**.

C. Place the component in the Microsoft Transaction Server Explorer.

D. Create the public methods **SetComplete** and **SetAbort** for the component.

4. Which of the following is an appropriate way to store state for MTS objects?

A. Instance data within a transaction

B. NT Service

C. Shared Property Manager

D. All of the above

5. If an MTS object is marked as Requires a transaction, what creation method should you use so that it participates in the existing transaction?

A. Visual Basic's **CreateObject** function

B. The ObjectContext CreateInstance method

C. Visual Basic's **New** keyword

D. None of the above

Chapter 5:
Accessing Data from the Middle Tier

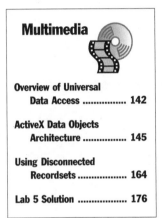
In this chapter, you will learn how to use ActiveX Data Objects (ADO) from within your MTS component. First, you will learn about the Universal Data Access strategy and the data access components within it. Then, you will learn about the ADO object model. You will review the use of ADO to establish a database connection, and retrieve and update records in a data source. You will also learn how to use ADO to take advantage of the features that are available when using an SQL database as your data source. Finally, you will review techniques that will help make the MTS components you build use ADO more efficiently in enterprise solutions.

Objectives

After completing this chapter, you will be able to:

♦ Describe Microsoft's Universal Data Access strategy and data access technologies available in enterprise development.

♦ List and describe the objects in the ActiveX Data Objects (ADO) object hierarchy.

♦ Write an MTS component in Visual Basic that retrieves and updates records in an SQL database.

♦ Use ADO to call a stored procedure.

♦ Create a disconnected recordset and perform batch updates.

♦ Choose the appropriate cursor locations, cursor types, and lock types for different enterprise scenarios.

ActiveX Data Objects

In this section, you will learn about Microsoft's Universal Data Access architecture and the Microsoft Data Access Components. You will also learn about the ADO object model.

ADO is a database programming model that enables you to write applications or components to access and manipulate data from a variety of data sources. Its goal is to supersede the Data Access Objects (DAO) and Remote Data Objects (RDO) models. ADO is a collection of Automation objects that can retrieve, update, and create records in any OLE DB or ODBC data source.

Universal Data Access

Universal Data Access (UDA) is a platform for developing multi-tier enterprise applications that require access to diverse relational or nonrelational data sources across intranets or the Internet. UDA consists of a collection of software components that interact with each other using a common set of system-level interfaces defined by OLE DB.

The strategy of UDA is to enable developers to access diverse types of data, from both relational and nonrelational data sources, while enabling them to work with familiar tools. Nonrelational data sources are data such as document containers (such as Internet Explorer), e-mail, and file systems.

The UDA strategy is based on COM. As a result, the UDA architecture is open and works with tools or programming languages that support COM. Thus, you do not need to use new tools to work with UDA.

 To see the expert point-of-view "Overview of Universal Data Access," see the accompanying CD-ROM.

The following illustration shows the Universal Data Access architecture.

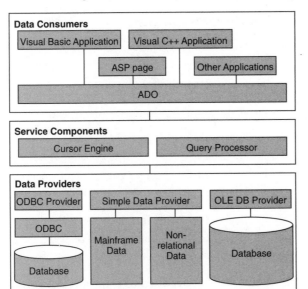

All interactions among components in the illustration can occur across process and machine boundaries through network protocols such as Microsoft's Distributed COM (DCOM) or HTTP. Transacted interactions among components are possible through MTS.

The previous illustration shows three general kinds of database components:

◆ Providers

Data providers are components that represent data sources such as SQL databases, indexed sequential files, and spreadsheets. Providers expose information uniformly using a common abstraction named the rowset.

◆ Services

Services are components that consume and produce OLE DB data. For example, a cursor engine is a service component that can consume data from a sequential, forward-only data source to produce scrollable data.

◆ Consumers

Consumers are components that consume OLE DB data. Examples of consumers include services such as a query processor; high-level data access models such as ADO; business applications written in languages like Visual Basic, Visual C++, or Java; and development tools themselves.

Microsoft Data Access Components

Microsoft Data Access Components (MDAC) is the practical implementation of UDA. The following table describes the four distinct technologies in MDAC Version 2.0.

MDAC technology	Description
ActiveX Data Objects (ADO)	Language-neutral object model that exposes data raised by an underlying OLE DB Provider.
OLE DB	Open specification designed to build on the success of ODBC by providing an open standard for accessing data.
ODBC Version 3.5	Common interface for accessing heterogeneous SQL databases based on SQL as a standard for accessing data.
Remote Data Service (RDS)	Service used to transport ADO recordsets from a server to a client computer. The resulting recordset is cached on the client computer and disconnected from the server.

This chapter focuses on ADO. For more information about MDAC, go to the Universal Data Access Web site at msdn.microsoft.com/data/.

ADO Object Model Overview

ADO is a high-level, language-independent data access interface. It is an automation interface that provides a layer between your application and the underlying data source.

ADO provides an object-oriented programming interface for accessing a data source by using an OLE DB data provider. OLE DB provides access to both SQL-based and non-SQL-based data. If a data source provides an OLE DB provider, ADO communicates directly with the provider. If the data source provides an ODBC driver, ADO communicates through MSDASQL.DLL to the driver.

The ADO object model is based on three major object types, **Connection, Command**, and **Recordset**, and four collections of objects.

In ADO, you create only those objects that are required to perform the desired task. For example, when performing an update on a data source, you only require a **Command** object. In this case, ADO implicitly creates a **Connection** object by using the connection information you provide.

In other situations you may create several independent objects and use them in a specialized manner. For example, you may create one **Connection** object and then have several **Command** objects use that one connection for interacting with the data source.

To see the animation "ActiveX Data Objects Architecture," see the accompanying CD-ROM.

The following illustration shows the objects and collections in the ADO object hierarchy.

ADO 2.0 Object Model

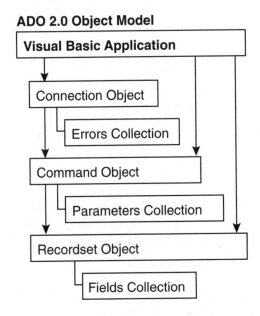

The following table describes the role of each object type and collection.

ADO object type and collection	Description
Connection object and **Errors** collection	The ADO **Connection** object represents a single session with the data source. The **Connection** object defines properties of the connection, provides a central location for retrieving errors, and provides a point for executing schema queries. Any errors that occur during the session are stored in the **Errors** collection.
Command object and **Parameters** collection	The ADO **Command** object specifies a data-definition or data-manipulation statement to be executed. In the case of a relational provider, this is an SQL statement. The **Command** object allows you to specify parameters in the **Parameters** collection and customize the behavior of the statement to be executed.
Recordset object and **Fields** collection	The ADO **Recordset** object is the actual interface to the data, whether it is the result of a query or generated in some other fashion. The **Recordset** object exposes a collection of **Field** objects that contain the metadata about the columns in the recordset, such as the name, type, length, and precision, as well as the actual data values themselves.

Each of the top-level ADO objects contains a collection of **Property** objects. The **Property** object allows ADO to dynamically expose the capabilities of a specific provider. Because not all data providers and service components have the same functionality, it is important for the ADO model to allow you to access provider-specific settings in a dynamic way. This also prevents the ADO model from being cluttered with properties that are available only in certain circumstances.

Using ADO with a Data Source

In this section, you will learn how to use ADO objects to create a connection to a data source. You will also learn how to execute commands, such as SQL statements. You will learn how to retrieve, navigate, and modify data. Finally, you will learn how to perform error handling for your ADO code.

Establishing a Database Connection

A **Connection** object represents an open connection to a data source. You can use the **Connection** object to run commands or queries on the data source. When a recordset is retrieved from the database, it is stored in a **Recordset** object.

Establishing a Connection to a Data Source

The following table summarizes the steps necessary to establish a connection with a data source.

Step	Description
Set a reference to the ADO Object Library.	To set a reference to the Microsoft ActiveX Data Objects Library in Visual Basic, click the **Project** menu, and click **References**. Then select the appropriate reference.
Declare a **Connection** object.	After setting a reference, declare a **Connection** object in your application. Using the **Connection** object, you can then create a **Command** or **Recordset** object.
Specify an OLE DB data provider.	Once you instantiate a **Connection** object, specify an OLE DB provider by setting the **Provider** property. For ODBC data sources, do not modify this property. Instead, enter the connection information for the ODBC data source in the next step.
Pass connection information.	Specify connection information by setting the **Connection** object's **ConnectionString** property using the **User ID**, **Password**, **Data Source**, and **Initial Catalog** properties.
Open a connection.	Use the **Open** method to establish a connection to the data source.

The following sample code creates a connection to a Microsoft SQL Server database named Classifieds on a server named MyServer using the SQL Server OLE DB data provider. To copy this code for use in your own projects, see "Creating a Connection to a Microsoft SQL Server Database" on the accompanying CD-ROM.

```
'Declare a Connection object
Dim conn As ADODB.Connection
Set conn = New ADODB.Connection
'Establish a connection
With conn
    .Provider = "SQLOLEDB"
    .ConnectionString = "User ID=sa;Password=;" & _
                        "Data Source=MyServer;" & _
                        "Initial Catalog=Classifieds"
End With

'Open the connection
conn.Open
```

Note Unless you are using both ADO and DAO in the same application, you do not need to use the prefix "ADODB" before ADO data types.

After the **Open** method succeeds in connecting with the data source, you can run commands or queries across the connection.

Closing a Connection

When you have finished working with the database, use the **Close** method of the **Connection** object to free any associated system resources. Closing a connection also closes any active recordsets associated with the connection. Using the **Close** method does not remove the object from memory. You can change the object's properties and then use the **Open** method to open it again. To completely remove an object from memory, set the object variable to **Nothing**.

This example code closes a data connection and removes the object from memory:

```
conn.Close
Set conn = Nothing
```

Note If you do not close a **Connection** object, it closes automatically when the connection variable goes out of scope or is Set to **Nothing**.

Executing a Command

The **Command** object contains a definition of a command that you want to run against a data source. For a data source that supports SQL, this is an SQL statement. For example, you can execute an SQL statement that returns a recordset, updates a database, calls a stored procedure, or manipulates the structure of the database.

When using ADO, you don't have to create a **Connection** object before using the **Command** object. However, if you do not associate the new **Command** object with an active connection, a new implicit **Connection** object is created automatically. If you have multiple **Command** objects, consider creating a single **Connection** object to associate with all of them. Otherwise each has a separate implicit **Connection** object, using additional server resources.

Using a Command with a Connection

Although an existing active connection is not required, it is more efficient to create **Command** objects from established connections. Once the **Command** object has been created, it can be used to execute the specified command or build a recordset.

The following sample code uses a **Connection** object and a **Command** object to execute an SQL command that modifies a customer's balance. To copy this code for use in your own projects, see "Using a Connection Object and a Command Object" on the accompanying CD-ROM.

```
Dim cmd As ADODB.Command
Set cmd = New ADODB.Command
With cmd
    'An existing Connection object is referenced
    Set .ActiveConnection = conn
    .CommandText = "UPDATE Customers SET Balance = Balance -" & _
                   "0.10*Balance"
End With

cmd.Execute
```

Creating a Stand-Alone Command Object

Because ADO provides a flat object model, you do not have to explicitly create a **Connection** object. Instead, you can pass the required connection information to the **ActiveConnection** property of the **Command** object. Then, when you use the **Execute** method to run the SQL command, a connection is established for you. However, using this technique, you cannot access the **Connection** object from your Visual Basic code.

The following sample code uses a **Command** object to execute an SQL command that modifies a customer's balance. To copy this code for use in your own projects, see "Using a Command Object to Execute an SQL Command" on the accompanying CD-ROM.

```
Dim cmd As Command
Set cmd = New Command
With cmd
    'No Connection object is used
    .ActiveConnection = "Provider=SQLOLEDB;" & _
                        "User ID=sa;" & _
                        "Data Source=MyServer;" & _
                        "Initial Catalog=Classifieds"
    .CommandText = "UPDATE Customers SET Balance = Balance -" & _
                   "0.10*Balance"
End With

cmd.Execute
```

Parameter Object

A **Parameter** object represents a parameter or argument associated with a **Command** object based on a parameterized query or stored procedure.

Many providers support parameterized commands, where the desired action is defined once, but variables (or parameters) are used to alter some details of the command. For example, an SQL SELECT statement could use a parameter to define the matching criteria of a WHERE clause, and another to define the column name for a SORT BY clause.

With the collections, methods, and properties of a **Parameter** object, you can set or return the name, value, or characteristics of a parameter. You can pass long binary or character data to a parameter, as well.

For more information about using the **Parameter** object and stored procedures, see "Executing Stored Procedures from the Command Object" on page 170 in this chapter.

Creating and Navigating Recordsets

The **Recordset** object enables your application to access data returned from an SQL query or stored procedure. Using the **Recordset** object, you can navigate through the records that have been returned, or edit their values.

Like the **Command** object, you don't have to create a **Connection** object before using the **Recordset** object. However, if you do not associate the new **Recordset** object with an active connection, a new implicit **Connection** object is created automatically. If you have multiple **Recordset** objects, consider creating a single **Connection** object to associate with all of them. Otherwise each has a separate implicit **Connection** object, using additional server resources.

Creating a Recordset

To retrieve records from a database, create a **Recordset** object. Use properties and methods of the **Recordset** object to manipulate the data in the recordset.

There are three ways that you can create a recordset:

◆ Create an instance of a **Recordset** object using the **New** operator, and then use the **Open** method to retrieve records.

◆ Call the **Execute** method on a **Connection** object.

◆ Call the **Execute** method on a **Command** object.

The following sample code creates a recordset from a **Connection** object. To copy this code for use in your own projects, see "Creating a Recordset from a Connection Object" on the accompanying CD-ROM.

```
' Declare the object variables
Dim connBookstore As ADODB.Connection
Dim rsBookPrices As ADODB.Recordset

' Instantiate the variables
Set connBookstore = New ADODB.Connection

' Establish a connection
With connBookstore
  .Provider = "SQLOLEDB"
  .ConnectionString = "User ID=sa;Password=;" & _
                      "Data Source=MSERIES1;" & _
                      "Initial Catalog=Bookstore"
  .Open
End With

' Build the recordset
Set rsBookPrices = connBookstore.Execute ("Select Title,
                                          "Price From Books")
```

Tip SQL Server allows a batch of queries to be issued and executed. When a batch of queries is executed, more than one recordset can be generated. For example, you can execute the SQL string "Select * from Sales; Select * from Stores" to retrieve sales records, then retrieve the stores records into the same **Recordset** object.

When multiple recordsets are generated, you fetch one recordset at a time until no more recordsets are available. The **NextRecordset** method of the **Recordset** object allows you to fetch any subsequent recordsets. If no more recordsets are available, the returned **Recordset** object is set to **Nothing**.

Choosing a Cursor Location and Type

The functionality of the recordset you create is determined by the values specified for the **CursorLocation** and **CursorType** properties. Server-side cursors are the default in ADO. If the data source you are connecting to does not support server-side cursors, a client-side cursor must be created. To explicitly specify the creation of a client-side cursor, set the **CursorLocation** property of the **Recordset** object to **adUseClient**.

For more information about cursors, see "Introduction to Cursors" on page 158 in this chapter. For information about disconnected recordsets, see "Disconnected Recordsets Defined" on page 163 in this chapter.

Navigating Recordsets

Of the ADO objects, only the **Recordset** object allows users to navigate through a set of records. Only one record within a recordset is current at a given time. Therefore, the **Recordset** object supports a number of properties and methods that allow users to navigate through the recordset.

The following table describes properties of the **Recordset** object that are used to navigate a recordset. For a complete listing of **Recordset** object properties, read the article "ADO Properties" in Platform SDK Help.

Property	Description
AbsolutePage	Sets or returns the absolute page in which the current record exists.
AbsolutePosition	Sets or returns the absolute position of the current record (this can be affected by record additions or deletions).
BOF	Indicates if the record pointer has moved before the first record.
Bookmark	Returns a unique identifier for the current record. Setting this property to a specific record's bookmark moves the record pointer to that record.
EOF	Indicates if the record pointer has moved past the last record.

The following table describes methods of the **Recordset** object that are used to navigate through a recordset. For a complete listing of **Recordset** object methods, read the article "ADO Methods" in Platform SDK Help.

Method	Description
Move	Moves a specified number of records forward or back.
MoveFirst	Moves to the first record.
MoveLast	Moves to the last record.
MoveNext	Moves to the next record.
MovePrevious	Moves to the previous record.

Modifying Data

When your application needs to update data in an external data source, you can either execute SQL statements directly or use a **Recordset** object and its various methods for modifying data.

If you do not need to create a recordset, you can use a **Command** object and execute an SQL **Insert**, **Update**, or **Delete** statement to add or modify records. Recordsets utilize cursors, which consume resources. Using an SQL statement such as **Insert** is more efficient than creating a recordset and using the **AddNew** method of the **Recordset** object in enterprise systems.

You can use either a **Connection** object or a **Command** object to execute SQL statements directly. Use a **Connection** object when the SQL command is only going to be issued once. Use the **Command** object for parameterized SQL statements or parameterized stored procedures. Both objects use the **Execute** method to send the SQL statement to the data source.

The following sample code executes an SQL **Update** statement using a **Connection** object to change the price of a book. To copy this code for use in your own projects, see "Updating a Record Using a Connection Object" on the accompanying CD-ROM.

```
' Declare and instantiate the object variable
Dim connBookstore As ADODB.Connection
Dim strSQL As String
Set connBookstore = New ADODB.Connection

' Establish a connection
With connBookstore
  .Provider = "SQLOLEDB"
  .ConnectionString = "User ID=sa;" & _
                      "Data Source=MSERIES1;" & _
                      "Initial Catalog=Bookstore"
  .Open
End With

' Build the SQL command
strSQL = "UPDATE Books SET Price = 39.95 WHERE Title =
'Programming Advanced ADO'"

' Execute the SQL command
connBookstore.Execute strSQL
```

If your application has already opened a recordset, you can modify data using the recordset's methods. Modifying records with a **Recordset** object is limited to a single addition, deletion, or update at a time. Consider using the **Connection** object's **Execute** method for performing multiple updates at once.

The following sample code creates a new **Recordset** object, navigates to the last record, and changes a book's title. To copy this code for use in your own projects, see "Creating a Recordset to Modify Data" on the accompanying CD-ROM.

```
Dim rsBooks as Recordset
Set rsBooks = New Recordset

'Use existing connection
Set rsBooks.ActiveConnection = connBookStore

'The following 2 lines of code create an updateable cursor
'Cursors are discussed in more detail later in this chapter
rsBooks.CursorType = adOpenKeyset
rsBooks.LockMode = adLockPessimistic

'Open recordset and change last book title
rsBooks.Open "Select Title from Books"
rsBooks.MoveLast
rsBooks!Title = "Programming Advanced ADO"
rsBooks.Update
```

Error Handling

Each **Connection** object has an **Errors** collection associated with it. Operations involving ADO objects can generate one or more OLE DB provider errors and warnings. For each error, an **Error** object is created, initialized with the appropriate error information, and then appended to the **Errors** collection.

If ADO itself encounters an error, it does not populate the **Errors** collection; you have to use a native error mechanism to catch and display the error, such as the Visual Basic **Err** object. If the provider or underlying components generate an error, then these are populated in the ADO **Errors** collection. You need to check both the Visual Basic **Err** object and the ADO **Errors** collection.

The **Errors** collection is only accessible from the **Connection** object.

You can read an **Error** object's properties to obtain specific details about each error. The following table describes the details provided by each property.

Property	Description
Description	Contains the text of the error.
Number	Contains the **Long** integer value of the error constant.
Source	Identifies the object that raised the error. This is particularly useful when you have several **Error** objects in the **Errors** collection following a request to a data source.
Helpfile and **HelpContext**	Indicate the appropriate Windows Help file and Help topic, respectively, (if any exist) for the error.
SQLState and **Native Error**	Provide information from SQL data sources.

The following sample code creates an error handler to support errors that may be returned while connecting to an external data source. To copy this code for use in your own projects, see "Creating an Error Handler" on the accompanying CD-ROM.

```
' Declare a connection and error object
Dim conn As ADODB.Connection
Dim errItem as ADODB.Error

Set conn = New ADODB.Connection

'Enable the error trap
On Error Goto ErrorHandler

'Establish a connection
With conn
    .Provider = "SQLOLEDB"
    .ConnectionString = "User ID=sa;Password=;" & _
                        "Data Source=MSERIES1;" & _
                        "Initial Catalog=Classifieds"
    .Open
End With
Exit Sub

ErrorHandler:
'If an error occurs, loop through the collection
'There can be more than one error code for a single
'run time error
For Each errItem in conn.Errors
    'Show each error description to the user
    MsgBox errItem.Description
Next
```

As each error occurs, one or more **Error** objects are placed in the **Errors** collection of the **Connection** object. When another ADO operation generates an error, the **Errors** collection is cleared, and the new set of **Error** objects is placed in the **Errors** collection. The **Errors** collection on the **Connection** object is cleared and populated only when the provider generates a new error, or when the **Clear** method is called.

Any ADO operation generating an **Error** object then causes a run-time error within your application. This error is then exposed to the native error mechanism of the run-time environment. In the case of Visual Basic, the **Err** object is set with the error information and then the procedure's error handling routine is called. The **Err** object is always set with the first error from the **Errors** collection.

While OLE DB provider errors are stored in the **Errors** collection, ADO errors are written only to the **Err** object. In both cases, provide an error handler to respond to these errors.

Errors generated by a provider can be determined by iterating through the **Errors** collection and using the collection's **Count** property and **Item** method.

> **Note** The **Err** object is cleared when an ADO object is set to **Nothing**. If you plan to raise an error in your error handler, raise it after releasing your objects.

Using ADO from the Middle Tier

In this section, you will learn how to use ActiveX Data Objects (ADO) to take advantage of the features that are available when using an SQL database as your data source. You will learn how to use cursors to navigate through recordsets. You will also learn how to use lock types to control record modification. Then, you will learn how to use disconnected recordsets to minimize demand on the MTS and network servers. Finally, you will learn best practices with ADO related to issues involving performance and scaling.

Introduction to Cursors

A cursor is a database mechanism that allows a user to navigate and access data from a recordset. A cursor maintains the position of the current record and determines how you can move through the recordset. It also controls whether or not you can update data or see updates created by other users.

There are different types of cursors and each type consumes resources differently. You can avoid expending unnecessary resources by choosing the correct type of cursor for your three-tier application.

Updateable versus Non-updateable Cursors

Updateable cursors give the user the capability to make changes to the data in a recordset and have those changes propagate back to the data provider of the cursor. You can think of this as having write privileges on the original data. However, updateable cursors require that additional metadata be downloaded by the cursor engine, which can be expensive to retrieve.

In a non-updateable (read-only) cursor, the user cannot make changes to the recordset. Non-updateable cursors offer better performance because they allow the data provider to offload the data to the cursor once and then essentially forget about it. The data provider can then continue servicing other requests, free from concerns about concurrency problems.

Scrollable Cursors

Cursors in all forms use the concept of a current record. The current record is the record in the recordset that is currently being pointed at by the cursor. When the user retrieves a field value from the recordset, the value is returned from the current record.

A cursor is scrollable if the user can change the current record, such as through the ADO **MoveNext** or **MovePrevious** methods. Nonscrollable cursors can only provide data in a first-in, first-out (FIFO) format as data is requested. Nonscrollable cursors are more efficient because they do not require additional resources to support backwards scrolling. In many situations, a nonscrollable cursor is useful because often data is simply read from the beginning of the recordset to the end.

Cursor Types

You can create four different types of cursors using ADO and SQL Server: Forward Only, Static, Keyset, and Dynamic. Each type has a different impact on the memory and network resources of your server.

To select the cursor type for a **Recordset** object, set the **CursorType** property to **adOpenForwardOnly**, **adOpenStatic**, **adOpenKeyset**, or **adOpenDynamic**.

The following table describes each cursor type and its impact on performance.

Cursor type	Description
Forward Only	Forward-only cursors require the least amount of overhead and are generally the fastest type of cursor. They retrieve each record one at a time from the beginning to the end of the recordset. They also allow updates to the data, although only one row at a time. Data changes by other users are not visible.
Static	Static cursors retrieve a copy of all the records requested in the query. They are fully scrollable and therefore consume more memory than forward-only cursors because the data for the entire recordset must be stored. Data changes by other users are not visible.

table continued on next page

Cursor type	Description
Keyset	Keyset cursors build keys for each record in the query. When you read records from the recordset, the keys are used to retrieve the actual record values. This results in less overhead than static or dynamic cursors because keys are being stored rather than the full record values. These cursors are scrollable. Deletions and updates to data by other users are visible; however, insertions by other users are not visible.
Dynamic	Dynamic cursors offer the most flexibility and functionality. However, they also consume the most memory and network resources. They are scrollable, and all insertions, deletions, and changes to the data by other users are visible in the recordset.

For information about choosing the proper cursor type for three-tier applications, see "Choosing Cursor Types" on page 162 in this chapter.

Cursor Location

When using ADO and SQL Server, you can choose to have the cursor exist on either the SQL Server computer or the client computer. The client computer of the database in a three-tier scenario is the server running MTS, and the clients are the MTS objects. SQL Server has built-in cursor functionality. By using SQL Server cursors, you can increase performance in several areas, mainly because the server is doing the caching required of a cursor instead of downloading records to be cached at the client.

Using a server-side cursor is useful when working with large recordsets in which you only update or read a few records. By caching the records on the server, you avoid sending them across the network. However, running many queries that build server-side cursors can quickly overload the server. In general, try to avoid server-side cursors unless they truly offer a performance benefit.

To specify the cursor location for a **Recordset** or **Connection** object, set the **CursorLocation** property to one of the following values:

Cursor location	Description
adUseClient	Uses client-side cursors supplied by a local cursor library. Local cursor engines often allow many features that server-supplied cursors may not, so using this setting may provide an advantage with respect to features that are enabled. For backward-compatibility, the synonym **adUseClientBatch** is also supported. ADO's client cursor engine only supports static cursors.
adUseServer	Default. Uses data provider- or server-supplied cursors. These cursors are sometimes very flexible and allow for some additional sensitivity to reflecting changes that others make to the actual data source. However, some features of the Microsoft Client Cursor Provider (such as disconnected recordsets) cannot be used with server-side cursors; these features are unavailable with this setting.

By default, the cursor location is at the server. To change the cursor location, modify the **CursorLocation** property of the **Connection** or **Recordset** object before calling the **Open** method. The following example code sets the location of the cursor to the client:

```
Dim rs As ADODB.Recordset
Set rs = New ADODB.Recordset
rs.CursorLocation = adUseClient
rs.CursorType = adOpenStatic
rs.Open "Select * from Categories", "DSN=Classifieds;UID=sa;PWD"
```

Lock Types

The **LockType** property of the **Recordset** object determines the type of lock placed on the data of the underlying database during editing. By default, an ADO recordset is set to a read-only lock, allowing no modification to the data. To change the lock type, modify the **LockType** property before opening the recordset.

The different lock types are:

Lock type	Description
adLockReadOnly	The default lock type. Read-only. Data cannot be altered.
adLockPessimistic	Pessimistic locking — the data is locked immediately upon editing.
adLockOptimistic	Optimistic locking — the data is locked when the **Update** method is called.
adLockBatchOptimistic	Optimistic batch update — this locking mode is required when using the **UpdateBatch** method.

If you are not going to update the data, opening the recordset as read-only reduces the overhead consumed by the recordset.

Pessimistic and optimistic locking have the same effect inside MTS transactions. This is because MTS transactions communicate to resource managers such as SQL Server through the Distributed Transaction Coordinator (DTC). MTS declares DTC transactions as serializable, which is similar to pessimistic locking.

The following example code opens a read-only keyset cursor recordset:

```
Dim rs As ADODB.Recordset
Set rs = New ADODB.Recordset
rs.LockType = adLockReadOnly
rs.CursorType = adOpenKeyset
rs.Open "Select * from Categories", "DSN=Classifieds;UID=sa;PWD"
```

Choosing Cursor Types

In an enterprise solution, you need to choose the right kind of cursor for the task at hand. The cursor type, location, and lock type have implications on how network and memory resources are consumed. Following are some guidelines for using cursors in your applications. Ultimately, you need to apply performance testing to your applications to see which cursors work best given the workload handled by your applications.

Retrieving Read-Only Data

When you need to retrieve data and simply read it from beginning to end, consider using a server-side, forward-only, read-only cursor. This is the most efficient cursor to use in terms of network bandwidth and memory utilization when retrieving data. It is often the fastest cursor as well. This cursor is useful when populating Web pages with data, performing calculations based on data, or making business-rule decisions based on data.

If you need a snapshot of the data that does not change, consider using a client-side, static, read-only cursor. These cursors are useful when you need an unchanging view of the data at a specific point in time. For example, a business object that retrieves all account balances to create a financial report must have all balances remain constant. Any balances that change while it is processing the recordset would cause the report to be inaccurate.

Also, if you need a snapshot, but don't need to scroll through the recordset, you can use a server-side, forward-only, read-only cursor. Changes to the data by other users are not seen by this cursor.

Retrieving Updateable Data

When you need to update data, consider using direct SQL statements through either the **Connection** object's **Execute** command or a **Command** object. This avoids the need to create cursors at all, and offers considerable savings in resources.

If you need to create an updateable recordset, use a client-side, static cursor.

In general, however, avoid using server-side cursors for updating data. In an enterprise application with many users, they can quickly overload a server. Also, avoid using dynamic cursors. Although they offer the most up-to-date view of the data, they are by far the most costly cursor to create in terms of network and memory resources consumed.

Disconnected Recordsets Defined

An advanced feature of ADO is the disconnected recordset. A disconnected recordset contains a recordset that can be viewed and updated, but it does not carry with it the overhead of a live connection to the database. This is a useful way to return data to the client that is going be used for a long time. While the client works on the data, the MTS server and database server are not tied up with any open connections.

The client can make changes to the disconnected recordset by editing the records directly, or adding or deleting them using ADO methods such as **AddNew** and **Delete**. All of the changes are stored in the disconnected recordset until it is reconnected to the database.

To see the animation "Using Disconnected Recordsets," see the accompanying CD-ROM.

Using Disconnected Recordsets in Three-tier Applications

In a three-tier scenario, the middle tier creates disconnected recordsets and returns them to the client. For example, a client may request a listing of all furniture inventory for a specific store. The user on the client computer may wish to compare the inventory against a physical inventory list and correct any inaccuracies. This process may take a substantial amount of time.

A disconnected recordset is ideal for this scenario. A good approach is to have the middle tier create the disconnected recordset and return it to the client. A **Furniture** MTS object can be created that exposes a **GetFurnitureList** method. When this method is called, it creates a recordset, populates it with the furniture records, and returns it to the client.

When the recordset is returned to the client, it is disconnected from the database. Now the client can work with the records as long as necessary without tying up an open connection to the database.

Later, when the user is ready to submit the changes, the client computer calls a **SubmitChanges** method on the **Furniture** object. The disconnected recordset is passed in as a parameter, and the **SubmitChanges** method reconnects the recordset to the database. Then **SubmitChanges** calls the recordset's **UpdateBatch** method. If there are any conflicts, **SubmitChanges** uses the existing business rules to determine the proper action.

Optionally, **SubmitChanges** could return the conflicting records to the client computer to let the user decide how to handle the conflicts. However, this scenario is more complicated. A separate recordset must be created, and returned to the client, that contains the conflicting values from the database. For more information about how to return conflicting records to a client, see Knowledge Base Article Q177720: "FILE: Rdsensub.exe with RDS Conflict Resolution Sample."

Creating and Using Disconnected Recordsets

To create a disconnected recordset, you must create a **Recordset** object that uses a client-side, static cursor with a lock type of **adLockBatchOptimistic**.

The **ActiveConnection** property determines if the recordset is disconnected. If you explicitly set it to **Nothing**, you disconnect the recordset. You can still access the data in the recordset, but there is no live connection to the database. Later, you can explicitly set **ActiveConnection** to a valid **Connection** object to reconnect the recordset to the database.

The following example code shows how to create a disconnected recordset:

```
Dim rs As ADODB.Recordset
Set rs = New ADODB.Recordset
rs.CursorLocation = adUseClient
rs.CursorType = adOpenStatic
rs.LockType = adLockBatchOptimistic
rs.Open "Select * From Authors", "DSN=Pubs"
Set rs.ActiveConnection = Nothing
```

If you return the disconnected recordset from a function, either as the return value, or as an out parameter, the recordset copies its data to the caller. If the caller is a client in a separate process, or on another computer, the recordset marshals its data to the client's process.

When the recordset marshals itself across the network, it compresses the data to use less network bandwidth. This makes disconnected recordsets ideal for returning large amounts of data to a client.

Tip You can make a disconnected recordset marshal just the modified records across the network by setting the **MarshalOptions** property to **adMarshalModifiedOnly**. This is useful when you are submitting a recordset from the client to an MTS object for updating changes. It avoids copying records that won't be used by the MTS object.

Submitting Changes from a Disconnected Recordset

While a recordset is disconnected, you can make changes to it by editing, adding, or deleting records. The recordset stores these changes so that you can eventually update the database. When you are ready to submit the changes to the database, you reconnect the recordset with a live connection to the database and call **UpdateBatch**. **UpdateBatch** updates the database to reflect the changes made in the disconnected recordset.

The following example code shows how to reconnect a disconnected recordset to the database and update the database with the changes:

```
Dim conn As ADODB.Connection
Set conn = New ADODB.Connection
conn.Open "DSN=Pubs"
Set rs.ActiveConnection = conn
rs.UpdateBatch
```

Note If the recordset is generated from a stored procedure, then you cannot call **UpdateBatch**. **UpdateBatch** only works for recordsets created from SQL statements.

Resolving Conflicts in Disconnected Recordsets

Before you call **UpdateBatch**, other users may have already changed records in the database. Depending on the business rules, you may not want to overwrite changes in the database with changes in the disconnected recordset. To guard against unwanted changes, the disconnected recordset contains three views of the data: original value, value, and underlying value. You can access these views by using the **Original**, **Value**, and **Underlying** properties of the **Recordset** object.

Recordset property	Description
Original	Accesses the original values in the recordset when it was first created.
Value	Accesses the current values in the recordset. These values reflect any changes you have made to the recordset.
Underlying	Accesses the underlying values in the recordset. These values reflect the values stored in the database. These are the same as the original values when you first create the recordset and are only updated to match the database when you call the **ReSync** method.

When **UpdateBatch** is called, it creates a separate SQL query for each changed record to modify in the database. Part of the SQL query checks to see if the record has changed since the recordset was first created. It does this by comparing the underlying value against the database value. If they are the same, then the database has not changed, and the update can proceed. If they are different, then someone has recently changed the database, and the update fails.

When a record fails to update because of a conflict with the database, **UpdateBatch** flags it by changing its **Status** property. After **UpdateBatch** returns, you can check to see if there were any conflicts by setting the recordset's **Filter** property to **adFilterConflictingRecords**. This forces the recordset to navigate only through conflicting records. If there are conflicting records, you can check the **Status** property to determine why the update failed. For more information about the **Status** property, search for "Status Property" in the ADO Programmer's Reference.

If there are conflicts, you must decide how best to resolve them. You can overwrite the conflicting records in the database, you can decide not to change the conflicting records, or you can take other action depending on the business rules. To help make this decision, you can update the underlying values in the disconnected recordset to examine the conflicting values in the database. To update the underlying values, call the **Resync** method with the **adAffectGroup** and **adResync UnderlyingValues** parameters.

The following example code shows how to resynchronize the underlying values in a recordset:

```
rs.Filter = adFilterConflictingRecords
rs.Resync adAffectGroup, adResyncUnderlyingValues
```

Once the underlying values are synchronized with the database, you can see the changes other users have made through the **Underlying** property, and decide if you want to overwrite them or not. If you decide to overwrite the conflicting records, simply call **UpdateBatch** again. Now that the underlying values match the database, there are no conflicts, and the updates occur.

Note When the disconnected recordset is passed from one process to another, it does not marshal the underlying values. Thus, if you return a disconnected recordset to a client for conflict resolution, you must pass the underlying values via another mechanism, such as a separate disconnected recordset containing just the underlying values. For more information about how to return conflicting records to a client, see Knowledge Base Article Q177720: "FILE: Rdsensub.exe with RDS Conflict Resolution Sample."

ADO Best Practices

There are issues involving performance and scaling that need to be considered when using ADO or any database access technology in a three-tier architecture. Here are some best practices that can help you write better code for working with databases.

♦ If your code retrieves field values repeatedly, consider binding object variables to the fields collection. This improves performance because you do not incur the overhead of looking up fields in the **Recordset.Fields** collection for each record in the recordset. To see an example of how to bind object variables to fields. To copy this code for use in your own projects, see "Binding Object Variables to the Fields Collection" on the accompanying CD-ROM.

```
Dim rs As Recordset
Set rs = New Recordset
Dim fldId, fldFName, fldLName

rs.ActiveConnection = "Provider=SQLOLEDB;Data
Source=MSERIES1;Database=pubs;User Id=sa;Password=;"
rs.Source = "select au_id, au_fname, au_lname from authors"
rs.Open

Set fldId = rs.Fields(0)
Set fldFName = rs.Fields(1)
Set fldLName = rs.Fields(2)

While Not rs.EOF
    Debug.Print fldId.Value, fldFName.Value, fldLName.Value
    rs.MoveNext
Wend
```

◆ ADO uses the **Recordset** object's **CacheSize** property to determine the number of rows to fetch and cache. While you are within the range of cached rows, ADO returns data from the cache. When you scroll out of the range of cached rows, ADO releases the cache and fetches the next **CacheSize** number of rows. By monitoring how your application uses data, you can tune the **CacheSize** property to reduce the number of network trips for data.

◆ Microsoft Data Access Components (MDAC) 2.0 ships with native providers for three SQL data sources: SQL Server, Oracle, and Jet (.mdb). In earlier versions, you had to go through the OLE DB provider for ODBC data, which in turn used the appropriate ODBC driver to access these data sources. With MDAC 2.0, you can use these native OLE DB providers to access your data faster and with lower disk and memory footprint.

◆ ADO 2.0 includes a new execution option called **adExecuteNoRecords**, which you should use for commands that do not return rows. When you specify this option, ADO does not create a **Recordset** object, and does not set any cursor properties. Also, the provider can optimize for this case by not verifying any rowset properties. The following sample code uses **adExecuteNoRecords**. To copy this code for use in your own projects, see "Using the adExecuteNoRecords Option" on the accompanying CD-ROM.

```
Dim conn As Connection
Set conn = New Connection

conn.Open "Provider=SQLOLEDB;Data
Source=MSERIES1;Database=pubs;User Id=sa;Password=;"
conn.Execute "insert into AddressBook values(5, 'Joe',
'Programmer')", , adExecuteNoRecords
```

◆ ADO 2.0 optimizes one-time command executions when done through **Connection.Execute**. This is a common scenario in Internet Information Server (IIS), Active Server Pages (ASP), and MTS environments where the code typically opens a connection, executes a row- or nonrow-returning command, processes results, and closes the connection. For such scenarios, use **Connection.Execute** instead of **Recordset.Open** or **Command.Execute**. When you use **Connection.Execute**, ADO does not preserve any command state information which improves performance. Note that you may still need to use **Recordset.Open** or **Command.Execute** if you need a more functional cursor, or if you need to use **Command.Parameters**.

- In general, acquire database resources such as connections and recordsets as late as possible, and release them as soon as possible. This means that connections and recordsets have a lifetime limited to the scope of the business or data object in which they were created.

- Be aware when using server-side cursors. Opening them in transactions can have locking implications such as blocking other users. They also consume server system resources. When possible, use a client-side cursor, or a disconnected recordset.

- Avoid transferring unnecessary data. For example, to insert a record into a table, you can execute an SQL **Insert** command rather than create a recordset and use the **AddNew** and **Update** methods. When you use the SQL **Insert** command, you do not create a recordset.

- Specify only those fields that you actually use when generating a **Recordset** object. Avoid **Select** * if you do not need all of the fields, as this returns unnecessary data over the network.

- Use the **MaxRecords** property of the **Recordset** object if you know how many records you are going to use. For example, set the property to 10 if you only want the first ten records of a given recordset.

Executing Stored Procedures from the Command Object

In this section, you will learn how to use stored procedures from the ADO **Command** object. Then, you will learn two ways to fill the **Parameters** collection. Finally, you will learn how to access output parameters and return values from stored procedures.

Executing Stored Procedures

Stored procedures are compiled collections of SQL statements and control-of-flow language that execute quickly. Executing a stored procedure is similar to executing an SQL command, except that the stored procedure exists in the database as an object, even after execution has finished. Stored procedures hide potentially complex SQL statements from the components that use them. Also, SQL Server compiles and stores stored procedures, which makes them run much faster than submitting the SQL statements as separate SQL queries.

To use a stored procedure, set the **CommandType** property of the **Command** object to the constant **adCmdStoredProc**, the **CommandText** to the name of the stored procedure, and then invoke the **Execute** method.

This example code retrieves a recordset by invoking the Island Hopper News **Customer_GetByEmail** stored procedure:

```
Dim cmd As ADODB.Command
Dim rs As ADODB.Recordset
Set cmd = New ADODB.Command
'Use a previously created connection
Set cmd.ActiveConnection = conn
cmd.CommandType = adCmdStoredProc
cmd.CommandText = "Customer_GetByEmail " & "someone@microsoft.com"
Set rs = cmd.Execute
```

Populating the Parameters Collection

Stored procedures may require that one or more parameters be passed to them. For each required parameter, a **Parameter** object should be created and appended to the **Parameters** collection of the **Command** object.

There are two approaches to populating the **Parameters** collection. For situations where access to the data source is fast, or for rapid development purposes, you can have the data source automatically populate the parameters by calling the **Refresh** method of the collection. The command must have an active connection for this to succeed. Once completed, you can assign values to the parameters and then run the stored procedure.

The following sample code shows how to call the Island Hopper News stored procedure **Customer_GetByEmail** using the **Refresh** method to fill the **Parameters** collection. To copy this code for use in your own projects, see "Using the Refresh Method to Fill the Parameters Collection" on the accompanying CD-ROM.

```
Dim conn As ADODB.Connection
Dim cmd As ADODB.Command
Dim rs As ADODB.Recordset

Set conn = New ADODB.Connection
Set cmd = New ADODB.Command
conn.ConnectionString = "DSN=Classifieds;UID=sa;PWD="
conn.Open
```

code continued on next page

code continued from previous page

```
Set cmd.ActiveConnection = conn
cmd.CommandType = adCmdStoredProc
cmd.CommandText = "Customer_GetByEmail"
cmd.Parameters.Refresh
cmd.Parameters(1) = "someone@microsoft.com"
Set rs = cmd.Execute
```

Using the **Refresh** method causes ADO to make an extra trip to SQL Server to collect the parameter information. You can increase the performance of your components by creating the parameters in the collection yourself, and avoid the extra network trip. To fill the **Parameter** collection, create separate **Parameter** objects, fill in the correct parameter information for the stored procedure call, and then append them to the collection using the **Append** method. For multiple parameters, you must append the parameters in the order that they are defined in the stored procedure.

The following sample code shows how to create parameters for the Island Hopper News **Customer_GetByEmail** stored procedure. To copy this code for use in your own projects, see "Creating Parameters for a Stored Procedure" on the accompanying CD-ROM.

```
Dim conn As ADODB.Connection
Dim cmd As ADODB.Command
Dim rs As ADODB.Recordset
Dim prm As ADODB.Parameter

Set conn = New ADODB.Connection
Set cmd = New ADODB.Command
conn.ConnectionString = "DSN=Classifieds;UID=sa;PWD="
conn.Open

Set cmd.ActiveConnection = conn
cmd.CommandType = adCmdStoredProc
cmd.CommandText = "Customer_GetByEmail"
Set prm = cmd.CreateParameter("vEmail", adVarChar, _
          adParamInput, 50, "someone@microsoft.com")
cmd.Parameters.Append prm
Set rs = cmd.Execute
```

Return Codes and Output Parameters

Stored procedures may contain input and output parameters and return values. For example, the **Customer_Remove** stored procedure contains the @vCount output parameter which is assigned the number of records in the customer table after a customer is removed. Also, if **Customer_Remove** can successfully find and remove the desired record, it returns a code of 1. Otherwise, it returns a code of 0. Because customer information is in both the CustomerPasswords and Customers tables, **Customer_Remove** must delete the information from both tables to completely remove the customer.

The following sample code shows the **Customer_Remove** procedure. To copy this code for use in your own projects, see "Customer_Remove Procedure" on the accompanying CD-ROM.

```
CREATE PROCEDURE Customer_Remove
    @vEmail varchar(30),
    @vCount int OUTPUT

AS

DECLARE @vCustomerID int

SELECT @vCustomerID = CustomerID FROM Customers
    WHERE Email= @vEmail
IF @vCustomerID IS NULL
    return (0)
ELSE
    begin
        DELETE FROM CustomerPasswords
            WHERE CustomerID = @vCustomerID
        DELETE FROM Customers
            WHERE CustomerID = @vCustomerID
        SELECT @vCount = COUNT(*) FROM Customers
        return (1)
    end
```

You can specify an input parameter for a stored procedure through the **Parameter** object. You must append the return parameter to the **Parameters** collection first. Then, you can obtain any output parameters by reading their values from the

Parameters collection. You can read the return code just like any other parameter because it is the first parameter in the **Parameters** collection. Be aware that the return code parameter is at index 0, instead of 1.

Note If you execute a stored procedure that returns a recordset and you assign the returned recordset to a **Recordset** object, you must close the **Recordset** object before you can read any return or output parameters. For more information, see Knowledge Base article Q167908, "PRB: Output Parameters Wrong after ADO Command.Execute Call."

The following sample code shows how to call the **Customer_Remove** stored procedure and access both the return code and the **vCount** output parameter after the call. To copy this code for use in your own projects, see "Using a Stored Procedure to Access a Return Code and Output Parameter" on the accompanying CD-ROM.

```
Dim conn As ADODB.Connection
Dim cmd As ADODB.Command
Dim prm As ADODB.Parameter

Set conn = New ADODB.Connection
Set cmd = New ADODB.Command
conn.ConnectionString = "DSN=Classifieds"
conn.Open
Set cmd.ActiveConnection = conn
cmd.CommandText = "Customer_Remove"
Set prm = cmd.CreateParameter("Return", adInteger, _
  adParamReturnValue, , 0)
cmd.Parameters.Append prm
Set prm = cmd.CreateParameter("@vEmail", adVarChar, _
  adParamInput, 30, "test@microsoft.com")
cmd.Parameters.Append prm
Set prm = cmd.CreateParameter("@vCount", adInteger, adParamOutput,
 , 0)
cmd.Parameters.Append prm
cmd.Execute
Debug.Print cmd("Return") 'Return Code
Debug.Print cmd("@vCount") 'Count
```

Stored procedures can return an integer value called a return status. This status indicates that the procedure completed successfully, or it indicates the reason for failure. SQL Server has a defined set of return values.

Value	Meaning
0	Procedure was executed successfully
-1	Object missing
-2	Datatype error occurred
-3	Process was chosen as deadlock victim
-4	Permission error occurred
-5	Syntax error occurred
-6	Miscellaneous user error occurred
-7	Resource error, such as out of space, occurred
-8	Non-fatal internal problem encountered
-9	System limit was reached
-10	Fatal internal inconsistency occurred
-11	Fatal internal inconsistency occurred
-12	Table or index is corrupt
-13	Database is corrupt
-14	Hardware error occurred

Lab 5: Using ADO to Implement Business Services

In this lab, you will implement the **ListByCustEmail** and **Update** methods of the **db_AdC** component. You will implement the **ListByCustEmail** method by using SQL statements to perform the required actions. Then you will test the **ListByCustEmail** method with a custom test client. Next you will implement the **Update** method to call a stored procedure to update an existing ad. Then you will modify the custom client to test the **Update** method as well.

To see the demonstration "Lab 5 Solution," see the accompanying CD-ROM.

Estimated time to complete this lab: **60 minutes**

To complete the exercises in this lab, you must have the required software. For detailed information about the labs and setup for the labs, see "Labs" in "About This Course."

Objectives

After completing this lab, you will be able to:

◆ Use SQL statements to retrieve and modify data on a data source.

◆ Use the ADO object model.

◆ Open a connection to a data source by using an ADO **Connection** object.

◆ Retrieve a set of records by using an ADO **Recordset** object.

◆ Use an ADO **Command** object to execute a SQL Server stored procedure.

◆ Use ADO **Parameter** objects to initialize parameters for a stored procedure.

Prerequisites

Before working on this lab, you should be familiar with the following:

◆ Adding and deleting components in MTS packages.

◆ Creating a COM DLL by using Microsoft Visual Basic.

Exercises

The following exercises provide practice working with the concepts and techniques covered in this chapter:

◆ Exercise 1: Using ADO to Execute Embedded SQL

In this exercise, you will use ADO and SQL statements to implement the **ListByCustEmail** method of the **db_AdC** component. The **ListByCustEmail** method returns a recordset containing all advertisements that match a specified e-mail name.

◆ Exercise 2: Testing the ListByCustEmail Method

In this exercise, you will test the **ListByCustEmail** method that you just implemented. First you will add the db_AdC.dll to the IsleHop_Classifieds package. Then you will create a custom test client to test the **db_AdC** component by retrieving ads for a given e-mail name. This method cannot be tested with the Island Hopper Visual Basic or Web clients.

◆ Exercise 3: Using ADO to Run Stored Procedures

In this exercise, you will implement the **Update** method of the **db_AdC** component to update an existing ad in the database by running a stored procedure. The Island Hopper implementation of **Update** uses an SQL command statement to perform the update, but you will use a stored procedure called **UpdateAd** instead.

◆ Exercise 4: Testing the Update Method

In this exercise, you will test the **Update** method that you just implemented. You will open the db_AdTest project you created in Exercise 2 and add an **Update** button. The **Update** button uses the **Update** method to update an existing ad in the database with the information on the form. This method cannot be tested with the Island Hopper Web client.

Exercise 1: Using ADO to Execute Embedded SQL

In this exercise, you will use ADO and SQL statements to implement the **ListByCustEmail** method of the **db_AdC** component. The **ListByCustEmail** method returns a recordset containing all advertisements that match a specified e-mail name.

▶ **Open the db_AdC project**

1. Start Visual Basic.

2. Open the **db_AdC** project located in Labs\Lab05\Exercise1 folder.

3. Open the Ad class module.

▶ **Implement the ListByCustEmail method**

1. In the code window, open the **ListByCustEmail** function.

2. Define two variables, a String variable called **strSQL** to hold the SQL command statement and a Recordset variable called **rs** to hold the resulting recordset:

```
Dim strSQL As String
Dim rs As ADODB.Recordset
```

3. Enable error trapping by adding an **On Error** statement:

```
On Error GoTo ErrorHandler
```

4. Initialize **strSQL** with an SQL **Select** statement to retrieve all records from the Advertisements table. Select those records that match the e-mail name passed in the **strEmail** parameter. To do this you will join the Advertisements table with the Customers table through the CustomerID field. Order the records by advertisement title.

To see an example of how your code should look, see Lab Hint 5.1 in Appendix B.

5. Instantiate the recordset. Using a local cursor, open the recordset with the IslandHopper file DSN as the connection source:

```
Set rs = New ADODB.Recordset
rs.CursorLocation = adUseClient
rs.Open strSQL, "FILEDSN=" & fileDSN, _
  adOpenUnspecified, adLockUnspecified, adCmdUnspecified
```

6. Call **SetComplete**.

7. Assign the recordset to the function and return to the caller.

8. Implement the error hander by clearing the **Recordset** object, aborting the MTS transaction, and then raising an error:

```
ErrorHandler:
  If Not rs Is Nothing Then
  Set rs = Nothing
End If
GetObjectContext.SetAbort
Err.Raise Err.Number, SetErrSource(modName, "ListByCustEmail"), _
  Err.Description
```

9. Save the project and build db_AdC.dll.

Exercise 2: Testing the ListByCustEmail Method

In this exercise, you will test the **ListByCustEmail** method that you just implemented. First you will add the db_AdC.dll to the IsleHop_Classifieds package. Then you will create a custom test client to test the **db_AdC** component by retrieving ads for a given e-mail name. This method cannot be tested with the Island Hopper Visual Basic or Web clients.

▶ **Register db_AdC.dll with MTS**

1. Start the MTS Explorer and remove the current db_AdC.dll by deleting it from the IsleHop_Classifieds package.

2. Add the db_AdC.dll you just created to the IsleHop_Classifieds package and set its transaction attribute to **Requires a transaction**. For more information on adding components, see "Adding Components to a Package" on page 82 in Chapter 3, "Introduction to Microsoft Transaction Server (MTS)."

▶ **Test with a custom client**

1. Create a new Standard EXE project in Visual Basic.

   Place controls on the form and set their properties as follows.

Control	Property	Value
Command button	Name	cmdRetrieve
	Caption	Retrieve Ads
Text box	Name	txtEmail
	Text	None
Text box	Name	txtTitle
	Text	None
Text box	Name	txtBody
	Text	None
Text box	Name	txtStartDate
	Text	None

table continued on next page

Control	Property	Value
Text box	Name	txtEndDate
	Text	None
Label	Caption	Email:
Label	Caption	Ads:
Label	Caption	Title:
Label	Caption	Body:
Label	Caption	StartDate:
Label	Caption	EndDate:
List box	Name	lstAds
Form	Name	frmAdClient
	Caption	db_AdC Custom Client

This illustration shows how your form should look.

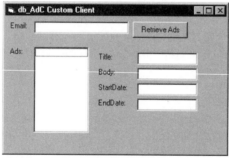

2. On the **Project** menu, click **References** and add a reference to the db_AdC.dll project. Also add a reference to the Microsoft ActiveX Data Objects 2.0 Library.

3. Save the new project and form as the files dbAdTest.vbp and dbAdTest.frm.

4. In the Declarations section, declare a variable **rs** of type **ADODB.Recordset**.

5. In the **cmdRetrieve_Click** event, declare a variable **objAd** of type **db_AdC.Ad**.

6. Set **objAd** equal to a new instance of **db_AdC.Ad**.

7. Call the **ListByCustEmail** method on **objAd** passing **txtEmail.Text** as the parameter. Set **rs** equal to the return value.

8. Use a loop to add the advertisement ID from each ad record to the lstAds list box:

```
While Not rs.EOF
  lstAds.AddItem rs("AdvertisementID")
  rs.MoveNext
Wend
```

9. In the **lstAds_Click** event, use the following code to find the advertisement ID that was clicked on in the recordset. Then populate the text boxes with the advertisement fields:

```
rs.MoveFirst
rs.Find "AdvertisementID=" & lstAds.List(lstAds.ListIndex)
txtTitle = rs("Title")
txtBody = rs("Body")
txtStartDate = rs("StartDate")
txtEndDate = rs("EndDate")
```

10. Save the project and run it. Test the **ListByCustEmail** method by typing in a valid e-mail name and pressing the **Retrieve Ads** button. You can enter "someone@microsoft.com" as a valid e-mail name to test with. The advertisement IDs should be displayed in the list box. When you click an advertisement ID, you should see the ad information displayed in the text boxes.

Exercise 3: Using ADO to Run Stored Procedures

In this exercise, you will implement the **Update** method of the **db_AdC** component to update an existing ad in the database by running a stored procedure. The Island Hopper implementation of **Update** uses a SQL command statement to perform the update, but you will use a stored procedure called **UpdateAd** instead.

▶ **Open the db_AdC project**

1. Start Visual Basic.

2. Open the db_AdC project you worked on in the previous exercise.

3. Open the **Ad** class module.

▶ **Implement the Update method to call a stored procedure**

1. In the code window, open the **Update** function.

2. Use the following code to declare **strSPCmd** and **param**, and instantiate **cmd** and **conn**. Cmd will execute the stored procedure. **Conn** will hold the connection to the database, and **StrSPCmd** will hold the name of the stored procedure. **Param** will append parameters to the **Command** object:

```
'Declare the variables
Dim strSPCmd As String
Dim param As ADODB.Parameter

'Instantiate the variables
Set cmd = New ADODB.Command
Set conn = New ADODB.Connection
```

3. Enable error trapping by adding an **On Error** statement:

```
On Error GoTo ErrorHandler
```

4. Set the **ActiveConnection** property of **cmd** equal to **conn**.

5. Open a connection with **conn** using the IslandHopper file DSN as the connection source:

```
conn.Open "FILEDSN=" & fileDSN
```

6. Set the **CommandText** property of the **cmd** object equal to **UpdateAd**.

7. Set the **CommandType** property of the **cmd** object equal to **adCmdStoredProc**.

8. Use the following code to create and append all the parameters for the **UpdateAd** stored procedure:

```
Set param = cmd.CreateParameter("Title", adVarChar, _
  adParamInput, 100, strTitle)
cmd.Parameters.Append param
Set param = cmd.CreateParameter("StartDate", _
  adDBTimeStamp, adParamInput, , varStartDateTime)
cmd.Parameters.Append param
Set param = cmd.CreateParameter("EndDate", _
  adDBTimeStamp, adParamInput, , varEndDateTime)
cmd.Parameters.Append param
Set param = cmd.CreateParameter("CustomerID", _
  adInteger, adParamInput, , lngCustomerID)
```

```
cmd.Parameters.Append param
Set param = cmd.CreateParameter("CategoryID", _
  adInteger, adParamInput, , lngCategoryID)
cmd.Parameters.Append param
Set param = cmd.CreateParameter("ModifiedDate", _
  adDBTimeStamp, adParamInput, , Date)
cmd.Parameters.Append param
Set param = cmd.CreateParameter("Body", adVarChar, _
  adParamInput, 1000, strBody)
cmd.Parameters.Append param
Set param = cmd.CreateParameter("AdID", adInteger, _
  adParamInput, , lngAdvertisementID)
cmd.Parameters.Append param
```

9. Execute the stored procedure.

10. Call **SetComplete**.

11. Save the project and build db_AdC.dll.

Exercise 4: Testing the Update Method

In this exercise, you will test the **Update** method that you just implemented. You will open the db_AdTest project you created in Exercise 2 and add an **Update** button. The **Update** button calls the **Update** method to update an existing ad in the database with the information on the form. This method cannot be tested with the Island Hopper Web client.

▶ **Modify the custom client**

1. Start Visual Basic and open the db_AdTest project you created in Exercise 2.

2. Add a button to the form and set its **Caption** property to **Update**. Set its **Name** property to **cmdUpdate**.

3. In the **cmdUpdate_Click** event, declare a variable **objAd** of type **db_AdC.Ad**.

4. Set **objAd** equal to a new instance of **db_AdC.Ad**.

5. Call the **Update** method, passing the text box values on the form for the **Title, Body, StartDate,** and **EndDate** parameters. Use the recordset to provide the other parameters:

```
objAd.Update rs("AdvertisementID"), txtTitle.Text, _
  txtBody.Text, rs("StartDate"), rs("EndDate"), _
  rs("CategoryID"), rs("CustomerID")
```

6. Save the project and run it. Test the **Update** method by retrieving advertisements for a specific e-mail name, changing some of the fields and clicking the **Update** button. You can use "someone@microsoft.com" as a valid test e-mail name. After you update an advertisement, you will need to retrieve the advertisements again to ensure that the update worked.

▶ **Test with the Visual Basic Island Hopper client (optional)**

1. Start the Island Hopper News Visual Basic client application.

2. Go to the **Ad Maintenance** section and retrieve any customer that has placed ads.

3. Double click an ad to bring up the **Ad Details** form. Change the ad and save it. The Visual Basic code that performs the save will ultimately call the **Update** method that you implemented.

Self-Check Questions

To see the answers to the Self-Check Questions, see Appendix A.

1. Which ActiveX Data Objects (ADO) are members of a collection?

   A. Field and Parameter only

   B. Field, Parameter, Property, and Error

   C. Field, Command, Parameter, and Property

   D. Field, Parameter, and Error only

2. List all ActiveX Data Objects (ADO) that can generate a recordset.

   A. Recordset object

   B. Recordset and Command objects

   C. Recordset, Command, and Connection objects

   D. Tabledef, Command, and Connection objects

3. True or False: The following example code creates a client-side, static cursor with a lock type of optimistic batch update.

```
Dim rs As ADODB.Recordset
Set rs = New ADODB.Recordset
rs.CursorType = adOpenStatic
rs.LockType = adLockBatchOptimistic
rs.Open "Select * From Authors", "DSN=Pubs"
Set rs.ActiveConnection = Nothing
```

A. True

B. False

4. What are the steps to create the parameters in the Parameters collection yourself when using stored procedures?

A. Create separate **Parameter** objects, fill in the correct parameter information for the stored procedure call, and then append them to the collection using the **Append** method.

B. Establish an active connection, call the **Refresh** method of the **Parameters** collection, assign values to the parameters, and then run the stored procedure.

C. Set the **CommandType** property of the **Command** object to the constant **adCmdStoredProc**, the **CommandText** to the name of the stored procedure, and then invoke the **Execute** method.

D. Append the return parameter to the **Parameters** collection, obtain any output parameters by reading their values from the **Parameters** collection, and then read the return code.

5. Which Recordset method would you use to update a database from a disconnected recordset?

A. Refresh

B. Update

C. UpdateBatch

D. Resync

Student Notes:

Chapter 6:
Building Stored Procedures with SQL

In this chapter, you will learn how to determine when it is appropriate to implement data services in Microsoft Transaction Server (MTS) objects or in an SQL Server database. You will learn how to implement data integrity and stored procedures. Finally, you will learn about SQL transactions and compare these transactions to those found in MTS.

Objectives

After completing this chapter, you will be able to:

◆ Choose when to implement services in database or MTS objects.

◆ Explain the role of data integrity when implementing data services in an enterprise solution.

◆ Implement business and data services by using stored procedures.

◆ Write a stored procedure that generates return parameters and can be used by other services, such as client applications written with Visual Basic.

◆ Debug a stored procedure.

◆ Write a stored procedure that uses advanced SQL programming constructs, such as conditional branching and looping structures.

◆ Describe the characteristics of SQL transactions and explain how they work with MTS transactions.

Implementing Business and Data Services with SQL Server

In traditional two-tier client/server database architecture, the database serves as the data repository and provides centralized business logic in the form of triggers and stored procedures.

In three-tier architecture, business logic is often placed in a business services tier separate from the client or database. However, it still makes sense to place some business logic in the data services tier. Such business logic still takes the form of triggers and stored procedures.

There are no hard rules about where to place business logic, but here are some guidelines for when to put business logic in the business services tier versus the data services tier.

◆ Place simple business logic in the data services tier.

Business logic should be placed in the data services tier when the logic involves operations such as simple inserts, updates, or deletes. Business logic that runs in the data services tier can take advantage of native database capabilities that may not be available from the business services tier. However, complex business logic can overburden the database server as the number of users increases, and should be placed in business services.

◆ In general, place business logic in the business services tier.

You have a greater degree of control when developing business logic, as database personnel often create stored procedures. You have more flexibility in the business services tier because you can write business logic in any language. By placing business logic in the business services tier, you can work with multiple resource managers.

This chapter focuses on building simple stored procedures and the issues involved with stored procedures. Although most often the database administrator creates and maintains stored procedures, it is important for you as a developer to understand the issues involved with data services and stored procedures. The more familiar you are with a database and its abilities, the better able you are to program against it and take advantage of its features.

Introduction to SQL Server

In this section, you will learn about the role of SQL Server and the benefits that it provides in an enterprise solution. You will also learn about the SQL Enterprise Manager and the Visual Basic Data View add-in tools by examining the Island Hopper News Classifieds database. Later in this chapter, you will use Data View to build stored procedures for use with SQL Server databases.

SQL Server in an Enterprise Solution

Microsoft SQL Server version 6.5 is a scalable, high-performance database management system designed specifically for distributed client/server computing. Its built-in data replication, powerful management tools, Internet integration, and open system architecture provide a superior platform for delivering cost-effective information solutions.

SQL Server provides excellent data services for an enterprise solution. It provides data integrity that is enforced through the implementation of procedural data integrity and/or declarative data integrity. It handles concurrent access from many applications and users to the data, and it provides stored procedures for running fast business logic and data access logic directly on the server.

Microsoft SQL Server is a high-end relational database management system (RDBMS). Its database architecture features include:

◆ A parallel, symmetric server architecture with automatic workload balancing across multiple processors.

◆ True multi-threaded kernel for improved transaction performance and scalability.

◆ Full online transaction processing with automatic rollback and roll-forward recovery.

◆ Enhanced, cost-based query optimizer with statistics-based query cost analysis for improved response.

◆ Improved checkpointing for better data throughput and response time.

◆ Asynchronous I/O support for parallel access to multiple disk devices for greater throughput.

◆ High-speed row- and page-level locking with configurable lock escalation; automatic deadlock resolution.

Examining the Classifieds Database

The structure of the Island Hopper Classifieds database can be viewed and managed with either the SQL Enterprise Manager or the Visual Basic Data View add-in.

The SQL Enterprise Manager is more suitable for database administrators, providing functionality to manage all aspects of SQL databases such as design, stored procedures, replication, security, and so on. The Visual Basic Data View add-in, on the other hand, contains tools more suitable for developers and database development, such as data access and stored procedures.

Enterprise Manager

The structure of the Classifieds database can be managed through the Server Manager window in SQL Enterprise Manager.

When you start SQL Enterprise Manager for the first time, you must register the SQL Server you are managing by specifying the name of the SQL Server and providing a login. Once you have registered the server, you can view information about the databases in that server. For example, if you expand the Databases folder and then expand the Classifieds folder, you can view information about tables, views, stored procedures, defaults, and user-defined data types in the Classifieds database.

The following illustration shows the Server Manager window in SQL Enterprise Manager.

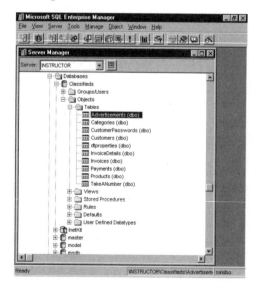

To see the demonstration "Using Enterprise Manager," see the accompanying CD-ROM.

Visual Basic Data Environment Designer and Data View

The Data Environment designer is an object you can add to your Visual Basic project that provides an interactive, design-time environment for creating objects that access data.

Use the Data Environment designer to:

◆ Add a Data Environment to your project.

◆ Add connections to databases.

◆ Add commands to retrieve and manipulate data.

Once you have added a Data Environment to a Visual Basic project and established a connection to a database, you can use the Data View window to view the structure and contents of the database.

▶ **To create a new Data Environment**

1. If the **Add Data Environment** command is not present on the **Project** menu, then click **Components** on the **Project** menu.

2. In the **Components** dialog box, click the **Designers** tab and select the **Data Environment** check box.

3. On the **Project** menu, click **Add Data Environment**.

4. Use the Properties window to set the **Name** property of the Data Environment to something appropriate for your application.

   This is the name you use to refer to the Data Environment programmatically.

When you add a Data Environment to your project, a **Connection** object named Connection1 is included by default. You can also create new connections at any time by choosing **Add Connection** from the Data Environment designer toolbar.

Setting Connection Properties

When you create a connection in the Data Environment you need to specify details about the data source to which you are connecting, for example, the SQL Server database. The details about this connection are collectively referred to as the **Data Link** properties.

Use the **Data Link Properties** dialog box to select the data provider and set the properties for a connection. To display the **Data Link Properties** dialog box, in the Data Environment window, right-click a connection name, and then click **Properties**.

Use the **Provider** tab of the **Data Link Properties** dialog box to select the OLE DB provider you want to use to connect to a data source. Use the **Connection** tab to provide the necessary connection information.

Viewing the Classifieds Database with Data View

Within Visual Basic, Data View enables you to access the structure of the Classifieds database and it provides a way of using the Data Environment to visually manipulate the structure. Although it does not appear in the **Add-Ins** menu, the Data View add-in is automatically loaded when you start Visual Basic. To display the Data View, click the **View** menu and then click **Data View Window**.

To see the demonstration "Viewing a Database with Data View," see the accompanying CD-ROM.

Similar to Enterprise Manager, Data View allows you to drill down into the structure of a database. Under each database, an Object folder can be expanded, revealing information about database diagrams, tables, views, and stored procedures.

The following illustration shows the Data View window.

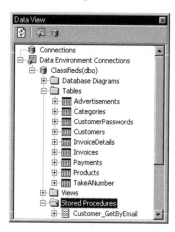

Using Data Integrity

In this section, you will learn about the different types of data integrity that can be implemented in SQL Server. You will also learn the different ways that declarative and procedural data integrity is enforced in SQL Server.

Introduction to Data Integrity

Data integrity refers to the consistency and accuracy of data stored in a database. Conventional database management systems require data integrity logic to be coded into each application. SQL Server stores this logic in the database itself, ensuring consistency and simplifying maintenance.

It is important that you understand how data integrity is enforced in an SQL Server database. Even if someone else, such as a database administrator, created the database, you should be familiar with the structure of a database if you plan to use it in your applications. You need to interpret the data integrity checks that are performed by the database management system so that you can possibly anticipate them in your application logic. Often, you can save time by performing some data integrity checks in your middle-tier components before the data is sent over the network to the database. You can also interpret errors that are generated when data integrity is violated and handle this situation more effectively in your code when you fully understand the database structure.

Data Integrity Types

The different types of data integrity are entity, domain, and referential.

Data integrity type	Description
Entity	Entity (or table) integrity requires that all rows in a table have a unique identifier, the primary key value. Whether the primary key value can be changed, or whether the whole row can be deleted, depends on the level of integrity required between the primary key and any foreign key references.

table continued on next page

Data integrity type	Description
Domain	Domain (or column) integrity specifies a set of data values that are valid for that column and determines whether null values are allowed. Domain integrity is often enforced through the use of "validity checking." It is also enforced by restricting the type (datatypes), the format (rules and constraints), or the range of possible values (rules, references, and check constraints).
Referential	Referential integrity ensures that the relationships among the primary and foreign keys are always maintained. A row in the referenced table cannot be deleted, nor the primary key changed, if a foreign key exists that refers to the row. A foreign key value cannot be inserted into the referencing table if no row with the corresponding primary key exists in the referenced table.

Enforcing Data Integrity

Implementing declarative data integrity and/or procedural data integrity enforces data integrity.

Declarative Data Integrity

Declarative integrity is defined directly on tables and columns as part of the database definition by using the SQL **Create Table** and/or **Alter Table** statements.

With declarative data integrity, integrity checking is performed automatically by the database management system. For this reason, it is more concise and less error prone than other implementations. The database management system — not the person responsible for writing rules, stored procedures, or triggers — is responsible for ensuring that data integrity checking is performed when needed.

Three ways that declarative data integrity is enforced are:

Declarative data integrity method	Description
Identity property	The SQL **Identity** property can be used to create columns (identity columns) that contain system-generated values that identify each row inserted into a table. SQL Server automatically generates a value based on the previous identity value and the increment that was specified for the column in the table definition. The **Identity** property can be placed on any column in any sequence, but only one identity column can be created per table.
Constraints	Constraints restrict the data values that can be inserted into a database as the result of an update. SQL Server provides Primary Key, Unique, Foreign Key, Default, Check, and Reference constraints.
Defaults and rules	Defaults and rules create database objects that are bound to a column or a user-defined data type. The default specifies a value to be inserted into the column to which the object is bound. Rules specify the acceptable values that can be inserted into that column. Although you may still use defaults and rules, the SQL Server 6.5 constraints **Default** and **Check** provide the same functionality as a default and rule and should be used instead.

Procedural Data Integrity

Procedural data integrity is implemented by using stored procedures and triggers, which use the data definition language combined with the Transact-SQL language on the server.

Stored Procedures

Stored procedures are precompiled SQL statements stored on the server. Stored procedures:

◆ Encapsulate business functionality for use by all applications, thus ensuring consistent data modification.

◆ Are checked for syntax and compiled the first time they are executed; the compiled version is stored in the procedure cache and used for subsequent calls, making execution faster and more efficient.

◆ Are usually invoked by an application, not automatically by SQL Server.

Triggers

A trigger is a special kind of stored procedure that is invoked (triggered) whenever an attempt is made to modify the data in the table it protects. This occurs whenever modifications are made to a table using the SQL **Insert, Update,** or **Delete** statements.

Triggers are often used to enforce business rules and data integrity, or for other complex actions, such as automatically updating summary data. Because cascading updates and deletes are not currently available with Declarative Referential Integrity (DRI), triggers are still necessary. Triggers allow you to perform cascading delete or update actions if a referential integrity violation occurs.

Comparing Triggers and Stored Procedures

From a procedural data integrity standpoint, only triggers enforce data integrity because they are automatically fired. Stored procedures do not directly support data integrity, but they play an important role in helping to maintain and support data integrity. Stored procedures can be used in combination with a trigger. For example, a trigger can call a stored procedure: the trigger providing data integrity automatically executes the stored procedure code. In addition, by placing the code in the stored procedure, this information is made available to both the user and the trigger. The user has the benefit of voluntarily executing the stored procedure.

Primary Key Constraint

The primary key is a column or combination of columns that uniquely identifies a row.

The **Primary Key** constraint automatically creates a **Unique** index. This index is not visible to the user and cannot be dropped directly. It is dropped when the **Primary Key** constraint is dropped.

Unique Constraint

The **Unique** constraint specifies that no two rows can have the same index value. The **Unique** constraint can be used for alternate candidate keys. This constraint is similar to the **Primary Key** constraint except that it allows **Nulls**. Though **Nulls** are allowed, it is not advisable to use them.

Foreign Key Constraint

The **Foreign Key** constraint defines a multicolumn, foreign key reference to another table. The **Foreign Key** constraint is used in conjunction with the **References** constraint when the key comprises more than one column.

Default Constraint

To supply a value (when a user does not enter one in a column), define a **Default** constraint or a default on that column. Unlike defaults, **Default** constraints do not need a binding step.

Check Constraint

A **Check** constraint determines the type of data that can be entered in a particular column or in a column that has a given user-defined datatype. The **Check** constraint is equivalent to a rule.

Reference Constraint

Reference constraints require that the data added to a table containing a **Reference** constraint must have a matching value in the table that it references. For example, assume that a **Reference** constraint is placed on the title_id column in the sales table in the Pubs database and it references the title_id column in the titles table.

Creating Stored Procedures

In this section, you will learn how to enforce procedural data integrity by building, executing, and debugging simple stored procedures in an SQL Server database. First, you will learn how to add a new stored procedure to a database by using the Visual Basic Data View add-in. You will then learn how write a stored procedure so that it accepts parameters from and returns parameters to the calling application. Finally, you'll learn how to debug a stored procedure by using the T-SQL Debugger in Visual Basic.

Using Data View to Create a Stored Procedure

Once you have added a Data Environment to your Visual Basic project and established a connection to an SQL Server database, you can use the Data View window to create a new procedure.

For more information about using the Data Environment designer, see "Examining the Classifieds Database" on page 190 in this chapter.

▶ **To create a new procedure using Data View**

1. In the Data View window, right-click the Stored Procedures folder and then click **New**.

2. In the New Stored Procedure window, create a stored procedure and provide a name for it.

3. Data View creates a template for the stored procedure that includes a **Create Procedure** statement. Add the parameters and the **Select** statement to the stored procedure.

4. Right-click the New Stored Procedure window and then click **Save to Database**.

5. Close the New Stored Procedure window.

The Create Procedure Statement

Stored procedures are created with the **Create Procedure** statement, which has the following syntax:

```
CREATE PROCEDURE [owner.]procedure_name[;number]
[(parameter1 [, parameter2]...[parameter255])]
[{FOR REPLICATION} | {WITH RECOMPILE}
[{[WITH] | [,]} ENCRYPTION]]
AS sql_statements
```

The following arguments are used in most stored procedures:

Argument	Description
procedure_name	Specifies the name of the new stored procedure. Procedure names must conform to the rules for identifiers and must be unique within the database and its owner. The complete name cannot exceed 20 characters.
parameter	Specifies a parameter in the procedure. One or more parameters can optionally be declared in a **Create Procedure** statement. The user must supply the value of each declared parameter when the procedure is executed (unless a default for the parameter has been defined). A stored procedure can have a maximum of 255 parameters.
sql_statements	Specifies the actions the procedure is to take.

For more information about these arguments and the other arguments in the **Create Procedure** statement, search for "Create Procedure statement" in Visual Basic Help.

The following example code creates a simple stored procedure called count_loanhist:

```
CREATE PROC count_loanhist
  AS
  SELECT count(*) FROM loanhist
```

Note The **Create Procedure** statement cannot be combined with other SQL statements in a single batch.

Adding Parameters to a Stored Procedure

Information is passed from the user to a stored procedure through parameters. You can also use parameter definitions to specify what information is returned to the user from the stored procedure once its work is complete.

You can declare up to 255 parameters for each stored procedure. Each parameter that you define has the following syntax:

parameter = @parameter_name datatype *[= default]* *[Output]*

The arguments for the *parameter* argument are:

Argument	Description
parameter_name	Specifies the parameter name, which must start with the @ symbol.
datatype	Specifies the datatype of the parameter. All datatypes except image are supported.
default	Specifies a default value for the parameter. If a default value is defined, a user can execute the procedure without specifying a value for that parameter.
Output	Indicates that the parameter is a return parameter. The value of this option can be returned to the **Execute** statement that called the procedure. Use return parameters to return information to the calling procedure.

The following example code creates a stored procedure named mathtutor that calculates the product of two input numbers @m1 and @m2, which are declared as datatype **smallint**. The **Output** parameter @result returns the result of the calculation.

```
CREATE PROCEDURE mathtutor
  @m1 smallint,
  @m2 smallint,
  @result smallint OUTPUT
AS
SELECT @result = @m1 * @m2
```

The following example code defines a stored procedure named **Customer_ListByLastName** that returns a result set rather than a single value as an **Output** parameter:

```
CREATE PROCEDURE Customer_ListByLastName
  @vLastName varchar(30)
AS
BEGIN
DECLARE @vLast varchar(31)
SELECT @vLast = @vLastName + '%'
SELECT LastName + ', ' + FirstName as FullName,
LastName, FirstName, Address, City, State, PostalCode, Country,
PhoneNumber, Balance, Email, CustomerID from Customers
WHERE LastName LIKE @vLast ORDER BY FULLNAME
END
```

A value is assigned to the @vLast parameter by concatenating the value of the input parameter @vLastName with the wildcard "%." The result set is created by a simple **Select** statement by using @vLast to specify the search criteria for LastName in the **Where** clause.

Note The **Declare** statement defines a variable in your SQL code. For more information about variables, see "Declaring Variables" on page 202 in this chapter.

Debugging a Stored Procedure

The Visual Basic T-SQL Debugger is installed with the Enterprise tools during Visual Basic setup. Using the Visual Basic T-SQL Debugger, you can interactively debug stored procedures written in SQL within the Visual Basic development environment.

▶ To use the T-SQL Debugger from Visual Basic

1. From the **Add-Ins** menu, click **Add-In Manager**.

2. From the list of available add-ins, click **VB T-SQL Debugger** and then click **OK**.

3. Select the **Loaded/Unloaded** checkbox to add the T-SQL Debugger to the **Add-ins** menu.

4. From the **Add-Ins** menu, click **T-SQL Debugger**. This displays the **Visual Basic Batch T-SQL Debugger** dialog box.

5. On the **Settings** tab, complete the necessary settings to connect to the SQL Server database that contains the stored procedures you want to debug.

6. On the **Stored Procedure** tab, select the stored procedure you want to debug. If there are parameters, provide a value for each one.

7. Click **Execute**. This displays the T-SQL Debugger.

You can also launch the T-SQL Debugger by using one of the following methods:

- Use the Data Environment designer.
- Right-click a stored procedure in the Data View window and choose the **Debug** command.
- Use the UserConnection designer.

Using the T-SQL debugger, you can:

- Display the SQL call stack, local variables, and parameters for an SQL stored procedure.
- Control and manage breakpoints.
- View local variables and parameters.
- View global variables.

To see the demonstration "Debugging a Stored Procedure," see the accompanying CD-ROM.

You can also display the T-SQL debugger for run-time debugging while you debug Visual Basic code. To set up the T-SQL debugger for run-time debugging, select **T-SQL Debugging Options** from the **Tools** menu. Then, select the checkbox to automatically step into stored procedures through RDO and ADO connections. If you then step into any ADO code that executes stored procedures, you step into the stored procedure itself inside the T-SQL Debugger.

> **Note** The T-SQL debugger does not work properly if SQL Server logs on as the SystemAccount. You can change this by opening the Services application in Control Panel and double-clicking the **MSSQLServer** service. If the service is set to run as the **SystemAccount**, change this so the server logs on to a specific account that is valid to the domain in which you are.

Programming with Transact-SQL

In this section, you will learn how to expand upon stored procedures that perform basic queries, to include variables and flow-of-control statements. You will also learn about SQL transactions and compare these transactions to those found in MTS.

Declaring Variables

You can declare and use local and global variables in your stored procedures. These can be used to store temporary results and values while the stored procedure runs.

Local Variables

Local variables can be used only within the stored procedure in which they are declared. They are declared in the body of a stored procedure with the **Declare** statement and are assigned values with a **Select** statement. Local variables are often used in a stored procedure as a counter for **While** loops or for **If...Else** blocks. All variables must be declared with a proceeding @ symbol. Local variables are preceded with a single @ symbol. For example, @vCount is a local variable (in this case, a counter.)

The **Select** statement is used to assign values to variables. If the **Select** statement returns more than one value, the variable is assigned the last value returned. If the **Select** statement returns no rows, the variable retains its present value unless the variable assignment is made with a subquery. Only if the subquery returns no rows is the variable set to **Null**. The **Select** statement that assigns values to variables cannot retrieve data in the same statement.

The following example code creates a local variable named @vLast that is assigned values using the **Select** statement. The @vLast variable has a % symbol appended to it, which established a search criteria. Then, the @vLast variable is used to find all last names beginning with the same characters stored in @vLast.

```
Create Procedure Customer_ListByLastName @vLastName varchar(30) as
begin
declare @vLast varchar(31)
Select @vLast = @vLastName + '%'
Select LastName + ', ' + FirstName as FullName,
LastName, FirstName, Address, City, State, PostalCode, Country,
PhoneNumber, Balance, Email, CustomerID from Customers
where LastName Like @vLast ORDER BY FULLNAME
End
```

Global Variables

You can declare user-defined global variables or use the predefined global variables that are provided by SQL Server. Predefined global variables can be used without being declared.

Global variables are distinguished from local variables by two @@ symbols preceding their names. Many of the global variables report on system activity since the last time SQL Server was started; others report information about a connection.

This example code returns the last error number generated by the system for the user connection:

```
Select @@error
```

For a complete list of the predefined global variables, search for "SQL Global Variables" in SQL Server: Platform SDK Help.

Using Flow-of-Control Statements

Flow-of-control statements control the flow of execution of SQL statements, statement blocks, and stored procedures. Without flow-of-control statements, separate SQL statements are performed sequentially, as they occur. Flow-of-control statements permit statements to be connected, related to each other, and made interdependent, using programming-like constructs.

Statement	Description
Declare	Declares local variables and cursors.
Return	Exits unconditionally.
RaiseError	Returns a sysmessages entry or a dynamically built message with user-specified severity and state.
Print	Prints a user-defined message on the user's screen.
Case	Allows an expression to have conditional return values.
Begin...End	Defines a statement block.
If...Else	Defines conditional execution, and optionally, alternate execution when a condition is false.
While	Repeats statements while a specific condition is true.
Break...Continue	**Break** exits the innermost **While** loop and **Continue** restarts a **While** loop.

The following sample code shows a stored procedure that uses an **If** block. To copy this code for use in your own projects, see "Using an If Block in a Stored Procedure" on the accompanying CD-ROM.

```
CREATE PROCEDURE Customer_Remove
    @vEmail varchar(30),
    @vCount int OUTPUT

AS

DECLARE @vCustomerID int

SELECT @vCustomerID = CustomerID FROM Customers
    WHERE Email= @vEmail
IF @vCustomerID IS NULL
    return (0)
ELSE
    begin
        DELETE FROM CustomerPasswords
            WHERE CustomerID = @vCustomerID
        DELETE FROM Customers
```

code continued on next page

```
code continued from previous page
        WHERE CustomerID = @vCustomerID
        SELECT @vCount = COUNT(*) FROM Customers
        return (1)
    end
```

In the stored procedure, **Customer_Remove,** an **If** block is used to determine if a customer exists before an attempt is made to remove the customer. The **Begin** block groups multiple statements together under the **Else** statement.

SQL Transactions

You have already seen how transactions work with MTS. Additionally, transactions can be created within SQL Server stored procedures to group sets of SQL statements into a transaction. In the event of power loss, system software failure, application problems, or transaction cancellation requests, the SQL Server database can be recovered. At recovery time, committed transactions are reflected in the database and uncommitted transactions are rolled back.

SQL Server Transactions

Transactions are implemented using the Transact-SQL statements **Begin Transaction, Commit Transaction,** and **RollBack Transaction.**

The following sample code shows the **Customer_Remove** stored procedure, which uses T-SQL statements to implement transactions. To copy this code for use in your own projects, see "Implementing Transactions in a Stored Procedure" on the accompanying CD-ROM.

```
CREATE PROCEDURE Customer_Remove
    @vEmail varchar(30),
    @vCount int OUTPUT

AS
DECLARE @vCustomerID int

SELECT @vCustomerID = CustomerID FROM Customers
    WHERE Email= @vEmail
IF @vCustomerID IS NULL
begin
    return (0)
end
```
code continued on next page

code continued from previous page

```
ELSE
    begin
        BEGIN TRANSACTION
        DELETE FROM CustomerPasswords
            WHERE CustomerID = @vCustomerID
        DELETE FROM Customers
            WHERE CustomerID = @vCustomerID
        SELECT @vCount = COUNT(*) FROM Customers
        SELECT * FROM Customers
        IF @@error = 0
        begin
            COMMIT TRANSACTION
            return (1)
        end
        ELSE
        begin
            ROLLBACK TRANSACTION
            return (0)
        end
    end
return (1)
```

When the **Customer_Remove** stored procedure attempts to remove a customer, it must delete the customer row from both the CustomerPasswords and Customers tables. Both deletes must happen successfully for the stored procedure to work correctly. These statements are executed inside a transaction block. If an error occurs, the stored procedure rolls back the transaction to undo the changes.

If a stored procedure such as **Customer_Remove** uses transactions, and it is called from an MTS object that is already inside a transaction, the stored procedure transaction is nested inside the existing transaction. Thus, the original transaction created in MTS must commit for the stored procedure transaction to commit. If the MTS transaction aborts, any stored procedures called are rolled back, even if they committed their nested transactions.

Lab 6: Creating and Debugging Stored Procedures

In this lab, you will implement the **UpdateAd** stored procedure used in Lab 5. In Exercise 1, you will implement the **UpdateAd** stored procedure by using the Data Environment designer tools in Visual Basic. In Exercise 2, you will implement the **UpdateAd** stored procedure by using SQL Server 6.5 Enterprise Manager.

To see the demonstration "Lab 6 Solution," see the accompanying CD-ROM.

Estimated time to complete this lab: **60 minutes**

To complete the exercises in this lab, you must have the required software. For detailed information about the labs and setup for the labs, see "Labs" in "About This Course."

Objectives

After completing this lab, you will be able to:

◆ Use the Data Environment designer to connect to a data source.

◆ Use the Data View to view database diagrams, tables, views, and stored procedures on a SQL Server database.

◆ Use the Data View to create stored procedures on a SQL Server database.

◆ Use the SQL Server Enterprise Manager to view and create stored procedures.

Prerequisites

There are no prerequisites for this lab.

Exercises

The following exercises provide practice working with the concepts and techniques covered in this chapter:

◆ Exercise 1: Implementing Stored Procedures with the Visual Basic Tools

In this exercise, you will use the Visual Basic Data Environment designer tools to implement the stored procedure **UpdateAd**. First, you will add a Database Environment to a Visual Basic project. Next, you will add a **Connection** object to the environment to view existing database diagrams, tables, views and stored procedures in the Classifieds database on SQL Server. Next, you will add new functionality to the Classifieds database by implementing a new stored procedure. Finally, you will use the Transact-SQL Debugger to walk through the execution of the stored procedure **UpdateAd**.

◆ Exercise 2: Using Enterprise Manager to Implement Stored Procedures

In this exercise, you will use SQL Server 6.5 Enterprise Manager to implement the stored procedure **UpdateAd**. First, you will use Enterprise Manager to view existing objects in the Classifieds database. Next, you will add new functionality to the Classifieds database by implementing a new stored procedure with Enterprise Manager. Finally, you will test the stored procedure **UpdateAd** by using the SQL Query Tool in Enterprise Manager.

Exercise 1: Implementing Stored Procedures with the Visual Basic Tools

In this exercise, you will use the Visual Basic Data Environment Designer tools to implement the stored procedure **UpdateAd**. First, you will add a Database Environment to a Visual Basic project. Next, you will add a **Connection** object to the environment to view existing database diagrams, tables, views and stored procedures in the Classifieds database on SQL Server. Next, you will add new functionality to the Classifieds database by implementing a new stored procedure. Finally, you will use the Transact-SQL Debugger to walk through the execution of the stored procedure **UpdateAd**.

▶ **Add a Database Environment and a Connection to a Visual Basic project**

1. Open a new Visual Basic Standard EXE project.

2. On the **Project** menu, click **Add Data Environment**.

3. Right-click **Connection1** and then click **Properties** to display the **Data Link Properties** dialog box.

4. On the **Provider** tab, select the **Microsoft OLE DB Provider for ODBC Drivers** option and click **Next**.

5. On the **Connection** tab, select **Use connection string**, and type **FILEDSN=dbAdC.DSN**.

6. In the next step of the **Connection** tab, type a user name of **sa** with no password. Select the **Blank password** checkbox. The initial catalog should be left blank.

7. Click **Test Connection** to ensure that the connection is working properly and then close the **Data Link Properties** dialog box.

The following illustration shows the **Data Link Properties** dialog box.

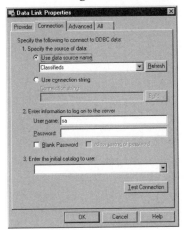

8. On the **View** menu, click **Data View Window**.

9. In the Data View window, expand the **Connection1**, **Tables**, and **Stored Procedures** folders.

This illustration shows the Data View window.

10. Right-click the **Advertisements** table and then click **Design**. In the Design Tables: Advertisement window you can make changes to the design of the Advertisements table without having to switch to the SQL Server Enterprise Manager. Close the Design Tables: Advertisement window.

▶ **Implement the UpdateAd stored procedure**

1. In the Data View window, delete any existing copy of **UpdateAd** (this was used in Lab 5).

2. In the Data View window, right-click **Stored Procedures**, and then click **New**.

3. In the New Stored Procedure window, create a stored procedure with the name **UpdateAd**.

4. Add the following parameter to the stored procedure.

Variable	SQL Server data type
@Title	varchar(100)
@StartDate	DateTime
@EndDate	DateTime
@CustomerID	Int
@CategoryID	Int
@ModifiedDate	DateTime
@Body	Text
@AdID	Int

5. Write a SQL **Update** statement that updates the Advertisement table. Do not update the Body column in the Advertisements table (this is a text data type and requires special handling). The search criteria in the **Where** portion of the statement should be based upon the AdvertisementID column in the Advertisements table:

```
UPDATE Advertisements
SET Title = @Title,
StartDate = @StartDate,
EndDate = @EndDate,
CustomerID = @CustomerID,
CategoryID = @CategoryID,
ModifiedDate = @ModifiedDate
Where AdvertisementID = @AdID
```

6. Declare a variable named **ptrval** of type **varbinary(16)**:

```
DECLARE @ptrval varbinary(16)
```

7. Write a **Select** statement that assigns the variable **ptrval** the pointer to the Body column of the Advertisements table. The search criteria in the **Where** portion of the statement should be based upon the AdvertisementID column of the Advertisements table:

```
SELECT @ptrval = TEXTPTR(Body)
FROM Advertisements
WHERE AdvertisementID = @AdID
```

8. Write a **WriteText** statement that updates the Body column of the Advertisements table using the variable **ptrval** and the parameter **@Body**. Use the **With Log** option:

```
WRITETEXT Advertisements.Body  @ptrval WITH LOG @Body
```

9. Right-click the New Stored Procedure window, and then click **Save to Database**.

To see an example of how your code should look, see Lab Hint 6.1 in Appendix B.

10. Close the New Stored Procedure window.

▶ **Debug the UpdateAd stored procedure**

1. Right-click the Data Environment window, and then click **Insert Stored Procedures**.

2. In the **Insert Stored Procedures** dialog box, select **dbo.UpdateAd** from the **Available** list and add it to the **Add** list. Click **Insert**.

This illustration shows the **Insert Stored Procedures** dialog box.

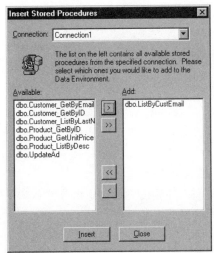

3. Close the **Insert Stored Procedures** dialog box.

4. In the Data Environment window, right-click **dbo_UpdateAd**, and then click **Debug**.

5. In the **Enter Unassigned Parameters** dialog box, enter the following values for each parameter, and then click **OK**.

Parameter	Value
Title	'Pellet Stove'
StartDate	'1/1/98'
EndDate	'1/7/98'
CustomerID	11901
CategoryID	1
ModifiedDate	'1/27/98'
Body	'TEXT data type update test'
AdID	5210

The following illustration shows the **Enter Unassigned Parameters** dialog box.

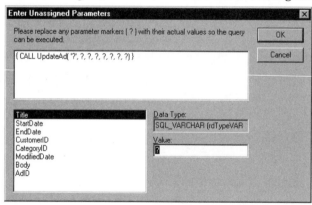

6. In the T-SQL Debugger window, position the cursor in front of the word Update.

7. On the **Edit** menu, click **Toggle Breakpoint**.

8. On the **Debug** menu, click **Step**. Note the local variable **@Title** has a value of **Pellet Stove**.

The following illustration shows the T-SQL Debugger window.

9. On the **Debug** menu, click **Go** to finish executing the stored procedure. A status of 0 (zero) will be returned in the output window.

Exercise 2: Using Enterprise Manager to Implement Stored Procedures

In this exercise, you will use SQL Server 6.5 Enterprise Manager to implement the stored procedure **UpdateAd**. First, you will use Enterprise Manager to view existing objects in the Classifieds database. Next, you will add new functionality to the Classifieds database by implementing a new stored procedure with Enterprise Manager. Finally, you will test the stored procedure **UpdateAd** by using the SQL Query Tool in Enterprise Manager.

▶ **Use SQL Enterprise Manager to view the Classifieds database**

1. Open SQL Server Enterprise Manager.

2. In the **Register Server** dialog box, click **Servers**. Select your server from the list of Active servers, and then click **OK**. Click **Use Standard Security**. The login ID is **sa**. There is no password. Click **Register**. Close the **Register Server** dialog box.

3. In the Server Manager window, expand the Server, Database, Classifieds database, and the Objects, Tables, and Stored Procedures folders.

The following illustration shows the Server Manager window.

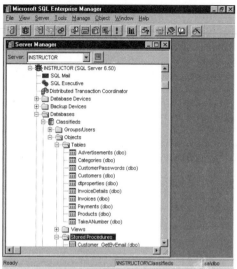

4. Double-click the Advertisements table. In the Manage Tables window, note that you can edit existing tables or create a new one. Close the Manage Tables window.

5. Double-click the **Customer_GetByEmail** stored procedure. In the Manage Stored Procedures window, note that you can edit existing stored procedures or create a new one. Close the Manage Stored Procedures window.

The following illustration shows the Manage Stored Procedures window.

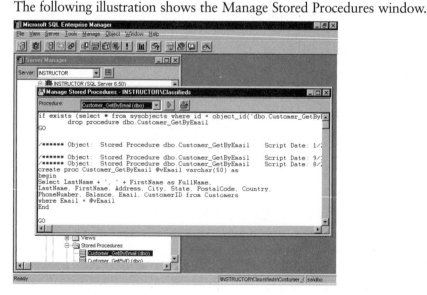

▶ **Implement UpdateAd by using Enterprise Manager**

1. Delete any existing copy of **UpdateAd** (this was used in Lab 5). You can delete a stored procedure by right-clicking on it and choosing **Drop**.

2. Right-click the Stored Procedures folder, and then click **New Stored Procedure**.

3. Replace <PROCEDURE NAME> with **UpdateAd**.

4. Add the following parameters to the stored procedure.

Variable	SQL Server data type
@Title	varchar(100)
@StartDate	DateTime
@EndDate	DateTime
@CustomerID	Int
@CategoryID	Int
@ModifiedDate	DateTime
@Body	Text
@AdID	Int

5. Write a SQL **Update** statement that updates the Advertisement table. Do not update the Body column of the Advertisements table (this is a text data type and requires special handling). The search criteria in the **Where** portion of the statement should be based on the AdvertisementID column of the Advertisements table:

```
UPDATE Advertisements
SET Title = @Title,
StartDate = @StartDate,
EndDate = @EndDate,
CustomerID = @CustomerID,
CategoryID = @CategoryID,
ModifiedDate = @ModifiedDate
Where AdvertisementID = @AdID
```

6. Declare a variable named **ptrval** of type **varbinary(16)**:

```
DECLARE @ptrval varbinary(16)
```

7. Write a **Select** statement that assigns the variable **ptrval** the pointer to the Body column of the Advertisements table. The search criteria in the **Where** portion of the statement should be based on the AdvertisementID column of the Advertisements table:

```
SELECT @ptrval = TEXTPTR(Body)
FROM Advertisements
WHERE AdvertisementID = @AdID
```

8. Write a **WriteText** statement that updates the Body column of the Advertisements table using the variable **ptrval** and the parameter **@Body**. Use the **With Log** option:

```
WRITETEXT Advertisements.Body  @ptrval WITH LOG @Body
```

9. Save the stored procedure by clicking the green triangle button.

   To see an example of how your code should look, see Lab Hint 6.2 in Appendix B.

▶ **Test the stored procedure by using the SQL Query Tool**

1. In Enterprise Manager, open the SQL Query Tool.

2. Select the Classifieds database from the DB drop-down list box.

3. Cut and paste the following Transact SQL into the Query window:

```
DECLARE @status int

EXECUTE @status = UpdateAd @Title = 'Pellet Stove',
@StartDate = '1/1/98',
@EndDate = '1/7/98',
@CustomerID = 11901,
@CategoryID = 1,
@ModifiedDate = '1/27/98',
@Body = 'TEXT data type update test',
@AdID = 5210

SELECT status = @status
```

4. Execute the stored procedure by selecting the green triangle command button. A status of 0 (zero) should be returned in the Results window.

Self-Check Questions

To see the answers to the Self-Check Questions, see Appendix A.

1. True or False: Always place business logic in the business services tier of a three-tier application.

A. True

B. False

2. Which type of data integrity is enforced through the use of validity checking, which restricts the type, the format, or the range of possible values in a column?

A. Entity

B. Referential

C. Unique

D. Domain

3. You can define a parameter for a stored procedure that returns a value to the calling application. What syntax is used in the Create Procedure statement to identify this type of parameter?

A. Output

B. Return

C. Input

D. None of the above

4. Which of the following statements defines a valid local variable in a stored procedure?

A. Dim LocalVariable

B. Declare @LocalVariable

C. Select @LocalVariable

D. Declare @@LocalVariable

Student Notes:

Chapter 7:
Implementing Security

In this chapter, you will learn how to implement security in an enterprise solution. First, you will learn how three-tier security is split into application and data security. Then you will learn about the security architecture in MTS and how to specify declarative security for components and packages. Next, you will learn how to set security on your SQL Server. You will also compare security in SQL Server to security provided by MTS. Then, you will learn how to set up SQL Server integrated security utilizing Windows NT and the SQL Security Manager. Finally, you will learn about best practices in managing security in enterprise solutions.

Objectives

After completing this chapter, you will be able to:

◆ List the advantages of three-tier security over two-tier security in enterprise solutions.

◆ Implement declarative security for MTS packages by using MTS roles and Windows NT user and group accounts.

◆ Describe the three security modes available in SQL Server.

◆ Assign permissions to a login using SQL Server Enterprise Manager.

◆ Implement integrated security by using Windows NT user accounts and SQL Security Manager.

◆ List best practices associated with implementing security in enterprise solutions.

Introduction to Security

A three-tier application must be secure against unauthorized access. More specifically, different groups of users have different privileges when using the application. For example, bank tellers can use an application to transfer money between accounts, but bank sales representatives can only create new accounts. An important aspect of security is how an application determines what group a user belongs to and, based on that group, what privileges the user has in the application.

Two-Tier Security

In a typical two-tier application, users log on to the database directly. Each user has a different login, and that information resides in the database. The database is protected from unauthorized access because users must supply a valid login to use the database. You can use more sophisticated databases, such as SQL Server, to create groups of users and manage privileges on a group basis. For example, you can create a bank teller group and assign the same privileges to all users who are bank tellers.

The following illustration shows how security works in a typical two-tier application.

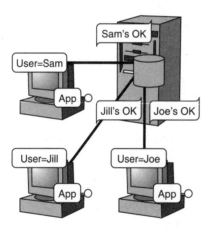

There are two drawbacks to security in two-tier applications:

◆ Scalability is reduced. There are a limited number of connections to the database, and if every user has a different login, the connections can be used up quickly.

◆ Applications cannot be integrated easily. If one application must call another to get work done, they must have a way of verifying the user's credentials. Often the user must log on again, or must start a new session with the second application.

Three-Tier Security

In a three-tier application, you separate business logic into a middle tier. Users no longer access the database directly from their client application. Instead, they access components running in MTS. The MTS objects then access the database and perform updates or retrievals on behalf of the users.

In this scenario, you split security into two types. The first type is application security. Application security involves authorizing users for access to the application code, or MTS packages. You implement application security in the middle tier by using MTS.

The second type is data security. This involves authorizing the various MTS packages for access to the database. You implement data security in the data services tier by using SQL Server.

The following illustration shows how security works in a three-tier application.

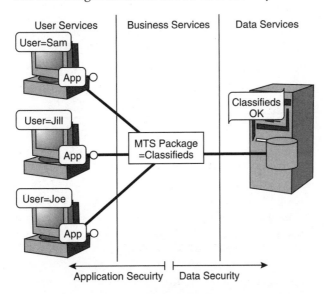

Application security involves authorizing users access to specific components and interfaces in MTS packages, limiting their capabilities. Thus, you map users to the application functionality that applies to them. For example, you might map bank sales representatives to a **CustomerAccounts** class that creates new accounts, while you map bank tellers to an **Accounts** class that performs money transfers.

Data security involves authorizing MTS packages access to the database. You assign each package an identity that SQL Server uses to authenticate the package, and then grants access to the database for that package.

Advantages of Three-Tier Security

There are five advantages to three-tier security:

◆ Because the user does not log on directly to the database, all database access can be totally encapsulated by the MTS components. This ensures data integrity.

◆ Because multiple concurrent users connect to the database with the same package identity, MTS can use connection pooling to reduce the load on the database. This improves scalability dramatically. For more information about connection pooling, see "Connection Pooling" on page 123 in Chapter 4, "Using MTS Transaction Services."

◆ Because each user does not need a login to the server, it reduces administration when setting up application access.

◆ Instead of thinking about end-user security in terms of databases and tables, you can use MTS to think about security in terms of the roles that an individual plays in the organization. This is a more efficient method of administering security.

◆ When one application package calls another application package, you do not need additional logins or sessions. You can configure MTS security to authenticate package-to-package calls.

Note In three-tier security you cannot perform database auditing because the database only tracks package identity rather than end user identity. However, you can perform auditing in MTS objects. For more information on designing auditing requirements in components, see "Security Best Practices" on page 247 in this chapter.

More planning is required when determining an application's security requirements in all three tiers. (more complicated in terms of understanding an application's security through all three tiers.

Implementing Security in MTS Applications

In this section, you will learn how to implement security in your MTS packages. First, you will see how MTS provides the security between the user and the middle-tier components through the use of MTS roles and Windows NT user and group accounts.

You will then learn how to implement security in MTS by creating roles and assigning them to packages and components. You will learn how to assign Windows NT user and group accounts to roles. Once roles have been defined and users have been assigned to them, you will enable security through package and component property settings.

Finally, you will learn about the role of package identity when using system resources such as databases.

MTS Security Overview

MTS provides two ways to implement security for MTS components:

◆ Declarative security

Use declarative security to define access privileges for users on a package level. Once you have declared security for a package, you can apply it to individual interfaces or components within that package.

◆ Programmatic security

Use programmatic security to define access privileges on a more granular level than that offered by declarative security. Using programmatic security, you can control user access to any part of your code.

This section focuses on declarative security. For more information about programmatic security, search for "Programmatic security" in Microsoft Transaction Server Help.

How Declarative Security Works

Declarative security is implemented through the use of MTS roles and Windows NT user and group accounts.

A role is a name that defines a group of related users for the set of components in a package. Each role defines which users are allowed to call interfaces on a component. Once roles have been created and populated with user accounts, an administrator grants access to the components in a package and its interfaces by using role membership. For example, the Island Hopper sample application contains a package named IsleHop Classifieds. This package might have Supervisors and OrderEntryClerks roles. The Supervisors role would grant its users access to all interfaces of all components. The OrderEntryClerks role would restrict access to just the bus_InvoiceC and bus_PaymentC components.

MTS uses roles to determine who can use a component whenever a call is made to an interface from outside the package. This includes method calls from an object in one package to an object in another package. MTS checks security on each method call because it's possible for an authorized client to pass an interface pointer to a client that is not authorized. If the unauthorized client calls a method on the interface pointer, it is denied access.

Method calls from one component to another inside a package are not checked because components in the same package trust each other.

The following illustration shows how MTS checks security. Any call from the client to the IsleHop Classifieds or IsleHop Utitilies packages is checked for access authorization. A method call from the bus_AdC component to the db_AdC component within the IsleHop Classifieds package is not checked, whereas a call from a component in this package to the WordCount.WordCount.1 component in the IsleHop Utilities packages is checked.

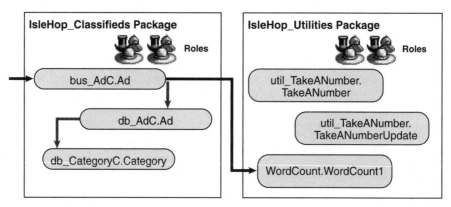

Note Because declarative security uses Windows NT accounts for authentication, you cannot use declarative security for packages running on computers that use the Windows 95 operating system.

Advantages of Declarative Security

Declarative security always uses roles to define which users can access components. It may seem easier to map Windows NT user accounts directly to components. However, MTS does not use this method because it is not effective for development and deployment of an MTS application.

Typically, MTS applications are developed on one set of computers and are deployed on another set of computers. The Windows NT user accounts for the two computer systems are likely to be different. Therefore, you do not have the information you need at development time to determine which Windows NT user accounts can access the components.

By creating roles, the developers can determine what categories of users can access components in each package. At deployment time, an administrator can then map specific Windows NT user accounts to the roles. The administrator can even create additional roles if needed. Roles provide an additional abstraction layer in security, which makes it easier to develop and deploy MTS applications.

Implementing Declarative Security

There are three main steps to implementing declarative security for a package:

1. Create the roles for the package and assign them to the components and interfaces in the package.

   You define roles at development time, when you often know the categories of users that will use the components, but you do not have specific information about user accounts.

2. Map Windows NT users and groups to roles.

   This step occurs when you deploy the package. The users that are assigned to a particular role at deployment time can be different for each installation of the package.

3. Enable security.

If you do not enable security for the package, MTS does not check roles for the components or interfaces in the package. In addition, if you do not enable security for a component, MTS does not check roles for the component's interface.

Creating and Assigning Security Roles

After you have created a package and added components to it, you can create roles for the package. You define roles at the package level and then map them to components or interfaces within the package.

To see the demonstration "Setting Security in MTS," see the accompanying CD-ROM.

▶ **To create a role**

1. In the left pane of the MTS Explorer, select the package that will include the role.

2. Double-click the Roles folder.

3. On the **Action** menu, click **New** and then click **Role.**

    −or−

    Right-click the Roles folder, click **New,** and then click **Role.**

4. Type the name of the new role and then click **OK.**

    The following illustration shows the **Roles** dialog box:

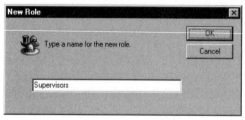

▶ **To assign roles to a component or interface**

1. In the left pane of the MTS Explorer, select the component or interface that will include the role.

2. Double-click the Role Membership folder.

3. On the **Action** menu, click **New**, and then click **Role**.

–or–

Right-click the Role Membership folder, click **New**, and then click **Role**.

4. In the **Select Roles** dialog box, select the roles you want to add to the component, and then click **OK**.

Mapping Users to Roles

When you install and distribute your application, you must map Windows NT users and groups to any existing roles. The roles determine which components and interfaces those users can access.

Using Windows NT Groups

The most flexible approach to administering security in MTS is to create a Windows NT group for each role in the MTS application. Then, assign each Windows NT group to its respective role. For example, if an MTS application has a role called OrderEntryClerks, you can create a Windows NT group called OrderEntryClerks. You can then assign the OrderEntryClerks group to the OrderEntryClerks role.

The following illustration shows two roles that have been created for the Accounting package: OrderEntryClerks and Supervisors. The Supervisors role can use any component in the Accounting package. The OrderEntryClerks role is limited to the bus_InvoiceC.Invoice and bus_PaymentC.Payment components.

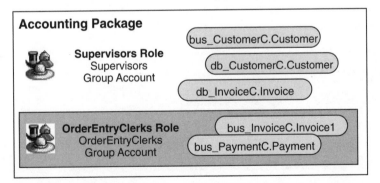

Once you have assigned Windows NT groups to all the roles in your MTS application, you can use the Windows NT User Manager application to add or remove users in each group. For example, adding a Windows NT user account named

"Joe" to the Windows NT group OrderEntryClerks effectively maps Joe to the Order Entry Clerks role.

With Windows NT groups, you can efficiently use one application to administer both Windows NT and MTS security.

Another benefit to using Windows NT groups is that if you are administering security remotely from another computer, you can add or remove users without having MTS installed. You can map Windows NT users directly to roles in an MTS application, but if you later decide to remove users from roles, you must do so through the MTS Explorer, which means that MTS must be installed.

▶ **To assign Windows NT groups to roles**

1. In the left pane of the MTS Explorer, open the package in which you want to assign Windows NT groups to roles.

2. Open the Roles folder and double-click the role to which you want to assign Windows NT groups.

3. Open the Users folder.

4. On the **Action** menu, click **New**, and then click **Users**.

   −or−

   Right-click the Users folder, click **New**, and then click **Users**.

5. In the **Add Users and Groups to Role** dialog box, add groups to the role.

   The following illustration shows the **Add Users and Groups to Role** dialog box.

6. Click **Show Users** or **Search** to locate a user or group account, and then click **OK**.

Note You must shut down the package process in the MTS Explorer before your security changes are reflected by MTS.

Enabling Security

In MTS, you enable security at two levels: package level and component level. You set package level security once. You set component level security for each component in the package.

Setting Package and Component Security

This table shows the implications of enabling or disabling authorization checking for packages and components.

Package security	Component security	Result
Enabled	Enabled	Enables security for the component.
Enabled	Disabled	Disables security for the component, but enables security for other components in the package that have security enabled.
Disabled	Enabled	Disables security for all components in the package.
Disabled	Disabled	Disables security for all components in the package.

Tip You can make it easier to test packages by disabling security at the package level. This disables security for all components in the package, regardless of the security settings at the component level. Then, you can test the components without the complication of security checks. However, disabling security at the package level or component level does not disable programmatic security in the components.

▶ **To enable or disable authorization checking for packages or components**

1. In the left pane of the MTS Explorer, click the package or component.

2. Right-click the package or component, and click **Properties**.

3. Click the **Security** tab.

4. Select or clear the **Enable authorization checking** check box.

For more information about setting properties for packages and components, see "Using the MTS Explorer" on page 76 in Chapter 3, "Introduction to Microsoft Transaction Server (MTS)."

System Package Security

The System package is automatically installed with MTS. MTS uses the components contained in the System package for internal functions. You can view but not set System component properties.

The System package has two default roles:

◆ Administrator

Users mapped to the Administrator role can use any MTS Explorer function.

◆ Reader

Users mapped to the Reader role can view all objects in the MTS Explorer hierarchy, but cannot install, create, change, or delete any objects, shut down server processes, or export packages.

When MTS is installed, the System package does not have any users mapped to the Administrator role. Therefore, security on the System package is disabled, and any user can use the MTS Explorer to modify package configuration on the MTS server. For this reason you should map a valid Windows NT user account to the Administrator role and enable security after MTS is installed.

Note If security is enabled and no users are assigned to the Administrator role, the MTS Explorer becomes unusable.

Setting Package Identity

When a package is set to run in a server process, it creates a server process to host any MTS objects created by clients. When the objects access resources such as files and databases, the objects are authenticated before being allowed access to those resources.

Traditionally, components are written to impersonate the calling client. For example, if a user named Joe calls a component on a remote computer, the component assumes the identity of Joe while doing its work. Thus, when the component is authenticated by Windows NT while accessing files, or authenticated by SQL Server while updating tables, it has userid Joe. This means that Joe must have appropriate privileges in Windows NT and SQL Server for the component to do its work successfully.

The following illustration shows how impersonation allows a component to use the identity of the calling client:

It is not recommended that you use impersonation when writing MTS components. Instead, MTS introduces the concept of package identity. Rather than impersonate the client, the package server process has its own identity in the form of a Windows NT user account. The MTS administrator generally creates these accounts at deployment time.

When any component in the package accesses files or databases, the package process uses the identity of the package. For example, if a package has an identity of Accounting, and Joe calls a component in the package, Windows NT and SQL Server identifies the component as userid Accounting, rather than userid Joe.

The following illustration shows how package identity gives components in a package a specific Windows NT user account name:

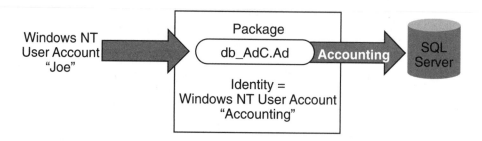

Setting Package Identity

There are two settings for establishing package identity:

◆ Interactive user (the default)

This setting allows the package to assume the identity of the currently logged-on user. However, if no user is logged on to the server when a client accesses the package, the package fails to create a server process. For this reason, you should establish a specific identity for each package.

◆ A specific Windows NT user account

This setting assigns a specific Windows NT user account to the package. When a client accesses the package, it creates a server process using this account as its identity. All components running in the package share this identity.

Tip The System package contains components that implement internal functionality for the MTS Explorer. If you want to administer MTS from a remote MTS computer, you need to give the System package a specific identity. This allows it to start as a server process and be accessible when you update packages and components from a remote MTS computer.

▶ **To set package identity**

1. Select the package whose identity you want to change.

2. On the **Action** menu, click **Properties**, and then click the **Identity** tab.

   −or−

   Right-click the package, click **Properties**, and then click the **Identity** tab.

3. To set the identity to a user account, click **This user** and enter the user domain followed by a backslash (\), user name, and password for the Windows NT user account.

   −or−

   To set the identity to Interactive User, select the **Interactive User** option.

For more information about setting package properties, see "Creating a Package" on page 79 in Chapter 3, "Introduction to Microsoft Transaction Server (MTS)."

Package Identity and Database Access

You can use package identity to pool database connections when your MTS components access databases. Connections are pooled based on userids and passwords, so if a process has many connections using the same userid and password, they can be pooled. If components impersonate clients, each userid is different and the connections cannot be pooled. By using package identity, each component can use the same userid and each connection can be pooled.

For more information, see "Connection Pooling" on page 123 in Chapter 4, "Using MTS Transaction Services."

Note If you want to use package identity to restrict access to a database, you must set database access privileges for the user account of that package. For more information, see "Using SQL Server Integrated Security" on page 244 in this chapter.

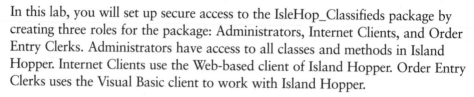

Lab 7.1: Implementing Security in MTS

In this lab, you will set up secure access to the IsleHop_Classifieds package by creating three roles for the package: Administrators, Internet Clients, and Order Entry Clerks. Administrators have access to all classes and methods in Island Hopper. Internet Clients use the Web-based client of Island Hopper. Order Entry Clerks uses the Visual Basic client to work with Island Hopper.

To see the demonstration "Lab 7.1 Solution," see the accompanying CD-ROM.

Estimated time to complete this lab: **45 minutes**

To complete the exercises in this lab, you must have the required software. For detailed information about the labs and setup for the labs, see "Labs" in "About This Course."

Objectives

After completing this lab, you will be able to:

◆ Create roles for a package and map them to classes.

◆ Create Windows NT groups and users and map them to roles.

◆ Enable security on a package.

Prerequisites

There are no prerequisites for this lab.

Exercises

The following exercises provide practice working with the concepts and techniques covered in this chapter:

◆ Exercise 1: Enabling Security in MTS

In this exercise, you will create three roles for the IsleHop_Classifieds package: Administrators, Internet Clients, and Order Entry Clerks. Next, you will create a Windows NT group named Order Entry Clerks and map it to the Order Entry Clerks role. Then, you will create two users named User1 and User2. You will place User1 in the Order Entry Clerks group, which effectively maps User1 to the IsleHop_Classifieds package. User2 will not be an Order Entry Clerk and will not have access to the IsleHop_Classifieds package. Finally, you will log on as each of these users to ensure that security is working properly on the IsleHop_Classifieds package.

Exercise 1: Enabling Security in MTS

In this exercise, you will create three roles for the IsleHop_Classifieds package: Administrators, Internet Clients, and Order Entry Clerks. Next, you will create a Windows NT group named Order Entry Clerks and map it to the Order Entry Clerks role. Then, you will create two users named User1 and User2. You will place User1 in the Order Entry Clerks group, which effectively maps User1 to the IsleHop_Classifieds package. User2 will not be an Order Entry Clerk and will not have access to the IsleHop_Classifieds package. Finally, you will log on as each of these users to ensure that security is working property on the IsleHop_Classifieds package.

▶ **Create roles**

1. Start the Microsoft Transaction Server (MTS) Explorer, and click the **Roles** folder of the IsleHop_Classifieds package.

2. On the **Action** menu, click **New**, and then point to **Role** to create a role called **Administrators**.

3. Create two additional roles called **Internet Clients** and **Order Entry Clerks**.

4. Click the Role Membership folder of the bus_AdC.Ad class.

5. On the **Action** menu, click **New**, and then point to **Role**. Click the Administrators, Internet Clients, and Order Entry Clerks roles, and then click **OK**.

6. Right-click **IsleHop_Classifieds** and click **Properties**.

7. On the **Security** tab, select **Authorization Checking**, and click **OK**.

▶ **Create Windows NT accounts**

1. Start the User Manager for domains. The User Manager is launched from the **Start** menu in the Programs, Administrative Tools folder.

2. Ensure that the User Manager has selected your computer name as the domain to administer. The computer name is displayed in the title bar. If a different name is displayed, change the domain to your computer name by choosing **User**, **Select Domain** from the menu.

3. Create a new local group.

   a. On the **User** menu, click **New Local Group**.

   b. Set **Group Name** to **Order Entry Clerks**.

   c. Set **Description** to **Order Entry Clerks**.

   d. Click **OK**.

4. Repeat Step 3 to create another local group called Internet Clients.

5. Create a new user.

    a. On the **User** menu, click **New User**.

    b. Set **Username** to **User1**.

    c. Set **Full Name** to **User1**.

    d. Set **Description** to **An Order Entry Clerk**.

    e. Set **Password** to **User1**.

    f. Set **Confirm Password** to **User1**.

    g. Select **User Cannot Change Password** and **Password Never Expires** and clear all other check boxes.

    h. Click **Add** to add the new user and click **Close**.

6. Repeat Step 5 to create a new user called User2. User2 is a regular user, and **Description** can be set to **Regular User** to describe this fact.

7. Select the **Order Entry Clerks** group.

8. On the **User** menu, click **Properties** to display the **Local Group Properties** dialog box.

9. Click **Add** to display the **Add Users and Groups** dialog box. Be sure to list the names from your computer.

10. Select **User1** and click **Add**. Click **OK** to close the **Add Users and Groups** dialog box.

11. Click **OK** to close the **Local Group Properties** dialog box.

12. Select the Internet Clients group.

13. Repeat steps 8 through 10 to add the IUSR_<MachineName> account for Internet Information Server to the Internet Clients group.

▶ **Map Windows NT accounts to roles**

1. In the MTS Explorer, expand the Roles folder for the IsleHop_Classifieds package and click the Users folder of the Administrators role.

2. On the **Action** menu, click **New**, and then point to **User**.

3. Add the Administrators group to the **Add Names** list and click **OK**. Be sure to select your computer name in the **List Names From** box.

4. Add the Administrators group and click **OK**.

5. Select the Users folder of the Internet Clients role.

6. Repeat steps 2 through 4 to add the Internet Clients group to the Internet Clients role.

7. Select the Users folder of the Order Entry Clerks role.

8. Repeat steps 2 through 4 to add the Order Entry Clerks group to the Order Entry Clerks role.

9. Log off the computer, and then log on as User1.

10. Run the Ad Test client that you built in Lab 4.1. If you haven't built the Ad Test client, you can run it from the \Labs\Lab07.1 folder.

11. Enter a valid Ad ID to retrieve, such as 5201. The ad should be retrieved successfully because User1 is in the Order Entry Clerks role.

12. Now log off the computer, and then log on as User2.

13. Again, run the Ad Test client and enter a valid Ad ID to retrieve. The application should fail because User1 is not in any roles on the IsleHop_Classifieds package.

14. Optionally, you can also run the Island Hopper Visual Basic client as User1 or User2 to test that application security is working. The Island Hopper Web client should always work because it accesses MTS through the Internet Clients group regardless of who the user is.

Overview of SQL Server Security

In this section, you will learn about the basics of security on SQL Server. You will learn about standard, integrated, and mixed security modes. Then, you will learn how permissions control the capabilities of each login. Finally, you will learn how to assign permission by using the SQL Enterprise Manager.

Security Modes

When you configure SQL Server security, you can choose one of the three available security modes.

◆ Standard

Standard security uses SQL Server's own login validation process for all connections. Connections validated by SQL Server are referred to as nontrusted connections.

◆ Integrated

Integrated security allows a SQL Server to use Windows NT authentication mechanisms to validate SQL Server logins for all connections. Connections validated by Windows NT Server and accepted by SQL Server are referred to as trusted connections. Only trusted connections are allowed.

◆ Mixed

Mixed security allows SQL Server login requests to be validated by using either integrated or standard security methods. Both trusted connections (as used by integrated security) and nontrusted connections (as used by standard security) are supported.

Standard Security

Standard security uses SQL Server's own login validation process for all connections. To log on to a SQL Server, each user must provide a valid SQL Server login ID and password. Standard security is useful in network environments with a variety of clients, some of which may not support trusted connections. Also, standard security provides backward compatibility for older versions of SQL Server.

The following illustration shows the steps involved for SQL Server to authenticate a login through standard security.

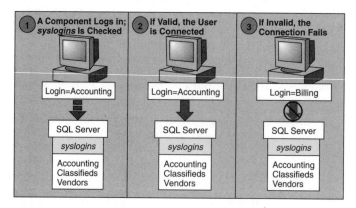

When a server's login security mode is set to standard, a component's login is validated as follows:

1. When a component attempts to log on to the server, SQL Server looks in the syslogins table for the component's login ID and password. A component supplies the login ID and password through the **ConnectionString** property of the ADO **Connection** object.

2. If the login ID and password are valid, the component is connected to SQL Server.

3. If the login ID and password are invalid, the component cannot connect to SQL Server even though the component may be logged on to Windows NT Server with the user account specified in its package's **Identity** property. The Windows NT user account name and password are inconsequential.

Integrated Security

Integrated security allows a SQL Server to use Windows NT authentication mechanisms to validate SQL Server logins for all connections. Using Integrated security means that users have one login ID and password for both Windows NT and SQL Server. Integrated security should be used in network environments where all clients support trusted connections. The clients of SQL Server in a three-tier application are MTS components. Later in this chapter, you will learn how MTS components and packages can be configured to take advantage of integrated security.

The following illustration shows the steps involved for SQL Server to authenticate a login through integrated security.

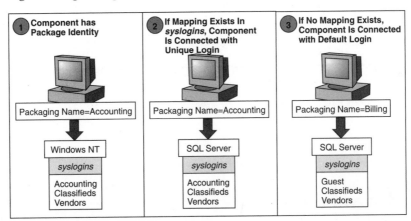

When a server's login security mode is set to integrated, a component's login is validated as follows:

1. To access SQL Server, a component first obtains a valid Windows NT user account. MTS components use the Windows NT user account specified in their package's **Identity** property.

Windows NT user account is on a:	Result
Domain	The user name and password are validated by the domain controller's security accounts database when the MTS package EXE launches.
Windows NT workgroup	The user name and password are validated by the local security accounts database.

2. The component connects to SQL Server, and SQL Server looks in the syslogins table for a mapping to a SQL Server Login ID. This mapping is created as part of the configuration process as follows:

Mapping	Result
Exists	The component is logged in to SQL Server with the privileges associated with that login ID.
Does not exist	The component is logged in to SQL Server using the default SQL Server Login ID (usually called guest) or, if the component's Windows NT user account has administrative privileges on Window NT, to SA.
Does not exist, and there is no default login	The component is denied access to SQL Server.

3. Once the login process is complete, access to individual SQL Server tables is managed through the permissions granted within a SQL Server database.

Mixed Security

When you use mixed security, SQL Server validates login requests using either integrated or standard security methods. Both trusted connections (as used by integrated security) and nontrusted connections (as used by standard security) are supported. Mixed security proves useful in network environments that have a mix of clients. For those clients that support trusted connections, Windows NT validates logins. For clients that only support nontrusted connections, SQL Server validates logins.

The following illustration shows the steps involved for SQL Server to authenticate a login through mixed security.

When you set a server's login security mode to mixed, a component's login is validated as follows:

1. When a component attempts to log on to the server over a trusted connection, SQL Server examines the login name.

   If this login name matches the component's network user name, or if the login name is blank or spaces, SQL Server uses the Windows NT integrated login rules (as for integrated security).

2. If the requested login name is any other value, the component must supply the correct SQL Server password, and SQL Server uses its own login validation process (as for standard security).

   If the login attempt is not over a trusted connection, the component must supply the correct login ID and password to establish the connection, and SQL Server uses its own login validation process (as for standard security).

Integrated or mixed security is recommended for enterprise solutions using Windows NT Server, MTS, and SQL Server. Integrated security makes management of logins easier because accounts can be administrated from one source in Windows NT. Also, you can avoid coding login IDs and passwords into your components, or placing them in ODBC DSNs. Any login changes under standard security would force components to be recompiled, or ODBC DSNs to be tracked down and updated.

Logins and Permissions

Logins are the core of SQL Server security. A login is an ID and password. A user or component must supply a login to establish a connection with SQL Server.

A component supplies its login through the **ConnectionString** property of the ADO **Connection** object. Or the login can be passed as a **ConnectionString** parameter to the **Open** method of the **Connection** or **Recordset** objects. If a component supplies a login ID and password, the component connects using standard security. If the component does not supply a login ID and password, the component connects using integrated security, and its package's identity is used as the login.

Tip If you are connecting through an OLE DB provider, you must notify the provider that you are connecting using integrated security. You do not provide a user ID or password, and you set the **Trusted_Connection** attribute as shown in the following example code:

```
Dim conn as ADODB.Connection
Set conn = New ADODB.Connection
conn.Provider = "SQLOLEDB"
conn.ConnectionString = "Data Source=MYSERVER;" & _
  "Initial Catalog=Pubs;Trusted_Connection=Yes"
conn.Open
```

Permissions

Regardless of whether you use standard security or integrated security to connect, SQL Server uses the login to identify the connection. Having a connection does not mean that the component has access to all of the database objects in SQL Server. The component must have permissions to perform any operations on the database. The component's permissions depend on its login.

You map each login to a set of permissions for each database object. The permissions are either enabled or disabled. For example, the login Joe may have **Select** permissions on the Authors table which allows Joe to perform **Select** statements on that table. But Joe may have no **Select** privileges on the Employee table, meaning he cannot get any data from that table.

You must grant permissions to a login before any components using that login can access databases or the objects inside those databases. The permissions describe the capabilities of each login. They describe what statements a login can issue against database tables, such as **Select, Insert, Update,** or **Delete.** They also describe whether or not a login can execute specific stored procedures.

If a login has execute permissions on a stored procedure, then that login may run the stored procedure. The stored procedure runs even if it performs actions for which the login has no permissions. For example, the login Joe may have execute permissions on a stored procedure named **AddCustomer.** Even though Joe does not have **Insert** permissions on the Customers table, the **AddCustomer** stored procedure can successfully execute an **Insert** statement to add the new customer.

You can provide better control over login capabilities by granting them execute permissions only on stored procedures. This forces logins to act within the capabilities of the stored procedures, rather than giving them unnecessary open capabilities on database objects, such as the capability to do any kind of **Update.**

▶ **To assign permissions**

1. Start the SQL Enterprise Manager.

2. Click the object to which you want to assign permissions, such as a table or stored procedure.

3. On the **Object** menu, click **Permissions.**

4. Select the permissions you want enabled for each user.

5. Click **Set** to assign the permissions.

The following illustration shows the **Object Permissions** dialog box.

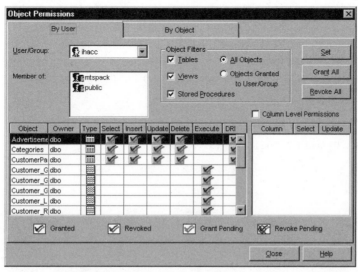

Using SQL Server Integrated Security

In this section, you will learn how to set up integrated security on SQL Server by using Windows NT accounts and the SQL Security Manager. You will learn how to create Windows NT user accounts for MTS packages. Then, you will learn how to create a Windows NT group account and add the user accounts for MTS packages to the group account. You will also learn how to create logins for the Windows NT user accounts in SQL Security Manager. Finally, you will learn how to create permissions for the logins.

Creating Windows NT Accounts

To set up a three-tier application to use SQL Server integrated security, create the necessary Windows NT user accounts for use by the MTS packages. When an MTS component connects to SQL Server, it is identified through integrated security as the Windows NT user account assigned to its package.

To see the demonstration "Configuring Integrated Security in SQL Server," see the accompanying CD-ROM.

▶ **To create a new Windows NT user account**

1. Start the User Manager for Domains. The User Manager is launched from the **Start** menu under the Programs, Administrative Tools folder.

2. On the **User** menu, click **New User**.

3. Enter the user name. You may want the user name to start with "MTS" to make it easier to recognize the account. Because this name will be used to create SQL logins later, keep the length under 30 characters. Do not use illegal SQL login characters, such as underscores. For example, **MTSAccounting** is a good user name for the IsleHop_Accounting package.

4. Set the account up as follows:

   • User cannot change password.

   • Password never expires.

   • Set and remember the password for this user.

5. Click the **Add** button to add the new user.

After you create a Windows NT user account for each package, create a group account called **MTS Packages**. Then add all the package accounts to this group account. This makes it easier to create logins for the packages in SQL Server.

▶ **To create a new Windows NT group account**

1. Start the User Manager for Domains.

2. On the **User** menu, click **New Local Group**.

3. Set the Group Name to **MTS Packages** or a name easily recognized as containing all the package accounts.

4. Click the **Add** button to add the existing package-user accounts you just created.

5. Click the **Remove** button to remove any non-package-user accounts that do not belong to this group.

6. Click **OK** to create the new group account.

Windows NT User Accounts and Package Identity

Now that you have created the Windows NT user accounts for MTS, you need to set up the packages to use the accounts. Do this by setting the package identity for each package to the Windows NT user account you created for it. For more information about setting package identity, see "Setting Package Identity" on page 232 in this chapter.

Once the package identity is established, the packages are ready to use integrated security. The final step for MTS is to set up the components to use integrated security. If they are already compiled to supply logins for standard security, they must be recompiled to use no logins. If they are connecting using connection information stored in ODBC DSNs, you need to modify the ODBC DSNs to use integrated security. This can be done through the ODBC Data Source Administrator available on the Control Panel.

Using the SQL Security Manager

Each Windows NT user account must have a corresponding SQL Server login in order for integrated security to work properly. Use the SQL Security Manager to create logins for the Windows NT Accounts.

▶ **To create logins for Windows NT user accounts**

1. Start the SQL Security Manager and connect to SQL Server as the system administrator.

2. On the **View** menu, click **User Privilege**. For almost all MTS packages you will want to grant user privileges.

3. On the **Security** menu, click **Grant New**. This displays up the **Grant User Privilege** dialog box.

4. Choose the Windows NT group you want to grant privileges. This is **MTS Packages** unless you chose a different name when you created the package group.

5. Choose to add login IDs for group members. This is important because this step creates the logins for each member of the **MTS Packages** group. Each Windows NT user account in the group must have a corresponding login ID.

6. Click **Add Users to Database** and choose which database to add the users to. If you do not select an option, then Master is the default.

7. Click **Grant**, and the logins are generated for the users on the selected database.

After you create the logins, you must set permissions for each new login, thus setting permissions for each package. This is what determines the capabilities of each package in the database.

▶ **To set permissions for logins**

1. Start the SQL Enterprise Manager and connect to SQL Server as the system administrator.

2. Select the database object on which you want to set permissions, such as a table.

3. On the **Object** menu, click **Permissions**.

4. You can now see the logins that were added by the SQL Security Manager. Select the permissions you want for each login on that object, and click **Set**.

5. Repeat steps 2 through 3 for any other objects that are accessed by the new logins.

Security Best Practices

Security can be complex to implement, test, and manage. Following are some best practices to help you implement security in your applications.

- ◆ Set up SQL Server for integrated (or mixed) security, when possible.

  By using integrated or mixed security, you avoid coding login IDs and passwords directly into MTS components or ODBC DSNs. It is a more flexible approach to security, because you can change security credentials by modifying a package's Windows NT user accounts, rather than recompiling the components in the package.

- ◆ Use stored procedures for all data access.

  This allows you to assign execute permissions on stored procedures for packages rather than try to determine all the different types of permissions each package should have. Also, stored procedures run much faster than submitting SQL statements from the components.

- ◆ Stage applications on a Quality Assurance (QA) server before moving them to production.

  The QA server should have the same security settings as the production server on which the application will ultimately run. These security settings include NTFS permissions, MTS roles, and SQL Server users. Without such a server, there is a chance that an application that runs fine on a developer's machine will encounter permission problems when put into production.

  When testing an application on the QA server, be sure to log on as a user that is not a member of the Administrators group.

- ◆ Grant end users access to resources through group accounts rather than individual accounts.

  The end users of an application should gain access to all resources through membership of a Windows NT group, rather than through granting them direct access to any resource (databases, files, or MTS components). This makes managing end-user security easier because you can control security at one point, the Windows NT groups, rather than tracking down each resource to which they have been granted access and making changes.

- ◆ Create at least one Windows NT group account for each application.

  If there are differing roles in an application that require different levels of access to resources, then there should be a Windows NT group for each of these roles, such as Bank Tellers and Bank Managers.

♦ Create at least one role for each MTS package.

If there are different levels of access, then there must be a role for each type of access, such as Tellers and Managers on the Bank package. Thus, there is a one-to-one relationship between Windows NT groups and roles: Bank Tellers to Tellers, and Bank Managers to Managers.

♦ Design auditing requirements into your business and database components.

Database auditing does not work as expected under the three-tier security model because all users access the database through the same user ID (the package's account). To implement logging on your MTS component, use the **GetOriginalCallerName** method. This returns the Windows NT name of the end user, even if the MTS component was called directly by another component. For example, if the **Customer** component keeps a log of all modifications to business data, it can use **GetOriginalCallerName**. The return value is the name of the end user, not the name an MTS package, which is the direct caller. The call might look like this:

```
Dim strModifiedBy as String
strModifiedBy = GetObjectContext().Security.GetOriginalCallerName()
```

Lab 7.2: Implementing Security in SQL Server

In this lab, you will modify the IsleHop_Classifieds package to use integrated security with Microsoft SQL Server. First you will create a new Windows NT user account that IsleHop_Classifieds will use as its identity. You will modify the ODBC file DSNs for the IsleHop_Classifieds package to use integrated security. Then you will use the Microsoft SQL Security Manager to create a login in SQL Server that matches the new Windows NT user account. Finally, you will set permissions for the new login and run the Ad Test client from Lab 4.1 to verify that integrated security is working properly

To see the demonstration "Lab 7.2 Solution," see the accompanying CD-ROM.

Estimated time to complete this lab: **60 minutes**

To complete the exercises in this lab, you must have the required software. For detailed information about the labs and setup for the labs, see "Labs" in "About This Course."

Objectives

After completing this lab, you will be able to:

♦ Create Windows NT user accounts and groups for Microsoft Transaction Server (MTS) packages.

♦ Set package identity on an MTS package to use a specific Windows NT user account.

♦ Modify ODBC file DSNs to use integrated security.

♦ Use the Microsoft SQL Server Security Manager to map Windows NT user accounts to logins.

♦ Use the Microsoft SQL Enterprise Manager to assign permissions on logins.

♦ Use the Microsoft SQL Trace application to monitor connections established by MTS components.

Prerequisites

Before working on this lab, you should be familiar with the following:

♦ Setting properties on MTS packages.

Exercises

The following exercises provide practice working with the concepts and techniques covered in this chapter:

♦ Exercise 1: Configuring Integrated Security for MTS

In this exercise, you will create a new Windows NT group called MTS Packages. Then you will create a new Windows NT user account called MTSClassifieds and add this account to the MTS Packages group. Then you will set the IsleHop_Classifieds package identity to be the MTSClassifieds account so that IsleHop_Classifieds no longer runs as an interactive user. Finally, you will modify the ODBC file DSNs used by IsleHop_Classifieds to use integrated security.

♦ Exercise 2: Configuring Integrated Security for SQL Server

In this exercise, you will use the Microsoft SQL Security Manager to grant user privileges to the MTS Packages group for the Classifieds database. Then you will use the Microsoft SQL Enterprise Manager to set permissions for the MTSClassifieds login so that it can access all tables and stored procedures in the Classifieds database. Finally, you will verify that integrated security is working by running the Ad Test application.

Exercise 1:
Configuring Integrated Security for MTS

In this exercise, you will create a new Windows NT group called MTS Packages. Then you will create a new Windows NT user account called MTSClassifieds and add this account to the MTS Packages group. Then you will set the IsleHop_Classifieds package identity to be the MTSClassifieds account so that IsleHop_Classifieds no longer runs as an interactive user. Finally, you will modify the ODBC file DSNs used by IsleHop_Classifieds to use integrated security.

▶ **Create a new local group**

1. Start the User Manager for Domains. The User Manager is launched from the **Start** menu in the Programs, Administrative Tools folder.

2. Ensure that the User Manager has selected your computer name as the domain to administer. The computer name appears in the title bar. If a different name appears, change the domain to your computer name by choosing **User, Select Domain** from the menu.

3. Create the new local group.

    a. On the **User** menu, click **New Local Group**.

    b. Set **Group Name** to **MTS Packages**.

    c. Set **Description** to **MTS Packages**.

    d. If there are any members listed, remove them by clicking **Remove**.

    e. Click **OK**.

▶ **Create a new user**

1. On the **User** menu, click **New User**.

2. Set **Username** to **MTSClassifieds**.

3. Set **Description** to **MTS Classifieds Package ID**.

4. Set **Password** and **Confirm Password** to **ihpwd**.

5. Select the **User Cannot Change Password**, and **Password Never Expires** check boxes. Make sure all other check boxes are cleared.

6. Click **Add** to add the new user.

7. Click **Close**.

▶ **Add the user to MTS Packages**

1. Select the MTS Packages group. On the **User** menu, click **Properties**.

2. Click **Add** and add the **MTSClassifieds** user name to the MTS Packages group. Be sure to list the names from your computer when searching for MTSClassifieds.

3. Click **OK** to close the **Add Users and Groups** dialog box. Then click **OK** to close the **Local Group Properties** dialog box.

▶ **Set package identity**

1. Start the MTS Explorer and select the IsleHop_Classifieds package.

2. On the **Action** menu, click **Properties**. This displays the **IsleHop_Classifieds Properties** dialog box.

3. On the **Identity** tab, set the user to **MTSClassifieds** and enter the password **ihpwd**.

4. Click **OK** to close the **IsleHop_Classifieds Properties** dialog box.

▶ **Update the ODBC file DSNs**

1. On the Control Panel, launch the ODBC applet.

2. On the **File DSN** tab, select **dbAdC.dsn** and click **Configure**. This displays the **Microsoft SQL Server DSN Configuration** dialog box.

3. Click **Next** to move to the next set of options.

4. Select **With Windows NT authentication using the network login ID**.

5. Click **Next** until you reach the last set of options. Then click **Finish**.

6. Click **OK** to close the **ODBC Microsoft SQL Server Setup** dialog box.

7. Select **dbCategoryC.dsn** and click **Configure**. Then repeat steps 3 through 6 to configure the dbCategoryC.dsn file to use integrated security.

8. Click **OK** to close the ODBC Data Source Administrator.

Exercise 2:
Configuring Integrated Security for SQL Server

In this exercise, you will use the Microsoft SQL Security Manager to grant user privileges to the MTS Packages group for the Classifieds database. Then, you will use the Microsoft SQL Enterprise Manager to set permissions for the MTSClassifieds login so that it can access all tables and stored procedures in the Classifieds database. Finally, you will verify that integrated security is working by running the Ad Test application.

▶ **Grant user privileges using SQL Security Manager**

1. Start the Microsoft SQL Security Manager.

2. Enter your computer name for the server and log on as **sa** with no password.

3. On the **View** menu, click **User Privilege**.

4. Grant User privileges for the MTS Packages group.

    a. On the **Security** menu, click **Grant New**.

    b. Select the **Local Groups** check box.

    c. Select the MTS Packages group.

    d. Select the **Add login IDs for group members** check box.

    e. Select the **Add Users to Database** check box. Set the database to **Classifieds**.

    f. Click **Grant** to grant privileges.

    g. Click **Done** when the grant operation is complete. Then click **Done** to close the **Grant User Privilege** dialog box.

▶ **Set database permissions**

1. Start the Microsoft SQL Enterprise Manager.

2. If you haven't already done so, register your SQL Server.

    a. Enter the server name, which is your computer name.

    b. Select **Use Standard Security**. This is the security method that SQL Enterprise Manager will use to log on.

    c. Set the **Login ID** to **sa**.

    d. Leave the **Password** field blank.

    e. Click **Register** to register your server.

3. In the Classifieds database, select the Advertisements table.

4. On the **Object** menu, click **Permissions**.

5. On the **By User** tab, change the **User/Group** to the MTSClassifieds login.

6. Click **Grant All** to grant all privileges on the Classifieds database to MTSClassifieds, then click **Set** to enact the change.

7. Click **Close** to close the **Object Permissions** dialog box.

▶ Test integrated security

1. Run the Microsoft SQL Trace application.

2. Enter your computer name for the server, and log on as **sa** with no password.

3. Create a new filter.

    a. Set **Filter Name** to **IsleHop**.

    b. On the **Events** tab, select the **Connections** check box and clear all other check boxes. This will allow you to trace just connection events.

    c. Click **Add** to add the filter.

4. Run the Ad Test client that you built in Lab 4.1. If you haven't built the Ad Test client, you can run it from the \Labs\Lab07.2 folder.

5. Enter a valid Ad ID to retrieve, such as 5201. After the ad is retrieved, look at SQL Trace to verify that the connection established used the **MTSClassifieds** login.

Note If you get a permission denied message, verify that you do not have **Enable Authorization Checking** enabled on the IsleHop_Classifieds package **Security** tab, or ensure that you are logged on as a valid user for the IsleHop_Classifieds package.

6. Optionally you can also run the Island Hopper Visual Basic client or Web client with SQL Trace to verify that integrated security is working properly.

Self-Check Questions

To see the answers to the Self-Check Questions, see Appendix A.

1. Which item is not an advantage of three-tier security?

A. All database access can be totally encapsulated by the MTS components. This ensures data integrity.

B. When one application calls another to get work done, it needs to verify the user's credentials, and the user logs on again, or starts a new session with the second application.

C. You can use MTS to think about security in terms of the roles that an individual plays in the organization. This is a more efficient method of administering security.

D. Because each user does not need a login to the server, it reduces administration when setting up application access.

2. When does MTS enforce declarative security on method calls to components?

A. Each call into a package from a client is checked. Calls between components in the same package are not checked. Calls between packages are checked.

B. Each call into a package from a client is checked. Calls between components in the same package are checked. Calls between packages are checked.

C. Each call into a package from a client is checked. Calls between components in the same package are not checked. Calls between packages are not checked.

D. Only the first call into a package from a client is checked. Calls between components in the same package are not checked. Calls between packages are checked.

3. True or False: Once SQL Server uses the login to identify the connection, the component has access to all of the database objects in SQL Server.

A. True

B. False

4. Choose the item that most completely describes integrated security.

A. It uses SQL Server's login validation process for all connections, and it is useful in network environments with a variety of clients.

B. Both trusted connections and nontrusted connections are supported, and it is useful in network environments that have a mix of clients.

C. Users have one login ID and password for both Windows NT and SQL Server, and it is useful in network environments where all clients support trusted connections.

D. Each user must provide a valid SQL Server login ID and password, and it provides backward compatibility for older versions of SQL Server.

5. True or False: Database auditing is an additional security option in the three-tier security model.

A. True

B. False

Student Notes:

Chapter 8:
Implementing COM with Visual Basic

In this chapter you will take a closer look at implementing COM objects with Visual Basic. Implementing interfaces in classes adds flexibility to your design. You can develop more complex applications that can adapt to changing user, business, and data requirements.

First, you will learn about creating and implementing interfaces for use in your own applications and by other developers. Then, you will learn about creating dual interfaces and how to access features in other applications for use in your own programs. Finally, you will learn how binding defines how a client connects to a particular object.

Objectives

After completing this chapter, you will be able to:

◆ Define, create, and implement an interface.

◆ Create multiple classes that use the same interface and multiple interfaces per class using Visual Basic.

◆ Describe the purpose of Interface Definition Language (IDL) files and use OLE/COM Object Viewer to view the contents of an IDL file.

◆ Describe how **IDispatch** is used to implement Automation to expose services to objects and how dual interfaces make the process more efficient.

◆ Describe the types of binding Visual Basic uses with objects, and choose the correct type of binding based on performance and flexibility requirements.

Interfaces

Many of the advantages COM brings to enterprise development occur through a mechanism known as interfaces. In this section you will learn about the attributes of interfaces and about the concept of an interface as a contract. You will learn about the base interface **IUnknown** that is supported by all interfaces. You will also learn about creating and implementing an abstract class and multiple interfaces. Finally, you will learn about the Interface Definition Language (IDL) used to define a new custom interface, and view IDL files using the OLE/COM Object Viewer.

Interfaces Defined

Interfaces are groups of functions that expose functionality through which clients and COM components communicate. Interfaces provide standardized access to the methods and properties (functionality) available from components. Further, they are a contract between the component author and the client developer that ensures consistent access to functionality. Finally, they structure that access so that components are easier to use.

The name of an interface is always prefixed with an "I" by convention, as in **IUnknown**. An interface defines what functions it supports, the names of those functions, the parameter types passed to each function, and the return type for each function. While the interface has a specific name (or type) and names of member functions, it defines only how you can use that interface and what behavior is expected from an object through that interface. Interfaces do not define any implementation. An object can have multiple interfaces to provide access to different sets of functionality.

To see the expert point-of-view "Using Interfaces in Enterprise Development," see the accompanying CD-ROM.

Attributes of Interfaces

Interfaces have four important points for you to understand:

◆ An interface is an abstract class.

An interface cannot be instantiated by itself because it carries no implementation. Another class must implement the interface.

◆ An interface is not an object.

An interface is a related group of functions with a specific signature that does not change over time. An interface is not an instance of a class. The object that supports a particular interface can be implemented in any language with any internal state representation, so long as it can provide pointers to interface member functions.

◆ Interfaces have a unique identifier.

Each interface needs its own unique identifier to eliminate any chance of a collision that would occur with human-readable names. Globally unique identifiers (GUIDs) are used to uniquely identify entries in the Windows registry. Visual Basic automatically generates a GUID for each public class and interface in your component. These are usually referred to as class IDs (CLSID) and interface IDs (IID). For more information, see "Version Compatibility" on page 53 in Chapter 2, "Building COM DLLs with Visual Basic."

◆ Interfaces are immutable.

Interfaces never change, thus avoiding versioning problems. A new version of an interface, created by adding or removing functions or changing semantics, is an entirely new interface and is assigned a new unique identifier. The implementation behind an interface can change (perhaps to improve performance) without changing the interface definition or affecting clients in any way. This is an ideal of COM, but in reality simply fixing a bug in a component or ActiveX Control can break clients. Another program relying on that bug, providing a solution or fix for the bug, could be broken, adversely affecting users.

Interfaces Are Contracts

An interface represents a contract between server and client so that an object always implements the functions for that interface in a standard way. The contract enables you to develop the object in any language so long as the object exposes interfaces according to the COM standard. By virtue of the contract, you know that:

◆ The interface has a globally unique interface identifier, or IID.

◆ The functions will occur in the same order in the declaration of the interface.

◆ The functions will take the same parameter types.

◆ The functions will return the same types.

◆ The functions will each be implemented to follow the semantics of the interface.

◆ The interface will always have the same set of functions. Functions cannot be added or deleted.

The encapsulation of functionality into objects accessed through interfaces makes COM an open, extensible system. It is open in the sense that anyone can provide an implementation of a defined interface and anyone can develop an application that uses such interfaces. As a developer using a component, you do not need to understand the internal implementation of its interfaces as long as you can read the interface specifications.

COM is extensible in the sense that new or extended interfaces can be defined without changing existing applications. Applications that understand the new interfaces can exploit them while older applications can continue to use the original interfaces.

The IUnknown Interface

In order to use an object, a client needs to know what interfaces that object supports.

The COM specification requires the following functionality of all objects:

◆ The object must be able to keep track of the number of connections made to it. When no longer in use, it must be able to destroy itself.

◆ The object must be capable of being queried by a client for additional interfaces that it may support.

In order to provide this functionality, all objects must support an interface named **IUnknown**. Furthermore, every other interface on the object must include the functionality provided by **IUnknown**. Although Visual Basic handles much of this behind the scenes, you should still understand what is going on in terms of reference counting and tracking objects. This will help you to troubleshoot and write the most efficient applications.

Functions of the IUnknown Interface

The **IUnknown** interface has three functions: **AddRef**, **Release**, and **QueryInterface**. The functions **AddRef** and **Release** are used to keep track of the creation and destruction of the object, and **QueryInterface** lets clients query for other interfaces provided by the object.

Traditionally clients destroy objects when they no longer need them. Because multiple clients from different processes and even different computers can connect to and use an object, any one client destroying the object would leave other clients hanging.

Therefore, a reference count is maintained so that when the count is greater than 0, the object stays alive. When the count goes to 0, the object destroys itself.

The following table describes the functions of **IUnknown**.

Function	Description
AddRef	Increments the usage count of the object when it assigns an interface pointer. **AddRef** is called when you use a **Set** statement to initialize an object variable.
Release	Decrements the usage count when a variable that points to the object goes out of scope. **Release** is called when you set an object variable to **Nothing**, or when the variable goes out of scope.
QueryInterface	Determines whether an object supports a specific interface. If an object supports an interface, **QueryInterface** returns a pointer to that interface. You then can use the methods contained in that interface to communicate with the object.

Querying Additional Interfaces

When a client contains an object variable that points to a valid COM interface, it can obtain any additional interfaces provided by the object with the **QueryInterface** method. Visual Basic provides this capability automatically through the **Set** and **TypeOf** statements, which you will learn to use in the next section.

Creating and Implementing Interfaces

An interface contains no code. It simply provides method declarations. Interfaces must be implemented by classes that wish to expose that set of methods.

When you publish an interface you are setting it out permanently. Interface immutability is an important principle of component design because it protects existing systems that have been written to an interface.

When an interface is clearly in need of change, a new interface should be created. This interface might be called **IInterface2**, to show its relationship to the existing interface.

While generating new interfaces too frequently can bulk up your components with unused interfaces, well-designed interfaces tend to be small and independent of each other, reducing the potential for performance problems.

For information about setting backward compatibility for components, see "Version Compatibility" on page 53 in Chapter 2, "Building COM DLLs with Visual Basic."

Defining an Interface

The purpose of an abstract class is to define an interface. An abstract class does not contain any implementation code. It contains the function signatures for the interface. The actual implementation of the interface occurs within other classes.

This Visual Basic example code defines an interface. The methods **GetByID** and **GetByEmail** are declared in a class module called **ILookup**. The instancing property of the **ILookup** class has to be set to **PublicNotCreatable**. **PublicNotCreatable** means that other applications can use objects of this class only if your component creates the objects first. In this example, an instance of the class would never be created because it has no implementation:

```
'A class module called ILookup
Function GetByID(ByVal lngID As Long) As Variant
End Function

Function GetByEmail(ByVal strEmail As String) As Variant
End Function
```

> **Note** Visual Basic creates classes in an ActiveX DLL project by using COM dual interfaces. For more information, see "Dual Interfaces" on page 272 in this chapter.

Implementing the Interface

Once an abstract class has been created or defined, you use it in a new class module by using the **Implements** keyword. To use the abstract class (interface), include the **Implements** keyword and the name of the abstract class in the Declarations section of other class modules. Then, you can implement each method in the abstract class by writing code for it.

The following sample code implements the **ILookup** interface in the **CCustomer** class. To copy this code for use in your own projects, see "Implementing the ILookup Interface in the CCustomer Class" on the accompanying CD-ROM.

```
'A class module called CCustomer
Implements ILookup
Private Function ILookup_GetById(ByVal lngID As Long) As Variant
  'implement GetByID
  'code segment
End Function

Private Function ILookup_GetByEmail(ByVal strEmail As String) As
Variant
  'implement GetByEmail
  'code segment
End Function
```

Notice that you must put the name of the abstract class in front of each method you implement. In the previous sample code, the **GetByEmail** method is named **ILookup_GetByEmail**.

As you learned earlier in this course, the class can be made available to other applications by compiling it into a COM DLL or COM EXE. Once a class has been compiled, a COM DLL or COM EXE can be added to MTS. For more information, see "Adding Components to a Package," on page 82 in Chapter 3, "Introduction to Microsoft Transaction Server (MTS)."

Using an Object's Interfaces

Once you implement an interface and develop the code for it, the next step is to use it from a client. The following example code shows the basic mechanics of creating an instance of the **CCustomer** class and accessing the object's **ILookup** interface:

```
Dim vInfo As Variant
Dim objLookup As ILookup
Dim objCustomer As CCustomer

Set objCustomer = New CCustomer
Set objLookup = objCustomer
vInfo = objLookup.GetByID (1001)
```

Examples later in this topic and the chapter expand upon the basic mechanics to implement more advanced features.

When you use the **Set** statement to assign a variable whose type is an interface definition, Visual Basic asks the object if it supports the interface. The method used for this is called **QueryInterface**. **QueryInterface** is a method of the **IUnknown** interface. In the previous example, **objLookup** is declared as type **ILookup**. When **Set** is used to assign **objLookup** to **objCustomer**, Visual Basic uses **QueryInterface** to determine if the **CCustomer** object referred to by **objCustomer** supports the **ILookup** interface. For more information, see "The IUnknown Interface" on page 260 in this chapter.

The intermediate step of creating the **objCustomer** variable in the previous example code is not necessary, but it helps make the flow of the example clearer. The previous example code could be rewritten as:

```
Dim vInfo As Variant
Dim objLookup As ILookup

Set objLookup = New CCustomer
vInfo = objLookup.GetByID(1001)
```

In this example, the **Set** statement creates the new **CCustomer** object, queries for the **ILookup** interface, sets the **objLookup** object variable to refer to the **ILookup** interface of the new **CCustomer** object, and sets the reference count of the new object equal to one.

If the answer to the **QueryInterface** method is no, that is, the object does not support the interface being requested, an error occurs. If the answer is yes, the object is assigned to the variable. You can only access the methods and properties of the interface through this variable.

Handling Errors from Set and QueryInterface

You have two alternatives to handle an error returned from the use of the **Set** statement. The first alternative is to use an error-handling routine to trap and respond to any error generated by **QueryInterface** when a class does not support an interface. The following sample code runs the error handler if the **objRef** object does not support the **ILookup2** interface. The **ILookup2** interface is an improved version of the **ILookup** interface, and the new client wants to take advantage of **ILookup2** if it is available. Otherwise, it falls back to the original **ILookup**. Note that in **ILookup2**, **GetByID** takes an extra parameter, perhaps to quicken the search for the particular record. To copy this code for use in your own projects, see "Using an Error Handler to Trap Errors from QueryInterface" on the accompanying CD-ROM.

```
Dim vInfo As Variant
Dim vOtherParam As Variant
Dim objLookup As ILookup
Dim objLookup2 As ILookup2
Dim objRef As Object 'objRef can refer to
                     'several types of objects.

On Error GoTo Handler

Set objRef = New CCustomer
Set objLookup2 = objRef 'Visual Basic calls QueryInterface.
vOtherParam = ... 'Initialize vOtherParam
vInfo = objLookup2.GetByID (1001, vOtherParam)
Exit Sub

Old:
    Set objLookup = objRef 'Visual Basic calls QueryInterface.
    vInfo = objLookup.GetByID (1001)

Handler:
    Resume Old
```

In the sample code, **objRef** is defined as an object and not a specific type, because it is used to refer to several different object types. If you declare **objRef** as a specific type, then Visual Basic ensures that **objRef** supports all the interfaces at compile time. However, you don't always know the types of objects you will be referring to at compile time. In addition, in Visual Basic Scripting Edition you cannot declare a variable as a specific object type. For example:

Note The **Set** statement in the previous error handler could fail as well. Depending on the scenario, you may need to trap the resulting error.

The second alternative is to explicitly check if a class supports an interface. You can use the **TypeOf** keyword to check if a class supports a particular interface. The following sample code uses the **TypeOf** keyword to check if the **objRef** object supports the **ILookup2** interface. To copy this code for use in your own projects, see "Using the TypeOf keyword in Error Handling" on the accompanying CD-ROM.

```
If TypeOf objRef Is ILookup2 Then 'Visual Basic calls
QueryInterface
    Set objLookup2 = objRef
    vInfo = objLookup2.GetByID (1001, vOtherParam)
Else
    If TypeOf objRef Is ILookup Then 'Visual Basic calls
QueryInterface
        Set objLookup = objRef
        vInfo = objLookup.GetByID (1001)
    Else
        'Handle case where object does not support ILookup2 or
ILookup.
    End If
End If
```

Applying Interfaces

One of the advantages of using abstract classes with **Implements** is that you can create polymorphism for clients. Polymorphism is the ability to call the same function name on two different objects and get two different behaviors. Polymorphism means that you can invoke **GetById** without knowing whether an object is a **Customer** or a **Vendor**.

For example, a client can create a single object variable of type **ILookup**. Then, the code executed by calling methods of the interface would depend on whether the object variable was referring to an object of type **CCustomer** or **CVendor**.

The following sample code calls the same function name on two different objects to get two different behaviors. To copy this code for use in your own projects, see "Using the Implements Keyword to Create Polymorphism" on the accompanying CD-ROM.

```
'Client code
Dim lngCustomerID As Long
Dim lngVendorID As Long
Dim vInfo As Variant

Dim objLookup As ILookup
Dim objCustomer As CCustomer
Dim objVendor As CVendor

Set objCustomer = New CCustomer
Set objVendor = New CVendor

Set objLookup = objCustomer
vInfo = objLookup.GetByID (ByVal lngCustomerID)

Set objLookup = objVendor
vInfo = objLookup.GetByID (ByVal lngVendorID)
```

In the sample code, the generic **objLookup** object is set to point at the **Customer** object and then the **Vendor** object. When the **GetById** method is called on each object, the objects get the appropriate information from the database. Even though **objLookup** is of the type **ILookup**, it always calls the code of the implemented class (**Customer** or **Vendor**). This is an example of polymorphism, and it allows a client to treat objects in a generic manner.

Multiple Interfaces

You can also implement multiple abstract classes or interfaces in a single class. Multiple interfaces allow you to develop applications that evolve interface by interface, or provide several types of functionality from the same class. For example, classes can begin small, with minimal functionality, and over time acquire additional features, as it becomes clear from actual use what features are important. Legacy code is protected by continuing to support old interfaces while implementing new ones.

The following sample code implements multiple interfaces in a single class. To copy this code for use in your own projects, see "Multiple Conversions in a Single Class" on the accompanying CD-ROM.

```
'CCustomer class implements ILookup and IChange interfaces
Implements ILookup
Implements IChange

Public Function ILookup_GetByID(...) As Variant
  'code statements
End Function

Public Function ILookup_GetByEmail(...) As Variant
  'code statements
End Function

Public sub IChange_Add(...)
  'code statements
End Sub

Public sub IChange_Remove(...)
  'code statements
End Sub
```

Some clients may wish to only use the **ILookup** interface, while other clients may use the **IChange** interface or both interfaces. This allows classes to be more versatile in what feature sets they expose and use.

Default Interface

When you compile an ActiveX DLL or EXE project, Visual Basic creates a default interface for each class. The default interface takes the name of the class preceded by an underscore. For example, the default interface for the **CCustomer** class is **_CCustomer**. Methods that are not part of another interface (preceded by InterfaceName_) become members of the default interface. This is all done behind the scenes by Visual Basic.

> **Note** Using **Set** to assign an object variable which is of a class type causes Visual Basic to **QueryInterface** for the **_CClassName** interface, which it will always find. For example:
>
> ```
> Dim objCustomer As CCustomer 'type is really _CCustomer
> Set objCustomer = New CCustomer 'QueryInterface for the
>                                 '_CCustomer interface
> ```

As a developer, you may never use interfaces other than the default interfaces provided by Visual Basic. How you choose to implement interfaces depends on the complexity of the application and design requirements.

Interface Definition Language

The Interface Definition Language (IDL) is a language for specifying an object's interfaces. The IDL is strictly for defining an interface's methods and parameters, and has nothing to do with an interface's implementation. COM uses IDL to describe interfaces. It lets you see what is going on behind the scenes when you build a component. Type libraries can be generated from IDL files, which, in turn, can be used at compile or run time. Defining interfaces in Visual Basic is done with abstract classes (or simply use the default interface) rather than IDL. Visual Basic creates type libraries and embeds them in components. There are tools, such as the OLE/COM Object Viewer, that allow you to reverse engineer any type library into IDL, including those built with Visual Basic. It is important to note that currently you cannot do everything available to you in IDL within Visual Basic.

To view the IDL from a Type Library, you can use the OLE/COM Object Viewer. The OLE/COM Object Viewer is an administration and testing tool you can use to view COM classes and Type Libraries on a system. It has many other features, in addition to viewing the IDL, that will not be used in this course.

To see the demonstration "Using OLE/COM Object Viewer," see the accompanying CD-ROM.

Clients and Interfaces

In this section you will learn how automation objects allow you to incorporate features of other applications into your own programs. You will look at the information that type libraries provide about automation objects. You will learn how the **IDispatch** interface allows clients to use object interfaces and how dual interfaces extend the capabilities of **IDispatch**. Finally, you will learn how binding determines the manner in which a client connects to an object.

COM Components and IDispatch

COM components that support **IDispatch** expose Automation services to other objects, programming tools and macro languages. Automation is a particularly attractive and powerful way to tie applications together for the following reasons:

- You have direct access to the other applications, including all their objects and commands.
- You can share data through properties so other applications can access them.
- You can control another application using the familiar properties and methods model.
- The Automation component does not necessarily need to be visible to the user when you invoke it. For example, a user can invoke a utility that compacts a customer database. The user invokes the utility through an option on the user interface and never sees the utility program.

Type Libraries

Clients get information about a COM component by inspecting its type library. Also known as an object library, a type library provides the following information:

- Definitions of interfaces supported by the object
- Descriptions of the properties, methods, and events provided by the object
- The return types and parameter types of the object's methods and events
- The Dispatch IDs these methods and properties use
- The names of the Help file and Help topics to be displayed about the object and its methods and properties

Type libraries are registered with the operating system. The registry keys for type libraries are located in HKEY_CLASSES_ROOT, in the TypeLib folder.

Type libraries can be stored as part of the .exe. or .dll file that they describe, or they can be stored as separate object library (.olb) or type library (.tlb) files. When you use Visual Basic to create a component, its type library is built into the component (COM EXE or COM DLL). Visual Basic also gives you the option to create a copy of the .tlb file outside the component. When you build a project in Visual Basic, you can select the **Remote Server Files** option in the **Component** tab of the **Project Properties** dialog box to create a copy of the .tlb file outside the component. The component still has the .tlb file embedded inside, as well.

The IDispatch Interface

The dispatch interface, **IDispatch**, is designed explicitly for exposing object methods and properties to a client. This interface contains four functions: **GetTypeInfoCount**, **GetTypeInfo**, **GetIDsOfNames**, and **Invoke**.

The functions **GetTypeInfoCount** and **GetTypeInfo** obtain information from the component's type library about the interfaces, methods, and properties that it supports.

The following table describes the functions in **IDispatch**.

Function	Description
GetTypeInfo	Retrieves the type information for an object, which can then be used to get the type information for an interface.
GetTypeInfoCount	Retrieves the number of type information interfaces that an object provides (either 0 or 1). If the object provides type information, the number is 1; otherwise the number is 0.
GetIDsOfNames	Takes one or more properties and/or methods, and returns their dispatch ID (**dispID**) values as defined in the type library. A **dispID** is a unique number assigned to every property and method in a type library.
Invoke	Takes a **dispID** and a variant array that contains the passed parameters, and executes the associated property or method.

The following illustration shows the functions contained in **IDispatch**, along with additional functions supported by the interface.

IDispatch

AddRef
Release
QueryInterface
GetTypeInfoCount
GetTypeInfo
GetIDsOfNames
Invoke

Note IDispatch inherits from the **IUnknown** interface so there are seven methods shown in the previous diagram.

Dual Interfaces

Although the **IDispatch** interface makes it easy for clients to access the methods in an object, it has a drawback. **IDispatch** is slow because it requires two function calls, one to **GetIDsOfNames** and one to **Invoke**, whenever a property or method is invoked. A client can obtain **dispIDs** in advance from the type library for an object to avoid calling **GetIDsOfNames**, but the **Invoke** call is still very slow.

The **Invoke** method also determines which method or property is being invoked, and then packs and unpacks the parameters in variant arrays. This is not the most efficient method of providing Automation.

Dual interfaces were created as a more efficient means of implementing automation. A dual interface is a custom interface defined by the component and derived from **IDispatch**. A dual interface contains all of the functions contained in **IDispatch**, as well as custom functions for each method and property defined for the class. A dual interface allows COM-compliant client applications the most efficient access to the methods and properties of COM components. Instead of using the **IDispatch** methods, a client can make a direct call to the method it wants to invoke.

The following illustration shows what a dual interface might look like. It contains all of the **IDispatch** functions and any custom functions for the properties and methods that the interface supports.

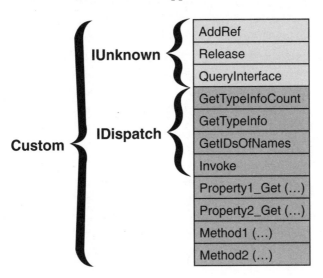

When a less sophisticated client, such as Visual Basic Scripting Edition, connects to an object that supports a dual interface, it uses the standard implementation of **IDispatch** to call **Method1** and **Method2** through the **Invoke** function.

A more advanced client, such as one written in Visual Basic, can call directly to the **Method1** and **Method2** functions in the interface. This more efficient form of access, known as **vtable** binding, is discussed in the next topic.

Introduction to Binding

For a client to use a method or property of an object, it must be bound to the object. Binding defines how a client connects to a particular object. There are two types of binding: late binding and early binding.

Late Binding

Late binding occurs whenever you declare variables of type Object. The compiler has no way of checking the methods, properties, types, or syntax of any object calls at compile time because a specific object type has not been declared.

The following example code results in the object **Customer** being late bound:

```
Dim objLookup as Object
Set objLookup = New CCustomer
objLookup.GetByID (1001), vInfo
```

When late binding is used, the client must make two calls to the object to access any method or property. The first call is made to the **GetIDsOfNames** method of the **IDispatch** interface to get the **dispID** for the particular method or property being invoked. The client then makes a second call to **Invoke**, passing the **dispID** to perform the desired action.

To see the animation "How Late Binding Works," see the accompanying CD-ROM.

An advantage of late binding is that the object to be created does not need to be known until run time. However, the disadvantage of late binding is that the compiler has no way to check the syntax. As a result, any errors, such as passing the wrong number of parameters or wrong parameter types, will not occur until run time. Late binding is less efficient because it requires calls to the **IDispatch** methods for each operation.

Early Binding

In contrast, early binding occurs when Visual Basic knows the type of Automation object variable at compile time. You establish early binding by declaring variables of a specific object type. When a variable is declared as a specific object type, the compiler will be able to check all object references using that variable against the information located in the type library. The type library will be either a stand-alone .tlb file or embedded in the component.

The example below results in the object **objLookup** being early bound:

```
Dim objLookup As CCustomer
Set objLookup = New CCustomer
objLookup.GetByID (1001), vInfo
```

Because the compiler has access to the object's type library, it can check the syntax of any calls that use that object variable, and notify you of any syntax errors at design time.

The compiler can also modify your code so that it optimizes execution speed when accessing the object. This optimization results in one of two early binding possibilities: **dispID** binding or **vtable** binding.

DispID Binding

DispID binding occurs whenever a variable is declared as a specific object type and the object does not support dual interfaces. With **dispID** binding, the compiler obtains the **dispID** from the object's type library and modifies all calls to the object with a call to **Invoke** with the appropriate **dispID**. This eliminates the need to call **GetIDsOfNames** for each method or property that is accessed.

To see the animation "How DispID Binding Works," see the accompanying CD-ROM.

DispID binding enhances performance by eliminating one call to the dispatch interface. It also permits syntax checking and code optimization. Because the object does not support dual interfaces, it is less efficient than **vtable** binding.

Vtable Binding

A faster form of early binding is known as **vtable** binding. **Vtable** binding is a more efficient form of binding because it completely avoids making the calls to **GetIDsOfNames** and **Invoke**. The client application accesses the methods and properties of an object directly.

Vtable binding occurs whenever a variable is declared as a specific object type and the object supports dual interfaces. Visual Basic builds clients that use **vtable** binding by default if the components being used support dual interfaces. All you need to do is create the reference to the type library and use the types for variable definitions. Using **vtable** binding to call a method or property in an in-process Visual Basic component does not require any additional overhead than that used by calling a function in a DLL. Components created with Visual Basic implement dual interfaces by default.

To see the animation "How Vtable Binding Works," see the accompanying CD-ROM.

Vtable binding provides the most efficient method of binding, providing syntax checking on object references and code optimization at compile time. It requires explicit object type declaration and that the object support dual interfaces.

Interfaces and Automation

Clients such as those built with Visual Basic Scripting Edition can only use late binding. In addition to that limitation, this type of client cannot specify a particular interface (other than the default interface) because it cannot call **QueryInterface**. If you want to build a class that has multiple interfaces and supports less sophisticated clients that cannot access interfaces other than the default, you must re-implement all your methods on the default interface.

The following sample code makes the functionality of the **ILookup** method, in the **CCustomer** class, available to Visual Basic Scripting Edition clients. To copy this code for use in your own projects, see "Re-implement Methods on a Default Interface" on the accompanying CD-ROM.

```
'CCustomer class
Implements ILookup

'ILookup interface
Private Function ILookup_GetByID(ByVal lngID As Integer)
As Variant
    ILookup_GetByID = GetByIDImplementation (ByVal lngID)
End Function

'default interface
Public Function GetByID(ByVal lngID As Integer) As Variant
    GetByID = GetByIDImplementation (ByVal lngID)
End Function

'Implementation code
Private Function GetByIDImplementation(ByVal lngID As Integer)
As Variant
' code segment
End Function
```

Lab 8: Interfaces

In this lab, you will examine how the classes within the Island Hopper News COM components use interfaces to group functionality. In addition, you will create the **ILookup** interface, as described in this chapter, implement the interface in a COM component class, and build a client application to test the interface. Next, you will move the new class into the Microsoft Transaction Server (MTS) environment and re-run the client application for more testing. You will also create a second class that will implement **ILookup** in a second COM component, move that COM component into MTS, and test polymorphism with an expanded client application.

To see the demonstration "Lab 8 Solution," see the accompanying CD-ROM.

Estimated time to complete this lab: **120 minutes**

To complete the exercises in this lab, you must have the required software. For detailed information about the labs and setup for the labs, see "Labs" in "About This Course."

Objectives

After completing this lab, you will be able to:

◆ Create an interface.

◆ Implement an interface in multiple classes in separate COM components.

◆ Insert the COM components in the MTS environment.

◆ Use COM components that implement interfaces in classes from client applications.

Prerequisites

Before working on this lab, you should be familiar with the following:

◆ Adding and deleting components in MTS packages.

◆ Creating a COM DLL by using Microsoft Visual Basic.

Exercises

The following exercises provide practice working with the concepts and techniques covered in this chapter:

◆ Exercise 1: Creating an Interface

In this exercise, you will use the MTS Explorer to see the interfaces implemented by some of the classes in the Island Hopper News components. Then, outside the scope of Island Hopper News, you will define an interface and implement that interface in a COM component. In order to focus on the interface issues, you will not include error handling, MTS service calls, or use true recordsets in the methods of the COM components you build.

◆ Exercise 2: Testing the Interface

In this exercise, you will create a test client to use the CustomerServer COM component that implements the **ILookup** interface. Then you will move the COM component into MTS and test it again using the same test client.

◆ Exercise 3: Re-implementing Interfaces

In this exercise, you will create the VendorServer COM component. This COM component will implement the **ILookup** interface in a new **CVendor** class. Both the **CCustomer** class and the **CVendor** class will than have the **ILookup** interface implemented.

◆ Exercise 4: Using Polymorphism

In this exercise, you will expand upon the InterfaceClient application that you built in Exercise 2. This new client will use both the **ILookup** methods of both the **CCustomer** and the **CVendor** classes.

Exercise 1: Creating an Interface

In this exercise, you will use the MTS Explorer to see the interfaces implemented by some of the classes in the Island Hopper News components. Then, outside the scope of Island Hopper, you will define an interface and implement that interface in a COM component. In order to focus on the interface issues, you will not include error handling, MTS service calls, or use true recordsets in the methods in the COM components you build.

▶ **Examine Island Hopper's use of interfaces to group functionality**

The Island Hopper News server components implement all of their interfaces in Interface Definition Language (IDL) and Visual C++ abstract classes rather than Visual Basic abstract classes. In this exercise, you will look at those interfaces as they appear in the MTS Explorer.

1. Run the MTS Explorer.

2. Locate the IsleHop_Accounting Package.

   If you need more information on using the MTS Explorer, see "Using the MTS Explorer" on page 76 in Chapter 3, "Introduction to Microsoft Transaction Server."

3. Expand the IsleHop_Accounting package, expand **Components**, expand **bus_CustomerC.Customer,** and then click **Interfaces.** You will see three interfaces:

   • _Customer (the default interface created by Visual Basic)

   • _IbusCustomerChange

   • IbusCustomerLookup

The following illustration shows the MTS Explorer, with the
bus_CustomerC.Customer interfaces displayed.

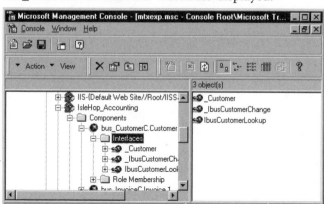

4. Expand the **IbusCustomerLookup** interface and examine the methods. You
will see the methods for **IUnknown** (**AddRef, Release** and **QueryInterface**),
IDispatch, (**GetTypeInfo, GetTypeInfoCount, GetIDsOfNames,** and **Invoke**),
and the methods **GetByID, ListByLastName,** and **GetByEmail.** The last three
methods relate to looking up customer information so they were grouped into
the **IbusCustomerLookup** interface.

▶ **Creating an interface**

1. Run Visual Basic and create a new ActiveX DLL project.

2. On the Project menu, click **Project1 Properties.** Set the following properties:

  • Set the project name to **CustomerServer.**

  • Enter a project description.

  • Select **Unattended Execution.**

  • Click **OK.**

3. Name the class module that was created **ILookup.**

4. Set the **Instancing** property to **PublicNotCreatable.**

5. Define two methods in the interface using the following code:

```
Function GetByID(ByVal lngID As Long) As Variant
End Function

Function GetByEmail(ByVal strEmail As String) As Variant
End Function
```

6. Save the project and class module as the files CustomerServer.vbp and ILookup.cls in a directory named Labs\Lab08\Exercise1.

▶ **Implementing the new interface in a separate class**

1. Create a new class in the CustomerServer project. Set the class name to **CCustomer** and in the declarations section, refer to the **ILookup** interface using the **Implements** keyword.

2. Create the **ILookup_GetByID** and **ILookup_GetByEmail** methods in the **CCustomer** class module. In the **ILookup_GetByID** method, simply append the `lngID` argument to the string "Customer ID: ". Return the concatenated string. Your code should appear as follows:

```
ILookup_GetByID = "Customer ID: " & lngID
```

3. In the **ILookup_GetByEmail** method, append the **strEmail** argument to the string "In Customer Email". Return the concatenated string. Your code should appear as follows:

```
ILookup_GetByEmail = "Customer Email: " & strEmail
```

4. Save your **CCustomer** class, as CCustomer.cls, and make the CustomerServer.dll. You will test your component in the next exercise.

Exercise 2: Testing the Interface

In this exercise, you will create a test client to use the CustomerServer COM component that implements the **ILookup** interface. Then you will move the COM component into MTS and test it again using the same test client.

▶ **Create a test client**

The test client will accept either an ID or an e-mail address and use the CustomerServer COM component methods, depending on the key the user enters.

1. Start Visual Basic and create a new Standard EXE project.

2. Set the name of the project to **InterfaceClient**.

3. Set a reference to the **CustomerServer** type library.

4. On the startup form, create the following controls with the properties listed.

Control	Name	Caption
Form	**frmInterface**	Interface Client
Text box	**txtIDorEmail**	None
Label	**lblIDorEmail**	ID or Email:
Command button	**cmdGetByID**	Get By ID
Command button	**cmdGetByEmail**	Get By Email

This illustration shows how your form should look. (Notice there is a little room at the top of the form for use in the next exercises.)

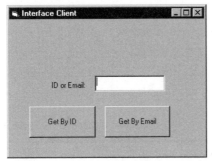

5. Save your project and form as the files InterfaceClient.vbp and frmInterface.frm in a folder named Labs\Lab08\Exercise2.

6. In the Declarations section of **frmInterface**, define a variable objILookup of type **ILookup.**

7. In the **cmdGetByID_Click** event procedure, set objILookup equal to a new **CustomerServer.CCustomer** object.

8. Next, call **GetByID** and pass it the value of the **txtIDorEmail** text box.

9. Display the return value from **GetByID** in a message box.

10. Finally, set **objILookup** to **Nothing** to clean up properly. Your code should appear as follows:

```
Set objILookup = New CustomerServer.CCustomer
MsgBox objILookup.GetByID(txtIDorEmail.Text)
Set objILookup = Nothing
```

11. Write the same code in the **cmdGetByEmail_Click** event procedure as you did for the **cmdGetByID_Click** event procedure. However, be sure to call **GetByEmail** rather than **GetByID**.

12. Create the InterfaceClient.exe file and run the application.

13. Test your CustomerServer COM component by entering either an ID or e-mail address and clicking the appropriate button. Because you have not completed error handling, entering a string and clicking the **GetByID** button will cause the application to fail.

    Make sure you have the InterfaceClient application and the CustomerServer COM component running properly before moving to the next exercise.

▶ Move the COM component into MTS

1. Once you are satisfied and have made whatever adjustments were necessary in the InterfaceClient and CustomerServer projects, go to the CustomerServer project, open the Project Properties window, and click **Component**.

2. Set **Version Compatibility** to **Binary Compatibility** and refer to the CustomerServer.dll file that was built in Exercise 1. This will ensure that Visual Basic will remind you any time you change the component in a way that is not binary compatible with this latest version. If you choose to make a DLL in the future that is not binary compatible, you must remember to recompile clients that rely on the older version.

3. Start the Windows NT Explorer and copy the CustomerServer.dll file to the Program Files\Mts\Packages folder.

4. Start the MTS Explorer.

5. Right-click **Packages Installed,** click **New,** and then click **Package**.

6. Create an empty package named Lab08 and set the package identity to **Interactive User**.

7. Click **Finish**.

8. Position the Windows NT Explorer and the MTS Explorer so you can see the complete contents of both windows.

9. In the MTS Explorer, click the **Components** folder under the Lab08 package. (This will display the contents of the Components folder of the Lab08 package, which is probably empty.)

10. Drag Program Files\Mts\packages\CustomerServer.dll from the Windows NT Explorer into the right pane of the MTS Explorer. This will add the CustomerServer COM component to the Lab08 package and adjust registry settings for the CustomerServer COM DLL.

   For more information about MTS and the registry, see "Adding Components to a Package" on page 82 in Chapter 3, "Introduction to Microsoft Transaction Server (MTS)."

11. In the MTS Explorer, click the Components folder under the Lab08 package.

12. Click **View**, and then click **Status**.

13. Run InterfaceClient.exe. You will see the number of objects and number of activated objects in the MTS Explorer. This gives you confirmation that the CustomerServer.dll is running in the MTS environment. The InterfaceClient application releases the object after the message box is displayed. If you examine the status of the components while the message box is displayed, you will see an object count of 1.

Exercise 3: Re-implementing Interfaces

In this exercise, you will create the VendorServer COM component. This COM component implements the **ILookup** interface in a new **CVendor** class. Both the **CCustomer** class and the **CVendor** class will then have the **ILookup** interface implemented.

▶ **Create the VendorServer COM component**

1. Create a new ActiveX DLL project in the Labs\Lab08\Exercise3 folder.

2. On the **Project** menu, click **Project1 Properties**. Set the following properties:

   • Set the **Project Name** to "VendorServer".

   • Add a project description.

   • Click **Unattended Execution**.

3. Set a reference to the CustomerServer type library.

   Notice that when you select the CustomerServer type library in the **References** dialog box, the location of the file is the MTS\Packages folder. Use the OLE/ COM Object Viewer to view the **ILookup** interface in the CustomerServer COM DLL and note the IID (you will use it later in this exercise.) The **ILookup** interface is found under the Interfaces folder in the OLE/COM Object Viewer.

To eliminate the dependency on the CustomerServer type library, you can create a type library that defines just the **ILookup** interface. Then, both the CustomerServer and VendorServer COM components will set references to the new type library.

4. Using the class that was created for you (Class1) in the ActiveX DLL project, set the class name to **CVendor**.

5. In the Declarations section of the **CVendor** class module, use the **Implements** keyword and refer to the **ILookup** interface.

6. Implement the **ILookup_GetByID** and **ILookup_GetByEmail** methods as they were implemented in the **CCustomer** class of the CustomerServer COM component. Make sure you change the methods to return vendor information instead of customer information.

To see and example of how your code should look, see Lab Hint 8.1 in Appendix B.

7. Save the project as VendorServer.vbp and create the VendorServer.dll.

8. Set binary compatibility and refer to the just compiled VendorServer.dll.

9. Copy VendorServer.dll to the Program Files\Mts\Packages folder.

10. As in Exercise 2, add VendorServer.dll to the Lab08 package so that the package has both the CustomerServer and VendorServer COM components.

11. In the MTS Explorer, you can verify that both **CCustomer** and **CVendor** implement the same interface. Under the **CustomerServer.CCustomer** component, click the **Interfaces** folder.

12. Click **View**, and then click **Property View**.

13. Look at the IID for the **ILookup** interface. It should match the IID you noted in Step 3.

14. Next, under the VendorServer.CVendor folder, click **Interfaces** folder. Use the **Property View** and note that the IID for the **ILookup** interface matches the IID from Step 3.

Exercise 4: Using Polymorphism

In this exercise, you will expand upon the InterfaceClient application that you built in Exercise 2. This new client will use both the **ILookup** methods of both the **CCustomer** and the **CVendor** classes.

▶ Create the new client

1. Open the InterfaceClient application from Exercise 2. You can copy the project in the Exercise 2 Solution folder if needed. Add a reference to the Vendor Server type library.

2. Add two option buttons to the top of the startup form (frmInterface). Set the properties of the option buttons as follows.

Caption	Property	Value
Customer	Name	optCustomer
	Value	True
Vendor	Name	optVendor
	Value	False

This illustration shows how your form should look.

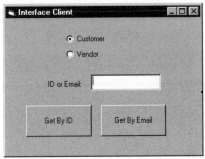

3. Edit the **cmdGetByID_Click** and **cmdGetByEmail_Click** event procedures to set **objILookup** to either a new **CustomerServer.CCustomer** object or a new **VendorServer.CVendor** object, depending on which option button is selected. The **If** statement should look similar to the following:

```
If optCustomer.Value = True Then
    Set objILookup = New CustomerServer.CCustomer
Else
    Set objILookup = New VendorServer.CVendor
End If
```

4. Compile and run the new InterfaceClient application. Be sure to alternate between the **Customer** and **Vendor** option buttons so that **objILookup** alternately refers to the **CCustomer** and **CVendor** objects. The **objILookup.GetByID** gets either a Customer ID or Vendor ID, depending on what object **objILookup** refers to. This is polymorphism with Visual Basic and interfaces.

5. Save the project as InterfaceClient.vbp in Labs\Lab08\Exercise 4 folder.

Self-Check Questions

To see the answers to the Self-Check Questions, see Appendix A.

1. Which item is not an attribute of interfaces?

A. Interfaces are immutable.

B. It is possible to create an instance of a class that defines an interface.

C. Interfaces are unique, each identified by an IID.

D. In Visual Basic, you define interfaces using abstract classes.

2. What is one advantage that interfaces provide the developer?

A. Interfaces make it easier to code.

B. Only the original developer of an interface defines its implementation.

C. There are no issues associated with supporting clients that have to use the default interface of a class.

D. Interfaces provide the ability to call the same function name on two different objects and get two different behaviors.

3. True or False: When defining and using an interface, set the instancing property of the interface class to Private.

A. True

B. False

4. Dual interfaces were created as a more efficient means of implementing automation. Which item most completely describes a dual interface?

   A. A custom interface that contains the **AddRef, Release,** and **QueryInterface** methods, and the custom functions for the properties and methods that the interface supports

   B. An interface that contains four functions: **GetTypeInfoCount, GetTypeInfo, GetIDsOfNames,** and **Invoke**

   C. An interface that contains the functions in the **IDispatch** and **IUnknown** interfaces

   D. A custom interface that contains all of the functions contained in **IDispatch,** as well as custom functions for each method and property defined for the class

5. Select the item that does not apply to early binding.

   A. The compiler obtains the **dispID** from the object's type library.

   B. The client makes a call to **GetIDsOfNames** for each method or property that is accessed.

   C. The client makes a call to **Invoke** with the appropriate **dispID.**

   D. The compiler provides syntax checking on object references.

Student Notes:

Chapter 9:
Advanced Client/Server Technologies

Multimedia

Using the MSMQ
Explorer 296

Lab 9 Solution 311

In this chapter, you will review the physical design of the Island Hopper solution and compare it to the techniques and technologies you practiced in this course. You will then learn about other business problems you may encounter in a corporate computing environment and other Microsoft technologies you can use to solve those problems.

Objectives

After completing this chapter, you will be able to:

◆ Describe a scenario where an asynchronous message queuing model is used.

◆ Using the Microsoft Message Queue (MSMQ) Explorer, create a new message queue and set properties for the queue, such as size and security.

◆ Write a Visual Basic application that sends messages to or receives messages from a message queue.

◆ Describe how Microsoft Cluster Server can be used to enhance the availability of server applications.

◆ List the Microsoft technologies that enable access to data in legacy database systems.

Overview of Advanced Client/Server Technologies

In this course, you learned how to build a three-tier client/server solution by developing the **bus_AdC** and the **db_AdC** components in Island Hopper News.

The following illustration shows the COM components for Island Hopper News.

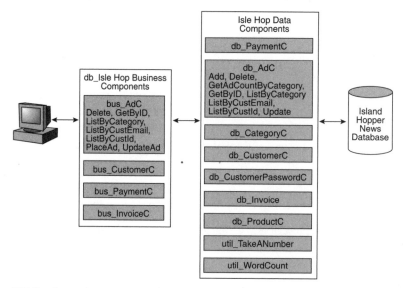

While the techniques you learned in class can be applied to many business problems, there are some problems that cannot be solved with MTS and SQL Server alone.

Unreliable or slow network connections, disconnected or remote users, heterogeneous application architectures, and legacy database systems all pose problems that require you to extend the solutions you have learned to build in this course.

In the sections that follow, you will learn more about some of the business problems that you may be facing now or in the future. You will also learn how technologies and products that run under the Windows NT Server 4.0 operating system address these problems and help you build robust, scalable applications.

Technologies that will be discussed include:

◆ Microsoft Message Queue (MSMQ)

◆ Microsoft Cluster Server

◆ Microsoft SNA Server

This is not a comprehensive list of the client/server technologies available. However, discussing these few technologies will provide a framework for future research and will help you identify when it is appropriate to apply these technologies.

Message Queuing

In this section, you will learn how Microsoft Message Queue (MSMQ) can help to solve the problems of unreliable or slow network connections, remote users, and heterogeneous application architectures. You will learn about asynchronous communication, how MSMQ provides asynchronous communication services for applications that run under Windows NT Server, and the basics of developing applications for MSMQ.

Introduction to Message Queuing

Applications that run on different computers can communicate with one another by passing messages and data. The information and data that are passed in a message can come in any form that is recognized by both the sender and the receiver of the message.

There are three possible scenarios when communication between two applications is attempted. An application sends a message to another application and:

◆ Expects and waits for an immediate response.

◆ Expects a response from the other application within a given timeframe, but continues to perform other work during that time.

◆ Does not expect a response.

The first scenario is an example of synchronous communication. The second and third scenarios are examples of asynchronous communication.

Synchronous Communication

When a sending application waits for a response from a receiving application, the applications can use DCOM or HTTP, and MTS for reliable and synchronous communications. Components assume that network connections and both parties in the communication process are always available. If one or more of these elements is unavailable, either an error occurs or, if an application participates in a transaction, the transaction rolls back; either everything happens or nothing happens. This is the environment under which Island Hopper operates. If for some reason communication is not established between the various parties and resources, the user is alerted and the operation does not take place.

The following illustration shows a tightly coupled, synchronous architecture, similar to that found in Island Hopper. This transaction spans two computers and two SQL Server data sources. A red "X" indicates each potential failure point in this architecture. A fault at any point in this architecture forces the entire transaction to fail.

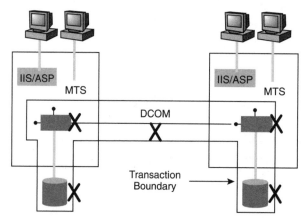

Asynchronous Communication

In an asynchronous communication model, an application sends a message and then continues with its work, without waiting for a response from the receiver of the message. The message goes into a message queue or holding area until the message receiver is ready to process it.

This is described as a loosely coupled communication model because various pieces of the communication process are independent of one another. The following illustration shows how the communication process can be broken up by transaction boundaries. A fault in one transaction does not necessarily mean that the entire process fails.

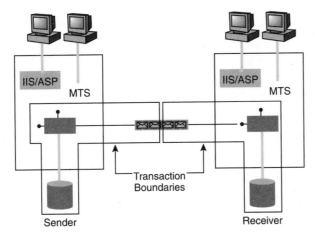

When an application uses asynchronous communication, it can either not expect a response or expect a response within a limited time frame.

One-Way Asynchronous Communication

When the sending application sends its message and never expects or receives confirmation from the receiving application, it uses one-way asynchronous communication. This is sometimes referred to as the business event push model. An example of one-way, asynchronous messaging is a retail point-of-sale application. Each time that a retail branch enters a sale, information about the sale is submitted to a receiving application in the form of a message. The receiving application is a sales-tracking application that collects the messages and processes the sales information for the marketing department.

This illustration shows a business event push model, where one-way asynchronous communication takes place. A business event, such as a retail sale, occurs and a message is pushed to the event consumer.

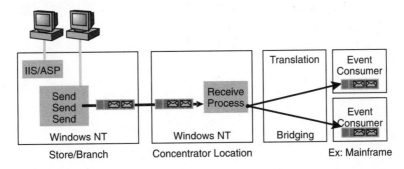

Request/Response Asynchronous Communication

When the sending application sends its message and expects a response from the receiving application within a specified length of time, it uses the request/response asynchronous communication model. For example, a stock-trading application accepts orders from customers and sends the trade information in the form of a message to a processing application. Two things can happen at this point. The message reaches the processing application and the trade is executed and recorded. Or, an amount of time passes (for example, three minutes) and the sending application does not receive a confirmation from the receiving application. In the second case, the sending application must reconcile the transaction by sending notification to the customer that the trade was not processed.

The benefit of this model is that system failures do not prevent the customer from entering a trade. The cost is that because the feedback is not immediate, as with synchronous communication, and the sending application does not wait to see if the trade actually occurs, the sender is then responsible for tracking the message and taking some action based on the outcome of the transaction.

The following illustration shows the request/response communication model.

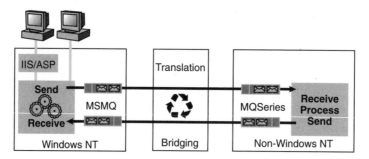

Note that this example shows communication between a Windows NT Server that uses MSMQ Server as the messaging software and a mainframe that uses IBM MQSeries, another messaging product. A third-party product named FalconMQ by Level 8 Systems provides the translation bridging between the two products.

Microsoft Message Queue (MSMQ)

By adding MSMQ to the Island Hopper sample application, you could easily incorporate the benefits of asynchronous messaging into the solution.

MSMQ is a product that enables applications to send and receive asynchronous messages. MSMQ is included as a feature of Microsoft Windows NT Server 4.0, both Standard and Enterprise Editions, and provides automatic integration with MTS.

MSMQ allows employees to submit advertisement information while they are disconnected from the corporate network. If Island Hopper components run from remote sites over weak or unreliable network connects, MSMQ would enable these components to run without interruption to the user.

For more information about MSMQ, go to the MSMQ Web site at http://www.microsoft.com/msmq.

How MSMQ Works

For each message, there is a sender and a receiver. The sender, an application on one computer, generates the message and then sends it to the MSMQ server. Messages are sent asynchronously, which means that once the message is sent, the sender can continue to work without waiting for the receiver of the message to respond. The message can contain text or binary data as defined by the sending application and can be up to 4 MB in size.

The message goes into a holding area on the server called a queue. When properly configured, the message queue is a safe and reliable storage area where the message and any data that it contains remains until the receiver is ready to retrieve it. In a distributed environment, it is possible that network connections may be unavailable or the receiving application may not be running, as is the case with applications that are used by remote or mobile users. The message queue stores the message until it receives a request from the receiver that indicates that it is ready to receive the message. It is also possible for a sending application to store messages locally if the network is unavailable. When the network becomes available, the messages will be forwarded automatically to the appropriate message queue server.

When the receiving application is ready to retrieve the message, it looks at the message queue for any messages that are addressed to it. Once it has received and processed the message, the receiver can respond to the sender or send messages of its own. It's up to the sender of the message to query the message queue for responses (or lack of responses, in some cases) and take appropriate action. The messages are destructively read, meaning they are removed from the queue once the receiving application retrieves the messages. Because of this, MSMQ can be used as a type of load balancer. Several servers can pull messages out of a single queue, retrieving new ones when ready to process the next message.

MSMQ Clients

MSMQ Server includes a server and two client configurations. The client configuration that you choose depends on the needs of your application and the characteristics of your platform.

- ◆ MSMQ independent clients

  Independent clients provide local queue management services to applications that run on the independent client computer.

  If the network between an independent client and other computers goes down (or doesn't exist in the case of a disconnected mobile user who logs on to the network periodically), local queue management services enable applications to continue to send and receive from local independent client queues. When the network connection is initiated or restored, the independent client forwards any messages stored in local queues that are destined for queues on another computer.

- ◆ MSMQ dependent clients

  Dependent clients provide all MSMQ application programming interfaces but require an available network connection to an MSMQ server in order to operate.

Dependent clients are easier to administer but independent clients do not require a constant network connection to operate, so they offer the most in terms of flexibility.

Using the MSMQ Explorer

You use the MSMQ Explorer to create, administer, and view sites, connected networks, computers, and queues on your MSMQ server.

To see the demonstration "Using the MSMQ Explorer," see the accompanying CD-ROM.

The following illustration shows the MSMQ Explorer window.

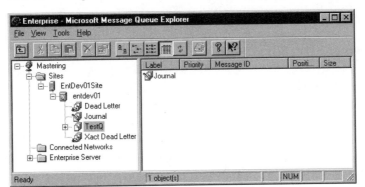

To create a new queue

1. In the MSMQ Explorer, double-click the Sites folder.

2. Right-click a computer, click **New**, and then click **Queue**.

3. In the **Name** box, type the new queue name.

4. Click **Transactional** to create a transactional queue. Select **Transactional** if you will use this queue with MTS applications.

Note Information displayed in the MSMQ Explorer may not be current and changes you make from within MSMQ Explorer may not be displayed. Click the **Refresh** button or press **F5** to refresh the information in the window.

For more information about using the MSMQ Explorer, see Microsoft Message Queue Help.

Sending and Receiving Messages

When two applications communicate using MSMQ, one must act as a sender and the other as a receiver. Once the sending application has sent a message, and the receiving application has received and processed the message, the two applications may reverse their roles. For example, the receiver may need to send confirmation to the original sender through another queue.

MSMQ provides an object model that enables you to program both the sending application and the receiving application. Most operations in MSMQ programming follow this basic process:

1. A send operation is performed.

2. The Queue Manager accepts the message and the send operation finishes.

3. The Queue Manager forwards the message to its destination queue.

4. The receiver retrieves the message from the destination queue.

The following illustration shows the architecture of the MSMQ programming model.

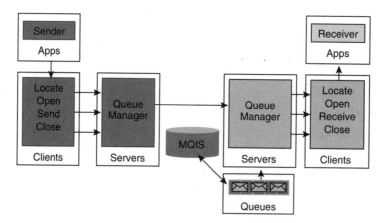

Using the MSMQ Object Model

The following illustration shows the three main objects in the MSMQ object model. Click each object to view a description of the object.

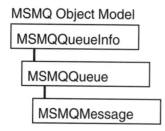

For more information about developing for MSMQ, see "Microsoft Message Queue Server (MSMQ)" under "Platform SDK," "Networking and Distributed Services" in Visual Studio Help.

▶ **To send a message by using MSMQ**

1. Create a reference to the **Microsoft Message Queue Object Library**.

2. Invoke the **Open** method of the **MSMQQueueInfo** object.

   Create an instance of an **MSMQQueueInfo** object, set the **PathName** property equal to the name of destination queue, and invoke the **Open** method on the object. For example:

```
Dim Qinfo as MSMQ.MSMQQueueInfo
Dim Q As MSMQ.MSMQQueue
Set Qinfo = New MSMQ.MSMQQueueInfo
Qinfo.PathName = "\\machinename\queuename"
Set Q = Qinfo.Open(MQ_SEND_ACCESS, MQ_DENY_NONE)
```

   The **MSMQQueue** object that is returned by the **MSMQQueueInfo** method is used only by MSMQ to identify the destination queue locally to the sending MSMQ Server. The Open operation does not establish an actual connection to the destination queue, and the destination queue does not have to be reachable over the network for the Open operation to be performed.

3. Create the message.

   Create an instance of an **MSMQMessage** object and provide values for the **Body** (which normally holds the application-specific content of the message) and **Label** (which describes the message and can be viewed by administrators through the MSMQ Explorer) properties. For example:

```
Dim Qmsg as MSMQ.MSMQMessage
Set Qmsg = New MSMQ.MSMQMessage
Qmsg.Label = "Message Label"
Qmsg.Body = "Message Body"
```

   If desired, you can set additional message properties, such as **MaxTimeToReachQueue**, **Delivery**, and **ResponseQueueInfo** (if required).

Tip Messages are sent to the message queue in UNICODE format. This is why the text in the **Body** property appears in the MSMQ Explorer interspersed with periods. For example:

M.e.s.s.a.g.e.B.o.d.y

4. Invoke the **Send** method of the **MSMQMessage** object.

Send the message by invoking the **Send** method on the message along with the **MSMQQueue** object representing the appropriate destination queue as a parameter. For example:

```
Qmsg.Send Q
```

5. Invoke the **Close** method.

Close the instance of the **MSMQQueue** object by invoking its **Close** method. For example:

```
Q.Close
```

If you anticipate sending additional messages to the same queue, you can leave the queue open and close it later. Avoiding frequent open and close calls to the same target queue improves application performance.

▶ To receive a message by using MSMQ

1. Create a reference to the **Microsoft Message Queue Object Library**.

2. Invoke the **Open** method of the **MSMQQueueInfo** object.

Create an instance of an **MSMQQueueInfo** object, set the **PathName** property equal to the name of queue from which to receive, and invoke the **Open** method on the object. For example:

```
Dim Qinfo as MSMQ.MSMQQueueInfo
Dim Q As MSMQ.MSMQQueue
Set Qinfo = New MSMQ.MSMQQueueInfo
Qinfo.PathName = "\\machinename\queuename"
Set Q = Qinfo.Open(MQ_RECEIVE_ACCESS, MQ_DENY_NONE)
```

To receive, the destination queue must be located on the same computer as the receiving application or be reachable over the network through an available network connection.

3. Invoke the **Receive** method on the **MSMQQueue** object. For example:

```
Dim Qmsg as MSMQ.MSMQMessage
Set Qmsg = Q.Receive(ReceiveTimeout:=1000)
```

The **Receive** method performs a synchronous read that will return immediately if a message is in the queue or wait indefinitely for the next message to be placed into the queue. Use the **ReceiveTimeout** property of the **MSMQQueue** object to set a timeout period (in milliseconds).

MSMQ passes back an instance of an **MSMQMessage** object containing the message at the head of the queue (or at the cursor position if cursors are being used). The object includes the body of the message (in the **Body** property) along with other information such as the name of any response queue.

It is the responsibility of the receiving application to decide what to do with all messages that it receives. This includes sending any required response messages or determining if the read will be destructive (the default) or not.

4. Invoke the **Close** method.

Close the instance of the **MSMQQueue** object by invoking its **Close** method. For example:

```
Q.Close
```

As before, if you anticipate receiving additional messages from the same queue, you can leave the queue handle open and close it later.

MSMQ supports a number of advanced receive options. For example, you can request nondestructive receives, and MSMQ returns an **MSMQMessage** object containing a copy of the message at the head of the queue but does not remove the message from the queue. This enables receivers to decide whether they want to process a given message or leave it for another application. MSMQ also supports blocking and nonblocking receives. With blocking receives, control is not returned to the requestor until a message is available in the queue. Using nonblocking receives enables applications to check for messages but continue processing if none are available.

MSMQQueueInfo provides queue management by enabling you to create a queue, open an existing queue, change a queue's properties, and delete a queue. The **Open** method of the **MSMQQueueInfo** object returns an **MSMQQueue** object.

MSMQQueue represents an MSMQ queue and provides the ability to traverse the messages in an open queue.

MSMQMessage provides properties that define MSMQ messages and a single method for sending the message to its destination queue.

MSMQ and MTS Integration

When MSMQ applications run under the MTS environment, these applications can automatically obtain some of the benefits provided by this environment, such as transactions and security.

MSMQ and MTS Transactions

All calls to MSMQ from transaction-enabled MTS components automatically join whatever transaction is active. As part of a transaction, messages can be committed or rolled back either in the component that sends the message or the component that receives the message. For example, if an application updates a database and sends a message to another application within a transaction, any abort condition causes the database updates to roll back. MSMQ also rolls back by canceling the send operation. MSMQ never completes a send operation until the transaction commits. This prevents receivers from getting messages from transactions that abort.

The following illustration shows the transaction boundary that includes the send operation.

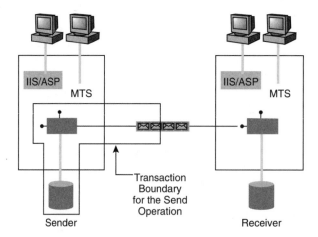

MSMQ takes similar actions when receive operations occur within a transaction. If the transaction aborts, MSMQ rolls back the receive operation by putting the received message back in its queue. This message becomes available for receipt by subsequent transactions.

The following illustration shows the transaction boundary that includes the receive operation.

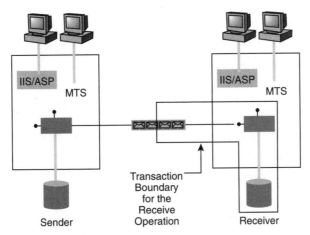

For more information about transaction processing in MTS, see Chapter 4, "Using MTS Transaction Services" on page 95.

MSMQ and MTS Security

MSMQ provides four types of security that work together to ensure that users attempting to use queuing services are authorized to do so.

Security type	Description
Access control	Restricts access to MSMQ resources, such as server administration tools and message queues.
Auditing	Records which users use each object in the MSMQ environment, which objects are used, and if access succeeds or fails.
Authentication	Provides verification that the message sender is authentic through the use of digital signatures.
Encryption	Encrypts or decrypts messages, which ensures they cannot be read or used by anyone not authorized to do so.

If a sending or receiving application runs under MTS, MSMQ uses the identity of the MTS package to determine who is attempting to use the message queue. This offers the same benefits to developers as it does with other types of resources, such as SQL Server. Applications can be developed more easily when access control is based on roles rather than specific Windows NT user or group accounts.

For more information about implementing security in MTS, see Chapter 7, "Implementing Security" on page 219. For more information about MSMQ security, see the MSMQ Administrator's Guide in Microsoft Message Queue Help.

Server Clustering

In this section, you will learn how to use Microsoft Cluster Server to improve the availability and reliability of your distributed applications. You will also learn about the tools you can use with Visual Basic to develop cluster-aware applications.

Introduction to Server Clustering

Through the use of components and MTS, Island Hopper presents a way that you can develop scalable and robust solutions. You can take this solution one step further by using server clustering. Server clustering enhances availability in mission-critical applications.

How Server Clustering Works

A cluster is a group of independent systems that work together as a single system. A client interacts with a cluster as though it were a single server. Cluster configurations are used to improve availability and manageability:

◆ Availability

When a system or application in the cluster fails or is taken down for maintenance or upgrades, the cluster software responds by restarting the failed application or dispersing the work from the failed or disabled system to the remaining systems in the cluster.

◆ Manageability

Administrators use a graphical console to move applications and data within the cluster to different servers. This is used for manually balancing workloads and for unloading servers for planned maintenance without downtime.

Clustering can take many forms. At the low end, a cluster may be nothing more than a set of desktop PCs connected by an Ethernet network. At the high end, the hardware structure may consist of high-performance symmetric multiprocessing (SMP) systems interconnected through a high-performance communications and I/O bus. In both cases, processing power for cluster-aware applications is increased in small increments by the addition of another computer. To a client, the cluster provides the illusion of a single server, or single-system image, even though it may be composed of many systems. Additional systems can be added to the cluster as needed to process increasingly complex or numerous requests from clients. If one system in a cluster fails, its cluster-aware workload can be automatically dispersed among the surviving systems. Frequently, this is transparent to the client.

When to Use Server Clustering

You can use server clustering to improve data availability, which protects applications from system failure.

In a retail operation, the point-of-sale system is the core of the business. Cashiers require ongoing access to the store's database of products, codes, names, and prices to keep the business logging sales. If the point-of-sale system fails, sales cannot be logged and the operation loses money and customers, as well as its reputation for quality service.

In this case, clustering technology can be used to deliver system availability. The clustering solution allows a pair of servers to access the multiport storage devices (disk array) on which the database resides. In the event of a server failure on Server 1, the backup system (Server 2) is automatically brought online, and end users are switched over to the new server without operator intervention. Thus, downtime is kept to a minimum. Industry standard fault-tolerant disk technology supported by Windows NT Server (striping, duplexing, and so forth) protects the disk array, but the addition of clustering technology ensures that the overall system remains online.

The following illustration shows the architecture at a retail branch, before a system failure.

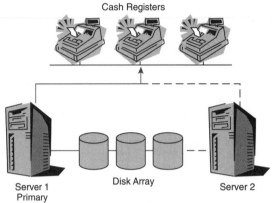

The following illustration shows the retail branch, after Server 1 fails.

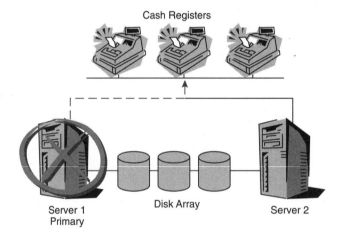

Microsoft Cluster Server

Clustering technology is available through Microsoft Cluster Server, a product of the Microsoft Windows NT Server, Enterprise Edition 4.0 operating system. In the past, clustering technology was available only through expensive proprietary hardware. Microsoft has been working with other vendors to develop a clustering technology that is based on open specifications and industry-standard hardware.

There are two phases in Microsoft Cluster Server:

◆ Phase 1: Two-Server Clusters for Availability and Manageability

This first phase is currently available in Windows NT Server Enterprise Edition, version 4.0.

A two-server cluster improves data and application availability by allowing two servers to trade ownership of the same hard disks within a cluster. When a system in the cluster fails, the cluster software recovers the resources and transfers the work from the failed system to the other server within the cluster. As a result, the failure of one system in the cluster does not affect the other systems, and in many cases, the client applications are completely unaware of the failure. This results in high server availability for the user. In addition, this two-server cluster system can be used for manual load-balancing and to unload servers for planned maintenance, without downtime.

◆ Phase 2: Multiple-Server Clusters for Enhanced Processing Power

The second phase will be available in a future version of Microsoft Cluster Server.

Phase 2 will enable more than two servers to be connected together for higher performance. As a result, when the overall load for a cluster-aware application or service exceeds the capabilities of the systems in the cluster, additional systems can be added to the cluster. This incremental growth will enable customers to add processing power as needed.

The current clustering capabilities of Windows NT Server Enterprise Edition 4.0 were architected for multiple nodes, but the initial delivery is limited to two nodes. This fully delivers the high availability most customers require from clusters, plus focuses the industry on quickly providing customers a wide choice of two-server cluster configurations validated for Microsoft Cluster Server. Both the Intel and RISC processor architectures (x86 and ALPHA) are supported. The second phase of Microsoft clustering development will increase the number of nodes supported and improve scalability by providing new services that simplify the creation of scalable, cluster-aware applications.

For more information about Microsoft Cluster Server, go to the Microsoft Cluster Server Web site at http://www.microsoft.com/ntserverenterprise/exec/overview/clustering/default.asp.

Developing for Microsoft Cluster Server

There are two ways that developers can take advantage of server clustering.

◆ Any server-based application that runs under Microsoft Cluster Server automatically obtains the benefit of availability, without requiring any additional programming.

◆ You can use a cluster API to develop cluster-aware applications, that is, applications that have been enhanced to detect component failures and initiate fast recovery.

However, not all server applications need to be cluster-aware to take advantage of cluster scalability benefits. Applications that build on top of cluster-aware core applications, such as large commercial database packages (for example, an accounting or financial database application built on top of SQL Server or MTS) will benefit automatically from cluster enhancements made to the underlying application. Many server applications that use database services, client/server connection interaction, and file and print services can benefit from clustering technology, without requiring application changes.

Using the Cluster Automation Server from Visual Basic

The Cluster Automation Server API is a COM-based dual interface used by cluster management applications written in Visual Basic or one of the scripting languages. The programmable objects provided by Cluster Server expose properties and methods that are specific to cluster management.

▶ **To prepare your environment to use the Cluster Automation Server with Visual Basic**

1. Install Microsoft Visual Basic version 4.0 or later.

2. Install the Microsoft Cluster Server SDK.

   To download the Microsoft Platform SDK Windows Base Services Components, which include the Microsoft Cluster Server SDK, go to the Microsoft Product Download site at http://www.microsoft.com/msdownload/platformsdk/winbase.htm.

3. Register MSCLUS.DLL, the dynamic-link library that contains the Cluster Automation Server. Typically you register when you install the SDK. However, if you need to manually register MSCLUS.DLL, use the system registry program REGSVR32.

To test your environment, launch Visual Basic and choose **References** from the **Projects** menu. If MSCLUS.DLL has been registered properly, it will appear in the list of components as MS Cluster 1.0 Type Library. Click the check box next to this item in the list to enable the Visual Basic Object Browser to include the programmable cluster objects. You now allocate instances of these objects, call their methods, and retrieve and set their properties.

For more information about using the methods exposed by the Cluster Server API, search for "Cluster Server Programming" in Visual Studio Help.

Accessing Mainframe Data

The Island Hopper application demonstrated several ways to access SQL Server databases from your Visual Basic applications. However, not all corporations have a homogeneous database environment. Legacy database systems in various mainframe environments are a common feature of corporate client/server architectures. From a cost standpoint, corporations want to embrace emerging technologies, while preserving investments that have been made in legacy systems. From a development standpoint, writing code that can work with any data source, regardless of its origin, in the same manner, is desirable. Microsoft addresses this problem with Windows SNA Server and other technologies targeted at providing access to mainframe data.

Windows SNA Server 4.0

SNA Server 4.0 provides easy and cost-effective means to integrate new applications with existing application logic in mainframe and AS/400 application environments, while providing a robust connectivity platform for access to legacy data.

SNA Server is more than just a traditional LAN-to-host SNA gateway. SNA Server extends the gateway platform by providing host integration services for building complete PC-to-host SNA applications and data integration solutions.

These solutions take advantage of MTS and its integration with Microsoft Internet Information Server (IIS). Since applications developed for MTS can be written once and used in many ways, you get the most from development investment. As an example, a component can be accessed from a Web application, a DCOM client application, or a SQL Server stored procedure. This flexibility provides the reusability that customers have been demanding.

SNA Server provides features that assist in integrating your applications with host data, including:

◆ COM Transaction Integrator for CICS and IMS

◆ OLE DB Provider for AS/400 and VSAM

◆ Microsoft Host Data Replicator (HDR)

For more information about Windows SNA Server, go to the Microsoft SNA Server Papers and Guides Web site at http://www.microsoft.com/sna/guide/jwp.asp.

COM Transaction Integrator for CICS and IMS (COMTI)

Microsoft COM Transaction Integrator for CICS and IMS (COMTI) provides client applications with access to the two most popular mainframe Transaction Processing (TP) environments: CICS and IMS/TM. Working in conjunction with MTS, COMTI makes CICS and IMS programs appear as typical MTS components that can be used with other MTS components for building distributed applications.

The COMTI Component Builder provides a COBOL Wizard that helps you determine what data definitions you need from the COBOL program, and generates a component library (.tlb file) that contains the corresponding automation interface definition. Because of the integration with MTS, when you drag the component library into the MTS Explorer, you create a COM object that exposes a method call that invokes the mainframe transaction. This allows you to build applications using Active Server technologies that can easily include mainframe transaction programs.

Similarly, in companies whose CICS and IMS applications are LU 6.2-enabled, you can easily integrate these applications with Microsoft Windows-based Internet and intranet applications. You do not have to learn new APIs, nor do you have to program custom interfaces for each application and mainframe platform. Because COMTI does all of its processing on the Microsoft Windows NT Server, there is no COMTI executable code required to run on the mainframe. Client applications simply make method calls to an automation server, and mainframe TPs respond as if called by another mainframe program. COMTI is the bridge between the two computing environments.

For more information about COMTI, go to the COM Transaction Integrator for CICS and IMS Web site at http://www.microsoft.com/sna/guide/comti.asp.

OLE DB Provider for AS/400 and VSAM

The OLE DB provider for AS/400 and VSAM allows record-level access to mainframe VSAM files and the AS/400 native file system. It provides record-level access to both physical and logical files on the AS/400. For the mainframe, you get record-level access to most variations of VSAM, and to PDS and PDSE files. If you are familiar with ActiveX Data Objects (ADO), you can use it without additional training.

For more information, go to the OLE DB provider for AS/400 and VSAM Web site at http://www.microsoft.com/sna/guide/snaoledb.asp.

Microsoft Host Data Replicator (HDR)

Microsoft Host Data Replicator (HDR) enables you to integrate data between Microsoft SQL Server and multi-platform DB2 databases by creating a bi-directional snapshot replication of data. HDR replicates the data from DB2 to SQL Server, which enables you to operate on the data in the Windows environment.

For more information, see the Microsoft Host Data Replicator Web site at http://www.microsoft.com/sna/guide/datarep.asp.

Lab 9: Using a Message Queue

In this lab, you will develop applications that send messages to and retrieve messages from a queue that you create with Microsoft Message Queue (MSMQ).

To see the demonstration "Lab 9 Solution," see the accompanying CD-ROM.

Estimated time to complete this lab: **60 minutes**

To complete the exercises in this lab, you must have the required software. For detailed information about the labs and setup for the labs, see "Labs" in "About This Course."

Objectives

After completing this lab, you will be able to:

◆ Create a new message queue using the MSMQ Explorer.

◆ Use objects from the MSMQ programming model to create applications that send and retrieve messages from a queue.

◆ Use the sending and receiving applications and the MSMQ Explorer to perform ad-hoc tests and see the impact on the queue.

Prerequisites

There are no prerequisites for this lab.

Exercises

The following exercises provide practice working with the concepts and techniques covered in this chapter:

◆ Exercise 1: Sending Messages to a Queue

In this exercise, you will use the MSMQ Explorer to create a new queue and develop an application that sends messages to the queue. Then, you will test the application and queue using the sending application and the MSMQ Explorer.

◆ Exercise 2: Receiving Messages from a Queue

In this exercise, you will develop an application that receives messages from a queue and test the sending and receiving applications using the MSMQ Explorer.

Exercise 1: Sending Messages to a Queue

In this exercise, you will use the MSMQ Explorer to create a new queue and develop an application that sends messages to the queue. Then, you will test the application and queue using the sending application and the MSMQ Explorer.

▶ **Create a new queue**

MSMQ is already installed on your computer, as part of the Windows NT Server 4.0 installation. The default site name is *computername*Site. Computers that are members of the site are listed below the site name and the list should include an entry for your computer. You will create a new queue on your computer.

1. Launch the MSMQ Explorer.

2. Open the Sites folder.

3. Click *computername*Site.

4. Click your computer name from the list of computers that are members of the *computername*Site.

5. Create a new queue called TestQ. Do not select the transactional option. The new queue is listed under *computername*.

6. Right-click the new queue, and then click **Properties**. Browse through the tabs to see the property options that are available.

▶ **Build the Send application**

1. Start Visual Basic and create a Standard EXE project. Name the project Send.

2. Add a reference to the **Microsoft Message Queue Object Library**.

3. Add controls to the default form and set their properties as follows.

Control	Property	Value
Label	**Caption**	Message Label:
Label	**Caption**	Message Body:
Text box	**Name**	txtLabel
	Text	None
Text box	**Name**	txtBody
	Text	None
Command button	**Name**	cmdAdd
	Caption	Add to Queue

The following illustration shows how your form should look.

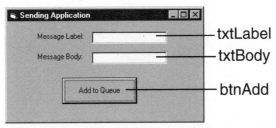

4. Declare the following variables in the General Declarations section of the form:

```
Dim Qinfo As MSMQ.MSMQQueueInfo
Dim Q As MSMQ.MSMQQueue
Dim Qmsg As MSMQ.MSMQMessage
```

5. In the **Form_Load** event procedure, create an instance of a **MSMQQueueInfo** object, set the **PathName** property equal to the name of the destination queue, TestQ, and invoke the **Open** method. Then, create an instance of an **MSMQMessage** object. This object will be used repeatedly to send messages to the queue.

To see an example of how your code should look, see Lab Hint 9.1 in Appendix B.

6. In the **cmdAdd_Click** event procedure, set the **Label** and **Body** properties of the **MSMQMessage** object using the contents of the text controls on the form.

To make the results of the Send application easier to see in the MSMQ Explorer, define a static variable that append a unique number onto the end of the label and body of each message. As you look through the list of messages in the Explorer, each message will have a unique number, reflecting each invocation of the Send application.

Then, send the message to the destination queue using the **Send** method of the **MSMQMessage** object, passing the **MSMQQueue** object as a parameter.

To see an example of how your code should look, see Lab Hint 9.2 in Appendix B.

7. In the **Form_Unload** event procedure, close the instance of the **MSMQQueue** object by invoking its **Close** method.

8. Save the project and form as Send.vbp and Send.frm. Then make the executable file.

▶ **Test the Send application**

1. Run the Send application and the MSMQ Explorer. Arrange your desktop so you can see the user interface of both applications.

The following illustration shows how your desktop should appear.

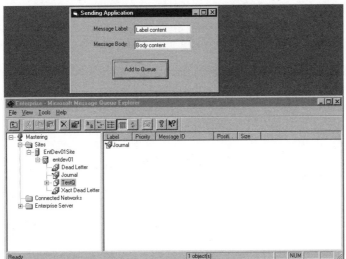

2. In the MSMQ Explorer, click the **TestQ** queue. The messages from the Send application will appear in the right pane.

3. In the Send application, enter the label and body for the new message. Click **Add to Queue** a number of times to add the message to the queue.

4. In the MSMQ Explorer, click the **Refresh** button, or press F5, to refresh the Explorer window.

5. On the **View** menu, click **Columns**. If Label and Body are not listed in the **Show the following** list, add them and then click **OK**.

6. In the right pane of the MSMQ Explorer, you will see a list of messages sent by the Send application.

Exercise 2: Receiving Messages from a Queue

In this exercise, you will develop an application that receives messages from a queue and test the sending and receiving applications using the MSMQ Explorer.

▶ **Build the Receive application**

1. Start Visual Basic and create a **Standard EXE Project.** Name the project Receive.

2. Add a reference to the **Microsoft Message Queue Object Library.**

3. Place controls on the form and set their properties as follows.

Control	Property	Value
Label	**Caption**	Message Label:
Label	**Caption**	Message Body:
Text box	**Name**	txtLabel
	Text	None
Text box	**Name**	txtBody
	Text	None
Command button	**Name**	cmdGetNext
	Caption	Get Next Message

The following illustration shows how your form should look.

4. In the General Declarations section of the form, declare the following variables:

```
Dim Qinfo As MSMQ.MSMQQueueInfo
Dim Q As MSMQ.MSMQQueue
Dim Qmsg As MSMQ.MSMQMessage
```

5. In the **Form_Load** event procedure, create an instance of an **MSMQQueueInfo** object, set the **PathName** property equal to the name of the destination queue, TestQ, and invoke the **Open** method of the object.

   To see an example of how your code should look, see Lab Hint 9.3 in Appendix B.

6. In the **cmdGetNext_Click** event procedure, invoke the **Receive** method of the **MSMQQueue** object. This returns an **MSMQMessage** object.

   Use the **Label** and **Body** properties of the **MSMQMessage** object to populate the controls in the Receive application.

   Set the **ReceiveTimeout** property of the **MSMQQueue** object to 1000 milliseconds and then trap the error that is generated if the timeout period expires.

   To see an example of how your code should look, see Lab Hint 9.4 in Appendix B.

7. In the **Form_Unload** event procedure, close the instance of the **MSMQQueue** object by invoking its **Close** method.

8. Save the project and form as Receive.vbp and Receive.frm. Then make the executable file.

▶ **Test the Receive application**

1. Run the Receive application and the MSMQ Explorer. Arrange your desktop so you can see the user interface of both applications.

2. In the MSMQ Explorer, click the **TestQ** queue. The right pane of the Explorer will display the messages that were generated by the Send application.

3. In the Receive application, click **Get Next Message**.

   This will retrieve the first message from the queue and destroy it from the queue. The label and body of the message will display on the Receive form. Continue receiving messages until the queue is empty and the error handler is called.

4. Click **Refresh** to refresh the Explorer window and note the effect of removing messages from the queue.

▶ **Test the Send and Receive applications together**

1. Run the Send and Receive applications, and MSMQ Explorer. Arrange your desktop so you can see the user interface of all of the applications.

The following illustration shows how your desktop should appear.

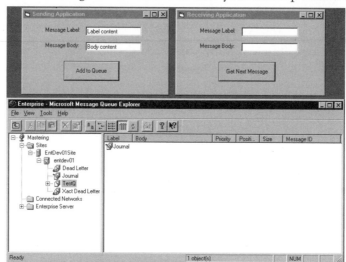

2. In the MSMQ Explorer, click **TestQ**.

3. Using the Send and Receive applications, send and receive messages to test the functionality of the queue. Refresh the MSMQ Explorer window to see the results.

Self-Check Questions

To see the answers to the Self-Check Questions, see Appendix A.

1. **True or False: One of the key features of MSMQ is Independent Clients, which enables client computers to store messages locally until they are reconnected to the network.**

    A. True

    B. False

2. **How are MSMQ and MTS integrated?**

    A. MSMQ and MTS are not integrated in any way.

    B. A send transaction is completed when the receiving application retrieves the message.

    C. A send transaction is completed when a reply message is sent by the receiving application.

   D. All calls to MSMQ from transaction-enabled MTS components automatically join whatever transaction is active.

3. True or False: Microsoft Cluster Server improves the availability, manageability, and performance of an application.

   A. True

   B. False

4. Which of the following technologies provide client applications with access to two of the most popular mainframe transaction processing environments?

   A. Microsoft SNA Server

   B. Microsoft COM Transaction Integrator for CICS and IMS (COMTI)

   C. The OLE DB Provider for AS/400 and VSAM

   D. Microsoft Host Data Replicator (HDR)

5. What happens when a message queue is opened with receive access and a receiving application calls the Receive method of the MSMQQueue object?

   A. The messages in the message queue remain there until the **Purge** method of the **MSMQQueue** object is called by the receiving application. This clears all messages from the queue.

   B. The first message in the queue is returned to the receiving application and is not removed from the message queue.

   C. The last message added to the message queue by the sending application is retrieved by the receiving application.

   D. Each message is deleted from the message queue as it is retrieved by the receiving application.

Student Notes:

Appendix A:
Self-Check Answers

Chapter 1

1. True or False: Application infrastructure is software that supports concurrent access to a shared service, usually business and data services.

A. True

   Correct

   For example, Microsoft Transaction Server (MTS) is software that works with the operating system to provide the application infrastructure for sharing business services implemented as components.

B. False

   Incorrect

   A server computer provides the centralized, multi-user functionality in a three-tier architecture. Other terms for this functionality are application infrastructure and plumbing. For example, access to stored procedures and data on a database server are controlled by a Relational Database Management System (RDBMS).

For more information, see *Client/Server Architecture and Terms*, page 2.

2. Which item is not defined in the COM specification?

A. How an object is created from a component

   Incorrect

   Object creation is covered in the COM specification.

B. How a client accesses features of the object

   Incorrect

   How to access objects and their features is covered in the COM specification.

C. The object's responsibility for destroying itself when it is no longer in use
Incorrect

Reference counting and object destruction are covered in the COM specification.

D. The suite of interfaces each component should support
Correct

The interfaces that are implemented are determined by the functionality requirements of the component, not the COM specification.

For more information, see *Implementation of COM*, page 11.

3. Choose the correct statement related to enterprise development.

A. Microsoft's Enterprise Development Strategy is only concerned with intranets and LANs.
Incorrect

Microsoft's Enterprise Development Strategy includes the Internet as well.

B. Components that execute in the middle tier can be accessed by ASP files and other COM clients such as applications built by using Visual Basic.
Correct

This is a key part of the development strategy. Work done in the middle tier can be implemented and used successfully across the LAN or Internet.

C. Stored Procedures can only be used to implement data services and never business services.
Incorrect

Even with MTS available, it still may make sense to implement some business services as stored procedures.

D. Visual Basic should always be used to build COM components which run in the middle tier.
Incorrect

Visual C++ gives programmers more control and speed. Developers frequently use Visual C++ to build COM components that run in the middle tier.

For more information, see *Microsoft's Enterprise Development Strategy*, page 12.

4. Select the statement that incorrectly describes a Microsoft development tool.

A. Visual Basic is a Rapid Application Development (RAD) tool.

Incorrect

Visual Basic is a RAD tool with enhanced data connectivity support.

B. Visual C++ is designed to help programmers build optimized, high-performing, enterprise solutions.

Incorrect

Visual C++ gives the ultimate level of control and speed.

C. Visual InterDev is a RAD tool used to build Web applications.

Incorrect

Visual InterDev is used to build Web applications, including ASP files.

D. Visual Basic can always be used without support of the other development tools to build Enterprise solutions.

Correct

The Microsoft development tools are applied together to build complete Enterprise solutions.

For more information, see *Microsoft Development Tools*, page 34.

5. What is the correct description of the development phase in the MSF Process Model?

A. You define a vision statement that articulates the ultimate goals for the product or service and provides clear direction.

Incorrect

This describes the Envisioning phase of the Process Model.

B. The development phase provides the opportunity for customers and end users, operations and support personnel, and key project stakeholders to evaluate all features of the product.

Correct

The Developing Phase culminates in the Scope Complete/First Use milestone.

C. Testing activities, bug finding, and fixing are the primary foci, and the product is formally turned over to the operations and support groups.

Incorrect

This describes the Stabilizing phase of the Process Model.

D. Customers and team agree on what is to be delivered, and how it will be built, reassess risk, establish priorities, and finalize estimates for schedule and resources.

Incorrect

This describes the Planning phase of the Process Model.

6. Which of the following is not a characteristic of services in the Application Model?

A. Services can be distributed across both physical and functional boundaries to support the needs of many different applications.

Incorrect

Tiers are a logical concept and do not imply physical deployment.

B. According to MSF, a service is always implemented as an API.

Correct

There are many ways to implement services besides an API.

C. COM components can be used to implement many services.

Incorrect

COM components are frequently used to implement services. ActiveX controls can be used to implement user services.

D. Stored procedures can be used to implement many services.

Incorrect

Stored procedures are frequently used to implement business or data services.

For more information, see *The Application Model and Services*, page 19.

Chapter 2

1. Which Visual Basic project template would you use to build an in-process COM component?

A. ActiveX Control

Incorrect

ActiveX controls are in-process, but they have a graphical interface and other features that are not necessary for a COM component.

B. ActiveX DLL

Correct

ActiveX DLLs are in-process, and can be used as COM components.

C. ActiveX EXE

Incorrect

The ActiveX EXE Visual Basic project template is an out-of-process COM component.

D. Standard EXE

Incorrect

A Visual Basic Standard EXE project template is a standard Windows application. It is not a COM component.

For more information, see *Choosing the Type of COM Component*, page 41.

2. How do you export a method from a class module in Visual Basic?

A. Mark the Visual Basic project for unattended execution.

Incorrect

In Visual Basic, unattended execution indicates that the project does not interact with the user, and makes the application apartment-threaded.

B. Set the **Instancing** property to **MultiUse**.

Incorrect

The **Instancing** property determines if one or multiple clients can use the same instance of a component.

C. Add the **Public** keyword before the method.

Correct

The **Public** keyword causes a method to be available outside the component.

D. Set the Visual Basic project type to **ActiveX DLL**.

Incorrect

Setting the project type does not enable methods to be exported.

The project type specifies whether the project is an ActiveX DLL, ActiveX EXE, or standard Windows program.

For more information, see *Creating Methods for Classes*, page 45.

3. What are all of the ways in which an in-process component can be registered?

A. When you run Setup for the component, when you run RegSvr32.exe, and when you compile the component with Visual Basic

Correct

You can register an in-process component by compiling it in Visual Basic, running RegSvr32.exe, or by running a Setup program for the component.

B. When you run Setup for the component, and when you compile the component with Visual Basic

Incorrect

You can register an in-process component by compiling it in Visual Basic, or by running a Setup program for it. However, you can also use other registration methods.

C. When you run RegSvr32.exe, and when you compile the component with Visual Basic

Incorrect

You can register an in-process component by compiling it in Visual Basic or by running RegSvr32.exe. However, you can also use other registration methods.

D. When you run Setup for the component, and when you run RegSvr32.exe

Incorrect

You can register an in-process component by running a Setup program for it or by running RegSvr32.exe. However, you can also use other registration methods.

For more information, see *Registering a COM DLL*, page 57.

4. How can you test an in-process component in Visual Basic so that you can trace into each method call as it runs?

A. Create a project group by adding a test project to the original component's project. Then add a reference to the component. Write code to call methods in the component and use the debugger to step into each method.

Correct

To test a component in Visual Basic so that you can trace into each method call as it runs, set up the test project and then use the debugging features in Visual Basic to step into the methods.

B. Create a separate test project and add a reference to the component project. Write code to call methods in the component and use the debugger to step into each method.

Incorrect

You must add the test project to the component project in order to test the component. It cannot be called from a separate project. Once it has been added, you can use the debugging features in Visual Basic to step into the methods.

C. In the component project, set breakpoints on the methods you want to step through. Run the component in the Visual Basic debugger, and then run a separate test project that calls the component.

Incorrect

You can use breakpoints to indicate that a component's method should break into debug mode. However, you must add the test project to the component project in order to test the component. It cannot be called from a separate project. Once it has been added, you can use breakpoints to invoke break mode and then to step into the methods.

D. In the component project, add a reference to a test project. Set breakpoints on the methods you want to step through, and run the component in the Visual Basic debugger. Then run the test project and call the methods.

Incorrect

Add a test project to the original component's project and then add a reference to the component. Write code to call methods in the component and use the debugger to step into each method.

For more information, see *Testing a COM DLL*, page 55.

5. To avoid generating new CLSIDs and other identifiers each time your component is built in Visual Basic, set the Version Compatibility option for the project to:

A. No Compatibility.

Incorrect

When the **No Compatibility** option is selected, each time you compile the component, the type library ID, CLSIDs, and IIDs are recreated. Because none of these identifiers match the ones existing clients are using, backward compatibility is not possible.

B. Project Compatibility.

Incorrect

With the **Project Compatibility** option selected, each time you compile the component, the CLSIDs and IIDs are recreated, but the type library remains constant. This is useful for test projects so you can maintain references to the component project. However, each compilation is not backward compatible with existing clients.

C. Binary Compatibility.

Correct

When the **Binary Compatibility** option is selected, each time you compile the component, Visual Basic keeps the type library ID, CLSIDs, and IIDs the same. This maintains backward compatibility with existing clients. However, if you attempt to delete a method from a class, or change a method's name or parameter types, Visual Basic warns you that your changes make the new version incompatible with previously compiled applications.

D. None of the above.

Incorrect

The correct Version Compatibility option is listed in the available choices.

For more information, see *Version Compatibility*, page 53.

6. True or False: When creating COM objects in code, the CreateObject function offers a slight performance improvement over using the New operator.

A. True

Incorrect

The **CreateObject** function is not faster than the **New** operator.

When you use the **New** operator, Visual Basic skips the step of calling **CLSIDFromProgID** at run time because it obtains the CLSID at design time. This makes the **New** operator slightly faster than the **CreateObject** function.

B. False

Correct

When you use the **New** operator, Visual Basic skips the step of calling **CLSIDFromProgID** at run time because it obtains the CLSID at design time. This makes the **New** operator slightly faster than the **CreateObject** function.

For more information, see *Activating a COM Object*, page 60.

Chapter 3

1. One difficulty in developing scalable distributed applications is programming your applications to handle simultaneous calls from multiple clients. How does MTS help you with this problem?

A. MTS provides a single-user concurrency model in which an activity defines the logical flow of work through components. You write components as if a single user will call them.

   Correct

   MTS handles thread management for you and provides a single-user concurrency model so that you can write components as though a single user calls them.

B. Each component can be written as apartment-threaded or free-threaded. You write free-threaded components and MTS dispatches multiple client calls simultaneously through the components.

   Incorrect

   MTS discourages multi-threaded component development. You should set MTS components as apartment-threaded and then write them as single-user components.

C. MTS contains a thread pool that dispatches a new thread for each client that calls. You write synchronization code in the components to handle the possibility of multiple client calls.

   Incorrect

   MTS handles thread management for you. There is no need to write synchronization code to handle multiple client calls.

D. MTS uses a single thread to process all client calls. Additional client calls are queued until the thread is free to process them. This allows you to write single-user components.

   Incorrect

   MTS uses a pool of threads to handle multiple client calls efficiently. However, only one thread is allowed to access your component at any given time, allowing you to program to a single-user concurrency model.

For more information, see *Overview of MTS*, page 70.

2. Which of the following is a characteristic of MTS packages?

A. MTS packages can contain any type of COM component.

Incorrect

An MTS package can only contain COM DLLs. COM EXEs cannot be added to MTS packages.

B. MTS components can run outside their MTS package, as long as the Unattended Execution option is set for those components.

Incorrect

MTS components must run inside an MTS package.

C. An MTS package can define a fault isolation boundary so that if a component fails in the package, it does not cause other packages to fail.

Correct

MTS packages can provide fault isolation to help ensure that component failures do not propagate to other packages.

D. You must design packages carefully because it is not possible to call a component in one package from another package.

Incorrect

Components in one package can call components in another package, as long as they are authorized to do so.

For more information, see *MTS Environment*, page 73.

3. What is the effect of setting a package's activation property to Server Package?

A. It runs as a server process and provides security for its components and fault isolation from other packages.

Correct

Setting the **Server Package** property for a package causes it to run in a server process and enables security and fault isolation.

B. It runs as a server process and provides security for its components.

Incorrect

Setting the **Server Package** property for a package also provides fault isolation from other packages.

C. It runs in the client's process and provides security for its components and fault isolation from other packages.

Incorrect

The **Server Package** property causes the package to run in a server process separate from the client process.

D. It runs in a server process and provides fault isolation from other packages.

Incorrect

Setting the **Server Package** property for a package also provides security for its components.

For more information, see *Creating a Package*, page 79.

4. Which of the following statements about the client application executable is false?

A. It extracts necessary type libraries and proxy stub DLLs from the client computer so the remote components can be accessed.

Incorrect

The client application executable copies the type libraries and proxy stub DLLs to the client computer.

B. It updates the system registry with the required entries for clients to use the server components remotely.

Incorrect

The client application executable updates the registry.

C. It registers the package application in the Add/Remove Programs option in the Control Panel so that the application can be uninstalled at a later date.

Incorrect

The client application executable registers the package application so that it can be uninstalled at a later date.

D. It copies all of the components in the package over to the client computer so they can be accessed locally.

Correct

Components remain on the server and are not copied to the client computer.

For more information, see *Configuring a Client to Use MTS Components*, page 88.

5. True or False: A resource dispenser is a service that manages nondurable, shared-state data on behalf of the components in a process. A resource manager is a system service that manages durable data.

A. True

Correct

Resource dispensers, such as the Shared Property Manager, manage nondurable data, while resource managers, such as Microsoft SQL Server, manage durable data.

B. False

Incorrect

Resource dispensers, such as the Shared Property Manager, manage nondurable data, while resource managers, such as Microsoft SQL Server, manage durable data.

For more information, see *Supporting Services*, page 74.

6. Which of the following modifications are made to the registry for each class in a component when it is added to an MTS package?

A. The InprocServer32 key for the component is modified to point to MTX.exe, which runs in place of the component when it is called from a client application.

Incorrect

The InprocServer32 key is cleared so that it has an empty value and no longer points to the location of the DLL.

B. A /p parameter is added to the path of the component listed in the InprocServer32 key, which specifies the identity of the package to run when the component is called.

Incorrect

The /p parameter specifies the identity of the package that contains the class, but it is not added to the InprocServer32 key.

C. The LocalServer32 key for the component is modified to point to MTX.exe, which runs in place of the component.

Correct

The LocalServer32 key contains the path of the MTS executable, MTX.exe. When the class is activated through COM, this executable launches in place of the component DLL. This ensures that the MTS executable hosts your DLL and that MTS services are available to your DLL.

D. None of the above.

Incorrect

One of the modifications listed is made to the registry.

For more information, see *MTS Components and the Registry,* **page 84.**

Chapter 4

1. How is an object deactivated with just-in-time activation?

A. When the transaction completes or when the object returns from a method call after calling **SetComplete** or **SetAbort**, MTS releases all references to the object by destroying it and making its resources available to other objects.

Correct

When the transaction completes or when the object calls **SetComplete** or **SetAbort**, the object is deactivated by MTS.

B. When the object returns from a method call after calling **SetComplete** or **SetAbort**, the client releases all references to the object, destroying it and making its resources available to other objects.

Incorrect

An object can also be deactivated if it participates in a transaction and the root object for the transaction calls **SetComplete** or **SetAbort**.

C. Each time the object returns from a method call, MTS releases all references to the object, destroying it and making its resources available to other objects.

Incorrect

MTS does not deactivate an object until the object calls **SetComplete** or **SetAbort**, or the root object for the transaction is deactivated.

D. The object calls the **DeActivate** method on the **ObjectContext** object. Then MTS releases all references to the object, destroying it and making its resources available to other objects.

Incorrect

The **ObjectContext** object does not have a **DeActivate** method.

MTS deactivates an object when the transaction completes, or when the object returns from a method call after calling **SetComplete** or **SetAbort**.

For more information, see *Calling SetComplete and SetAbort,* **page 104.**

2. If an object does not explicitly call SetComplete, SetAbort, EnableCommit, or DisableCommit, what is the default status of the object?

A. SetComplete

Incorrect

SetComplete is not the default status for objects.

B. SetAbort

Incorrect

SetAbort is not the default status for objects.

C. EnableCommit

Correct

EnableCommit is the default status for objects if no other method is called.

D. DisableCommit

Incorrect

DisableCommit is not the default status for objects.

For more information, see *Determining Transaction Outcome*, page 107.

3. How do you programmatically enable an object to participate in transactions on Microsoft Transaction Server?

A. Call the transaction functions **BeginTrans**, **CommitTrans**, and **Rollback**.

Incorrect

BeginTrans, **CommitTrans**, and **Rollback** are not functions in the MTS programming model.

B. Modify the component to call the methods **SetComplete** and **SetAbort**.

Correct

The **SetAbort** and **SetComplete** methods enable an object to participate in transactions on Microsoft Transaction Server.

C. Place the component in the Microsoft Transaction Server Explorer.

Incorrect

Placing a component in the Microsoft Transaction Server Explorer registers it with Microsoft Transaction Server, but does not modify the component to support transactions.

D. Create the public methods **SetComplete** and **SetAbort** for the component.

Incorrect

The **ObjectContext** object implements the methods **SetComplete** and **SetAbort**, so you do not need to implement them for the Transaction Server component.

For more information, see *Calling SetComplete and SetAbort*, page 104.

4. Which of the following is an appropriate way to store state for MTS objects?

A. Instance data within a transaction

Incorrect

This answer is partially correct. The advantages of stateless objects include all of the answers to the question.

B. NT Service

Incorrect

This answer is partially correct. The advantages of stateless objects include all of the answers to the question.

C. Shared Property Manager

Incorrect

This answer is partially correct. The advantages of stateless objects include all of the answers to the question.

D. All of the above

Correct

The advantages of stateless objects include all of the answers to the question.

For more information, see *Just-in-Time Activation*, page 113.

5. If an MTS object is marked as Requires a transaction, what creation method should you use so that it participates in the existing transaction?

A. Visual Basic's **CreateObject** function

Incorrect

CreateObject creates an MTS object, but that object does not inherit its context from the caller and it cannot participate in the existing transaction.

B. The ObjectContext CreateInstance method

Correct

Calling the **CreateInstance** method on the **ObjectContext** object causes MTS to automatically enlist the new object into the existing transaction.

C. Visual Basic's **New** keyword

Incorrect

Creating an object using the **New** keyword creates an MTS object, but that object does not inherit its context from the caller and it cannot participate in the existing transaction.

Also, you should never use the **New** keyword to create an MTS object, unless you are sure that the MTS object code is outside your Visual Basic project.

D. None of the above

Incorrect

The correct creation method is listed in the available choices.

For more information, see *Calling CreateInstance*, page 102.

Chapter 5

1. Which ActiveX Data Objects (ADO) are members of a collection?

A. Field and Parameter only

Incorrect

The **Property** and **Error** objects are also members of a collection.

B. Field, Parameter, Property, and Error

Correct

The **Field, Parameter, Property**, and **Error** objects are all members of a collection.

C. Field, Command, Parameter, and Property

Incorrect

The **Command** object is not a member of a collection. In addition, the **Error** object is a member of a collection.

D. Field, Parameter, and Error only

> **Incorrect**
>
> The **Property** object is also a member of a collection.

For more information, see *ADO Object Model Overview*, page 144.

2. List all ActiveX Data Objects (ADO) that can generate a recordset.

A. Recordset object

> **Incorrect**
>
> The **Command** and **Connection** objects can also generate a recordset.

B. Recordset and Command objects

> **Incorrect**
>
> The **Connection** object can also generate a recordset.

C. Recordset, Command, and Connection objects

> **Correct**
>
> The **Recordset**, **Command**, and **Connection** objects can all generate a recordset.

D. Tabledef, Command, and Connection objects

> **Incorrect**
>
> The **Recordset**, **Command**, and **Connection** objects can generate a recordset.

For more information, see *Creating and Navigating Recordsets*, page 151.

3. True or False: The following example code creates a client-side, static cursor with a lock type of optimistic batch update.

```
Dim rs As ADODB.Recordset
Set rs = New ADODB.Recordset
rs.CursorType = adOpenStatic
rs.LockType = adLockBatchOptimistic
rs.Open "Select * From Authors", "DSN=Pubs"
Set rs.ActiveConnection = Nothing
```

A. True

Incorrect

By default, the cursor location is at the server. The example code results in a server-side cursor. You would need to change the cursor location to client-side by modifying the **CursorLocation** property of the **Recordset** object to **adUseClient**.

B. False

Correct

By default, the cursor location is at the server. The example code results in a server-side cursor. To change the cursor location in the example code to client-side, you would need to modify the **CursorLocation** property of the **Recordset** object to **adUseClient**.

For more information, see *Introduction to Cursors*, page 158.

4. What are the steps to create the parameters in the Parameters collection yourself when using stored procedures?

A. Create separate **Parameter** objects, fill in the correct parameter information for the stored procedure call, and then append them to the collection using the **Append** method.

Correct

You can increase the performance of your components by creating the parameters in the collection yourself, and avoid the extra network trip. For multiple parameters, you must append the parameters in the order that they are defined in the stored procedure.

B. Establish an active connection, call the **Refresh** method of the **Parameters** collection, assign values to the parameters, and then run the stored procedure.

Incorrect

These steps describe using the **Refresh** method of the **Parameters** collection for situations where access to the data source is fast, or for rapid development purposes.

C. Set the **CommandType** property of the **Command** object to the constant **adCmdStoredProc**, the **CommandText** to the name of the stored procedure, and then invoke the **Execute** method.

Incorrect

These steps describe how to use a stored procedure.

D. Append the return parameter to the **Parameters** collection, obtain any output parameters by reading their values from the **Parameters** collection, and then read the return code.

Incorrect

These steps describe specifying an input parameter for a stored procedure through the **Parameter** object.

For more information, see *Populating the Parameters Collection*, page 171.

5. Which Recordset method would you use to update a database from a disconnected recordset?

A. Refresh

Incorrect

Refresh is not a recordset method. Use the **UpdateBatch** method to transmit all changes from a recordset to the underlying database.

B. Update

Incorrect

The **Update** method only affects the current record. Use the **UpdateBatch** method to transmit all changes from a recordset to the underlying database.

C. UpdateBatch

Correct

The **UpdateBatch** method is used to transmit all changes from a recordset to the underlying database.

D. Resync

Incorrect

Resync updates the recordset from the database. Use the **UpdateBatch** method to transmit all changes from a recordset to the underlying database.

For more information, see *Disconnected Recordsets Defined*, page 163.

Chapter 6

1. True or False: Always place business logic in the business services tier of a three-tier application.

A. True

Incorrect

While the business services tier is appropriate for many types of business logic, there are no rules that dictate that all business logic belongs there.

B. False

Correct

As a general rule, place business logic that is datacentric in the data services tier in the form of triggers and stored procedures, and business logic that performs calculations or nondatabase work, or involves interaction with other applications, in the business services tier.

For more information, see *Implementing Business and Data Services with SQL Server*, page 188.

2. Which type of data integrity is enforced through the use of validity checking, which restricts the type, the format, or the range of possible values in a column?

A. Entity

Incorrect

Entity (or table) integrity requires that all rows in a table have a unique identifier, the primary key value. Whether the primary key value can be changed, or whether the whole row can be deleted, depends on the level of integrity required between the primary key and any foreign key references.

B. Referential

Incorrect

Referential integrity ensures that the relationships among the primary and foreign keys are always maintained.

C. Unique

Incorrect

Unique is a constraint used to enforce data integrity.

D. Domain

Correct

Domain integrity specifies a set of data values that are valid for that column through the use of validity checking.

For more information, see *Introduction to Data Integrity*, page 193.

3. You can define a parameter for a stored procedure that returns a value to the calling application. What syntax is used in the Create Procedure statement to identify this type of parameter?

A. Output

Correct

The **Output** option indicates that the parameter is a return parameter.

B. Return

Incorrect

Return is not a valid option for parameter definitions.

C. Input

Incorrect

Input is not a valid option for parameter definitions.

D. None of the above

Incorrect

The correct answer is listed in the selections above.

For more information, see *Adding Parameters to a Stored Procedure*, page 199.

4. Which of the following statements defines a valid local variable in a stored procedure?

A. Dim LocalVariable

Incorrect

This is not a valid declaration for a local variable in a stored procedure.

B. Declare @LocalVariable

Correct

A local variable is defined by using the **Declare** statement, followed by a variable name that starts with a single @ symbol.

C. Select @LocalVariable

Incorrect

This is not a valid declaration for a local variable in a stored procedure.

D. Declare @@LocalVariable

Incorrect

This statement declares a global variable.

For more information, see *Declaring Variables*, page 202.

Chapter 7

1. Which item is not an advantage of three-tier security?

A. All database access can be totally encapsulated by the MTS components. This ensures data integrity.

Incorrect

In a three-tier application, you separate business logic into a middle tier. Users no longer access the database directly from their client application.

B. When one application calls another to get work done, it needs to verify the user's credentials, and the user logs on again, or starts a new session with the second application.

Correct

This is a drawback of two-tier security. Applications cannot be easily integrated, requiring additional work to maintain security.

C. You can use MTS to think about security in terms of the roles that an individual plays in the organization. This is a more efficient method of administering security.

Incorrect

In a three-tier application MTS objects access the database and perform updates or retrievals on behalf of the users, separating the users from the database.

D. Because each user does not need a login to the server, it reduces administration when setting up application access.

Incorrect

Application security involves authorizing users access to specific components and interfaces in MTS packages. You map users to the application functionality that applies to them.

For more information, see *Security Modes*, page 237.

2. When does MTS enforce declarative security on method calls to components?

A. Each call into a package from a client is checked. Calls between components in the same package are not checked. Calls between packages are checked.

Correct

MTS uses roles to determine who can use a component whenever a call is made to an interface from outside the package.

B. Each call into a package from a client is checked. Calls between components in the same package are checked. Calls between packages are checked.

Incorrect

Method calls from one component to another inside a package are not checked because components in the same package trust each other.

C. Each call into a package from a client is checked. Calls between components in the same package are not checked. Calls between packages are not checked.

Incorrect

Declarative security includes method calls from an object in one package to an object in another package. MTS checks security on each method call because it's possible for an authorized client to pass an interface pointer to a client that is not authorized.

D. Only the first call into a package from a client is checked. Calls between components in the same package are not checked. Calls between packages are checked.

Incorrect

MTS checks security on each method call into a package because it's possible for an authorized client to pass an interface pointer to a client that is not authorized.

For more information, see *MTS Security Overview*, page 223.

3. True or False: Once SQL Server uses the login to identify the connection, the component has access to all of the database objects in SQL Server.

A. True

Incorrect

The component must have permissions to perform any operations on the database. The component's permissions depend on its login. You map each login to a set of permissions for each database object.

B. False

Correct

Having a connection does not mean that the component has access to all of the database objects in SQL Server. You must grant permissions to a login before any components using that login can access databases or the objects inside those databases.

For more information, see *Logins and Permissions*, page 242.

4. Choose the item that most completely describes integrated security.

A. It uses SQL Server's login validation process for all connections, and it is useful in network environments with a variety of clients.

Incorrect

This is a description of standard security. Connections validated by SQL Server are referred to as nontrusted connections.

B. Both trusted connections and nontrusted connections are supported, and it is useful in network environments that have a mix of clients.

Incorrect

This is a description of mixed security. Mixed security allows SQL Server login requests to be validated by using either integrated or standard security methods. Both trusted connections (as used by integrated security) and nontrusted connections (as used by standard security) are supported.

C. Users have one login ID and password for both Windows NT and SQL Server, and it is useful in network environments where all clients support trusted connections.

Correct

Integrated security allows a SQL Server to use Windows NT authentication mechanisms to validate SQL Server logins for all connections. Connections validated by Windows NT Server and accepted by SQL Server are referred to as trusted connections.

D. Each user must provide a valid SQL Server login ID and password, and it provides backward compatibility for older versions of SQL Server.

Incorrect

This is a description of standard security. Connections validated by SQL Server are referred to as nontrusted connections.

For more information, see *Security Modes*, page 237.

5. True or False: Database auditing is an additional security option in the three-tier security model.

A. True

Incorrect

Database auditing is not useful under the three-tier security model because all users access the database through the same user ID (the package's account). If your application has any requirements for auditing, you must design for this in your business and database components.

B. False

Correct

Database auditing does not work as expected under the three-tier security model because all users access the database through the same user ID (the package's account).

For more information, see *Security Best Practices*, page 247.

Chapter 8

1. Which item is not an attribute of interfaces?

A. Interfaces are immutable.

Incorrect

Once published, interfaces can never change.

B. It is possible to create an instance of a class that defines an interface.

Correct

You never create an instance of a class that defines an interface. Instead, you refer to that class using Implements.

C. Interfaces are unique, each identified by an IID.

Incorrect

Each interface has a unique identifier (GUID or globally unique identifier) referred to as an interface ID or IID.

D. In Visual Basic, you define interfaces using abstract classes.

Incorrect

In Visual Basic you define interfaces in class modules using abstract classes with no implementation.

For more information, see *Interfaces Defined*, page 258.

2. What is one advantage that interfaces provide the developer?

A. Interfaces make it easier to code.

Incorrect

There is more effort required to create classes that support multiple interfaces.

For more information, see *Applying Interfaces*, page 266.

B. Only the original developer of an interface defines its implementation.

Incorrect

COM is an open, extensible system in the sense that anyone can provide an implementation of a defined interface, and anyone can develop an application that uses such interfaces.

For more information, see *Interfaces Defined*, page 258.

C. There are no issues associated with supporting clients that have to use the default interface of a class.

Incorrect

Supporting Visual Basic Scripting Edition and multiple interfaces requires reimplementing methods from other interfaces for the default interface.

For more information, see *Applying Interfaces*, page 266.

D. Interfaces provide the ability to call the same function name on two different objects and get two different behaviors.

Correct

Polymorphism is one of the design advantages realized by using interfaces.

For more information, see *Applying Interfaces*, page 266.

3. True or False: When defining and using an interface, set the instancing property of the interface class to Private.

A. True

Incorrect

Set the instancing property to **PublicNotCreatable** so you can refer to it but not create an instance.

B. False

Correct

PublicNotCreatable means that other applications can use objects of this class only if your component creates the objects first.

For more information, see *Creating and Implementing Interfaces*, page 261.

4. Dual interfaces were created as a more efficient means of implementing automation. Which item most completely describes a dual interface?

A. A custom interface that contains the **AddRef, Release,** and **QueryInterface** methods, and the custom functions for the properties and methods that the interface supports

Incorrect

In addition to the functions listed, a dual interface contains the four functions in the **IDispatch** interface.

For more information, see *Dual Interfaces*, page 272.

B. An interface that contains four functions: **GetTypeInfoCount, GetTypeInfo, GetIDsOfNames,** and **Invoke**

Incorrect

In addition to the functions listed for **IDispatch**, a dual interface also contains any custom functions for the properties and methods that the interface supports, and inherits the methods from the **IUnknown** interface.

For more information, see *Dual Interfaces*, page 272, and *COM Components and IDispatch*, page 270.

C. An interface that contains the functions in the **IDispatch** and **IUnknown** interfaces

Incorrect

A dual interface also contains the custom functions for each method and property defined for the class.

For more information, see *Dual Interfaces*, page 272.

D. A custom interface that contains all of the functions contained in **IDispatch,** as well as custom functions for each method and property defined for the class

   Correct

   A dual interface contains all of the **IDispatch** functions and any custom functions for the properties and methods that the interface supports. **IDispatch** also inherits the methods from the **IUnknown** interface.

   For more information, see *Dual Interfaces*, page 272, and COM *Components and IDispatch*, page 270.

5. Select the item that does not apply to early binding.

A. The compiler obtains the **dispID** from the object's type library.

   Incorrect

   In early binding the compiler obtains the **dispID** from the object's type library and modifies all calls to the object with a call to **Invoke** with the appropriate **dispID.**

B. The client makes a call to **GetIDsOfNames** for each method or property that is accessed.

   Correct

   When late binding is used, the first call is made to the **GetIDsOfNames** method of the **IDispatch** interface to get the **dispID** for the particular method or property being invoked.

C. The client makes a call to **Invoke** with the appropriate **dispID.**

   Incorrect

   With **dispID** binding, a form of early binding, the compiler obtains the **dispID** from the object's type library and modifies all calls to the object with a call to **Invoke** with the appropriate **dispID.**

D. The compiler provides syntax checking on object references.

   Incorrect

   Early binding permits syntax checking and code optimization at compile time.

For more information, see *Introduction to Binding*, page 273.

Chapter 9

1. True or False: One of the key features of MSMQ is Independent Clients, which enables client computers to store messages locally until they are reconnected to the network.

A. True

Correct

MSMQ does solve some of the problems associated with disconnected networks through Independent Clients.

B. False

Incorrect

Independent Clients enable client computers to store messages locally until they are reconnected to the network.

For more information, see *Introduction to Message Queuing*, page 291.

2. How are MSMQ and MTS integrated?

A. MSMQ and MTS are not integrated in any way.

Incorrect

MSMQ and MTS are tightly integrated.

B. A send transaction is completed when the receiving application retrieves the message.

Incorrect

A send transaction is completed when the message has been successfully sent to MSMQ. MSMQ immediately returns as soon as it gets the message from the sending application.

C. A send transaction is completed when a reply message is sent by the receiving application.

Incorrect

A send transaction is completed when the message has been successfully sent to MSMQ. MSMQ immediately returns as soon as it gets the message from the sending application.

D. All calls to MSMQ from transaction-enabled MTS components automatically join whatever transaction is active.

Correct

Transactional support is automatic in MSMQ whenever transaction-enabled MTS components are called.

For more information, see *Microsoft Message Queue (MSMQ)*, page 295.

3. True or False: Microsoft Cluster Server improves the availability, manageability, and performance of an application.

A. True

Incorrect

Microsoft Cluster Server improves availability and manageability, but application performance is not improved.

B. False

Correct

Microsoft Cluster Server improves availability and manageability, but application performance is not improved.

4. Which of the following technologies provide client applications with access to two of the most popular mainframe transaction processing environments?

A. Microsoft SNA Server

Incorrect

Microsoft SNA Server is designed to allow integration of new applications with existing application logic in mainframe and AS/400 application environments, while providing a robust connectivity platform for access to legacy data.

B. Microsoft COM Transaction Integrator for CICS and IMS (COMTI)

Correct

Microsoft COM Transaction Integrator for CICS and IMS (COMTI) provides client applications with access to the two most popular mainframe Transaction Processing (TP) environments: CICS and IMS/TM.

C. The OLE DB Provider for AS/400 and VSAM

Incorrect

The OLE DB Provider for AS/400 and VSAM allows record-level access to mainframe VSAM files and the AS/400 native file system.

D. Microsoft Host Data Replicator (HDR)

Incorrect

Microsoft Host Data Replicator (HDR) enables you to integrate data between Microsoft SQL Server and another type of database by creating a bi-directional snapshot replication of data.

For more information, see *Accessing Mainframe Data*, page 309.

5. What happens when a message queue is opened with receive access and a receiving application calls the Receive method of the MSMQQueue object?

A. The messages in the message queue remain there until the **Purge** method of the **MSMQQueue** object is called by the receiving application. This clears all messages from the queue.

Incorrect

The **Purge** method is not a valid method of the **MSMQQueue** object.

B. The first message in the queue is returned to the receiving application and is not removed from the message queue.

Incorrect

If a message queue is opened with receive access, the **Receive** method removes the message from the message queue after it has been retrieved by the receiving application.

To return the first message in the queue without removing from the message queue, use the **Peek**, **PeekNext**, or **PeekCurrent** methods of the **MSMQQueue** object.

C. The last message added to the message queue by the sending application is retrieved by the receiving application.

Incorrect

By default, MSMQ returns the first message added to the message queue by the sending application to the receiving application when the **Receive** method is called.

D. Each message is deleted from the message queue as it is retrieved by the receiving application.

Correct

By default, the **Receive** method performs a destructive read, which means that the message is deleted from the message queue after it has been received by the receiving application.

For more information, see *Sending and Receiving Messages*, page 297.

Appendix B:
Lab Hints

Lab Hint 2.1

```
Function SquareRoot(ByVal dblNumber As Double) As Double
    On Error GoTo ErrorHandler
    SquareRoot = Sqr(dblNumber)
    Exit Function
ErrorHandler:
    Err.Raise Err.Number, "Math Module: SquareRoot",
Err.Description
End Function
```

Lab Hint 2.2

```
Private Sub cmdSquareRoot_Click()
    On Error GoTo ErrorHandler
    txtAnswer.Text = objRoot.SquareRoot(txtNumber.Text)
    Exit Sub
ErrorHandler:
    MsgBox Err.Source & ", " & Err.Description, vbOKOnly, "Math
Error"
End Sub
```

Lab Hint 4.1

```
Dim objAd As db_AdC.Ad
Dim rs As New ADODB.Recordset

On Error GoTo ErrorHandler

' If this is a valid ad ID number, create an instance of
' the db_AdC.Ad object to retrieve the ad information.
If lngAdvertisementID >= 0 Then
    Set objAd = GetObjectContext.CreateInstance("db_AdC.Ad")
    Set rs = objAd.GetByID(lngAdvertisementID)
End If

' Allow MTS transaction set to proceed.
GetObjectContext.SetComplete

' Return the ad information in a recordset.
Set GetByID = rs
```

Lab Hint 4.2

```
Dim objAd As bus_AdC.Ad
Dim rs As ADODB.Recordset

On Error GoTo ErrorHandler

Set objAd = New bus_AdC.Ad
Set rs = objAd.GetByID(txtAdID)
MsgBox rs(1)
Exit Sub

ErrorHandler:
MsgBox "An Error Occurred: " & Err.Description
```

Lab Hint 4.3

```
'Attempt to create a new property group.  If property
'group of the same name already exists, this will
'retrieve a reference to that group.
Set spmGroup = spmMgr.CreatePropertyGroup(strPropGroupIn,
LockSetGet, Process, bResult)
```

Lab Hint 4.4

```
'Attempt to create new properties for the above group.
'This will set the individual property values to zero.
'If the group already exists, this will retrieve current
'value for the properties.
Set spmPropMaxNum = spmGroup.CreateProperty("MaxNumber", bResult)
Set spmPropNextNum = spmGroup.CreateProperty("NextNumber", bResult)

'If property group did not exist set next number to one.
If Not bResult Then
    spmPropNextNum.Value = 1
End If
```

Lab Hint 4.5

```
'The following if clause creates a new block of
'ID #'s if the maxnumber has been reached.
' The maxnumber represents the last number in a block of ID #'s.
'The nextnumber represents the current ID #. If they are the same
'it is time to issue a new block of numbers.
If spmPropNextNum.Value >= spmPropMaxNum.Value Then
    ' create an instanc of Util_takeANumber
    Set objTakeUpdate =
GetObjectContext.CreateInstance("util_TakeANumber.TakeANumberUpdate")
    'set NextNumber.  See TakeANumber code for specifics
    spmPropNextNum.Value = objTakeUpdate.Update(incQty,
strPropGroupIn)
    'Set new Max Number
    spmPropMaxNum.Value = spmPropNextNum.Value + incQty
End If
```

Lab Hint 5.1

```
strSQL = "SELECT * FROM Advertisements " & _
  "Join Customers " & _
  "On Advertisements.CustomerID = Customers.CustomerID " & _
  "WHERE Customers.Email = '" & strEmail & "' " & _
  "Order by Advertisements.Title"
```

Lab Hint 6.1

```
CREATE PROCEDURE dbo.UpdateAd
@Title  varchar(100),
@StartDate DateTime,
@EndDate DateTime,
@CustomerID Int,
@CategoryID Int,
@ModifiedDate DateTime,
@Body Text,
@AdID Int
As

UPDATE Advertisements
SET Title = @Title,
StartDate = @StartDate,
EndDate = @EndDate,
CustomerID = @CustomerID,
CategoryID = @CategoryID,
ModifiedDate = @ModifiedDate
Where AdvertisementID = @AdID

/* Write the Body portion of the Advertisement (TEXT data type) to
the database*/

DECLARE @ptrval varbinary(16)
SELECT @ptrval = TEXTPTR(Body)
FROM Advertisements
WHERE AdvertisementID = @AdID

WRITETEXT Advertisements.Body  @ptrval WITH LOG @Body
```

Lab Hint 6.2

```
CREATE PROCEDURE dbo.UpdateAd
@Title   varchar(100),
@StartDate DateTime,
@EndDate DateTime,
@CustomerID Int,
@CategoryID Int,
@ModifiedDate DateTime,
@Body Text,
@AdID Int
As

UPDATE Advertisements
SET Title = @Title,
StartDate = @StartDate,
EndDate = @EndDate,
CustomerID = @CustomerID,
CategoryID = @CategoryID,
ModifiedDate = @ModifiedDate
Where AdvertisementID = @AdID

/* Write the Body portion of the Advertisement (TEXT data type) to
the database*/

DECLARE @ptrval varbinary(16)
SELECT @ptrval = TEXTPTR(Body)
FROM Advertisements
WHERE AdvertisementID = @AdID

WRITETEXT Advertisements.Body  @ptrval WITH LOG @Body
```

Lab Hint 8.1

```
Function ILookup_GetByID(ByVal lngID As Long) As Variant
    ILookup_GetByID = "Vendor ID: " & lngID
End Function
Function ILookup_GetByEmail(ByVal strEmail As String) As Variant
    ILookup_GetByEmail = "Vendor Email: " & strEmail
End Function
```

Lab Hint 9.1

```
' The Form_Load event procedure for the Send application
Set Qinfo = New MSMQ.MSMQQueueInfo
Qinfo.PathName = ".\TestQ"
Set Q = Qinfo.Open(MQ_SEND_ACCESS, MQ_DENY_NONE)
Set Qmsg = New MSMQ.MSMQMessage
```

Lab Hint 9.2

```
' The cmdAdd_Click event procedure for the Send application
Static iCount As Integer
iCount = iCount + 1
Qmsg.Label = txtLabel.Text & " " & iCount
Qmsg.Body = txtBody.Text & " " & iCount
Qmsg.Send Q
```

Lab Hint 9.3

```
' The Form_Load event procedure for the Receive application
Set Qinfo = New MSMQ.MSMQQueueInfo
Qinfo.PathName = ".\TestQ"
Set Q = Qinfo.Open(MQ_RECEIVE_ACCESS, MQ_DENY_NONE)
```

Lab Hint 9.4

```
' The cmdGetNext_Click event procedure of the Receive application
On Error GoTo ErrorHandler
' Receive will wait indefinitely until the next message is
' placed into the queue unless a timeout is specified.
' If the timeout expires, an error is generated.
Set Qmsg = Q.Receive(ReceiveTimeout:=1000)
txtLabel.Text = Qmsg.Label
txtBody.Text = Qmsg.Body
Exit Sub

ErrorHandler:
      MsgBox "Message Queue is Empty."
Exit Sub
```

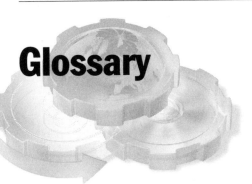

Glossary

abstract class
In Visual Basic, a class that is not instantiated but is used as a base from which other classes can be derived. An abstract class contains functions with no implementations.

ACID
The basic transaction properties of atomicity, consistency, isolation, and durability.

action query
A query that copies or changes data. Action queries include append, delete, make-table, and update queries. Delete and update queries change existing data; append and make-table queries move existing data. In contrast, select queries return data records. An SQL pass-through query may also be an action query.

action QueryDef
A data-access object that contains the definition of an action query. An action QueryDef object is used only with the Execute method, and it defines, moves or changes data instead of returning rows.

ActiveX
A set of technologies that enables software components to interact with one another in a networked environment, regardless of the language in which they were created. ActiveX is built on the Component Object Model (COM).

ActiveX DLL
See *COM DLL*.

ActiveX EXE
See *COM EXE*.

activity
A collection of Microsoft Transaction Server objects that has a single, distributed, logical thread of execution. Every Microsoft Transaction Server object belongs to one activity.

add-in
A customized tool that adds capabilities to the Visual Basic development environment. You select available add-ins by using the **Add-In Manager** dialog box, which is accessible from the **Add-Ins** menu.

administrator

A user that uses the Microsoft Transaction Server Explorer to install, configure, and manage Microsoft Transaction Server components and packages.

aggregate function

A function, such as **Sum**, **Count**, **Avg**, and **Var**, that you can use to calculate totals. In writing expressions and in programming, you can use SQL aggregate functions (including the four listed here) and domain aggregate functions to determine various statistics.

aggregation

A composition technique for implementing component objects whereby a new object can be built using one or more existing objects that support some or all of the new object's required interfaces.

apartment model multi-threading

The Component Object Model (COM) supports a form of multi-threading in Windows 95 and Windows NT called the apartment model. Apartment is essentially a way of describing a thread with a message queue that supports COM objects.

apartment thread

A thread used to execute calls to objects of components configured as "apartment-threaded." Each object "lives in an apartment" (thread) for the life of the object. All calls to that object execute on the apartment thread. This threading model is used, for example, for component implementations that keep object state in thread local storage (TLS). A component's objects can be distributed over one or more apartments. See also *main thread*.

append

Add objects, characters, or records to the end of a collection, recordset, or file.

append query

An action query that adds new records to the end of an existing table or query. Append queries do not return records (rows).

application architecture

A set of components, methods, and procedures to help application developers build business solutions. Each organization or department establishes its own enterprise application architecture to encourage consistency, interoperability, and reuse across applications.

application executable utility

A feature in the MTS Explorer that allows you to create an application executable by exporting a package.

application framework

A set of objects that provides packaged functionality and programming interfaces to accomplish specific tasks. For instance, the Microsoft Foundation Classes include a set of Microsoft Visual C++ classes optimized for writing Microsoft Windows-based applications and classes that make it easy to use many different computing resources. Frameworks are an important aspect of object technology because they can reduce development effort by providing interfaces that are easier to learn and use than low-level APIs. They also reduce the amount of code that needs to be written because the classes provide packaged functionality.

application model

A notation and rules for expressing the conceptual and implementation architectures of an application. The application model adopted by an enterprise strongly influences the character of its application architecture. An application model is to application design and development as a data model is to database design and development.

application object

The top-level object in an application's object hierarchy. The application object identifies the application to the system, and typically becomes active when the application starts.

application programming interface (API)

The set of commands that an application uses to request and carry out lower-level services performed by a computer's operating system.

application project

Visual Basic project that will be made into an .exe file.

architecture

A unified or coherent form or structure. An organized framework consisting of principles, rules, conventions, and standards that serves to guide development and construction activities so that all components of the intended structure work together to satisfy the ultimate objective of the structure.

asynchronous call

A function call whereby the caller does not wait for the reply.

asynchronous processing

A type of I/O in which some file I/O functions return immediately, even though an I/O request is still pending. This enables an application to continue with other processing and wait for the I/O to finish at a later time.

In asynchronous mode, the client issues a request but continues processing until a response is returned. The client may issue multiple requests and can field them in whatever order they return. Asynchronous communications are network independent, and clients can issue requests even if the network or remote system is down.

asynchronous query

A type of query in which SQL queries return immediately, even though the results are still pending. This enables an application to continue with other processing while the query is pending completion.

atomicity

A feature of a transaction that indicates that either all actions of the transaction happen or none happen.

attached table

A table in one database is linked to another database. Data for attached tables remains in the external database where it may be manipulated by other applications.

authentication

The process of determining the identity of a user attempting to access a system. For example, passwords are commonly used to authenticate users.

automatic transaction

A transaction that is created by the Microsoft Transaction Server run-time environment for an object based on the component's transaction attribute.

Automation object

An object that is exposed to other applications or programming tools through Automation interfaces.

Automation server

An application, type library, or other source that makes **Automation** objects available for programming by other applications, programming tools, or scripting languages.

base client

A client that runs outside the Microsoft Transaction Server run-time environment, but that instantiates Microsoft Transaction Server objects.

base process

An application process in which a base client executes. A base client runs outside the Microsoft Transaction Server run-time environment, but instantiates Microsoft Transaction Server objects.

bind

To associate two pieces of information with one another, most often used in terms of binding a symbol (such as the name of a variable) with some descriptive information (such as a memory address, a data type, or an actual value).

binding

The process of putting an object into a running state so that operations (such as edit or play) supplied by the object's application can be invoked. The type of binding determines the speed by which an object's methods are accessed by using the object variable. See also *early bound*, *late bound*.

Boolean

A true/false or yes/no value.

bound control

A data-aware control that can provide access to a specific column or columns in a data source through a **RemoteData** or **Data** control. A data-aware control can be bound to a **RemoteData** or **Data** control through its **DataSource** and **DataField** properties. When a **RemoteData** or **Data** control moves from one row to the next, all bound controls connected to the **RemoteData** or **Data** control change to display data from columns in the current row. When users change data in a bound control and then move to a different row, the changes are automatically saved in the data source.

browse

To walk through data a record or row at a time.

browse back

Button; looks like <<.

browse forward

Button; looks like >>.

browse mode

In VBSQL only, this mode supports the ability to perform updates while viewing data.

browse sequence

Order in which topics are displayed when user presses the >> button (forward) or the << button (backward).

browser

Software that interprets the markup of HTML, formats it into Web pages, and displays it to the user. Some browsers can also contain ActiveX components, and make it possible to play sound or video files.

business object

Representations of the nature and behavior of real-world things or concepts in terms that are meaningful to the business. For example, in an application, a customer, order, product, or invoice can be represented as a business object encapsulated for manipulation by users.

business rule

The combination of validation edits, login verifications, database lookups, and algorithmic transformations that constitute an enterprise's way of doing business. Also known as business logic.

business service

The logical layer between user and data services, and a collection of business rules and functions that generate and operate upon information. They accomplish this through business rules, which can change frequently, and are thus encapsulated into components that are physically separate from the application logic itself.

by reference

A way of passing the address of an argument to a procedure instead of passing the value. This allows the procedure to access the actual variable. As a result, the variable's actual value can be changed by the procedure to which it is passed. Unless otherwise specified, arguments are passed by reference.

Including bitmaps by reference refers to bitmaps not located in the directories specified in the ROOT or BMROOT option.

by value

A way of passing the value, rather than the address, of an argument to a procedure. This allows the procedure to access a copy of the variable. As a result, the variable's actual value can't be changed by the procedure to which it is passed.

caller

A client that invokes a method of an object. An object's caller isn't necessarily the object's creator. For example, client A could create object X and pass this reference to client B, and then client B could use that reference to call a method of object X. In this case, client A is the creator, and client B is the caller. See also *creator*.

calling convention

The coding convention used to make a function call.

catalog

The Microsoft Transaction Server data store that maintains configuration information for components, packages, and roles. You can administer the catalog by using the Microsoft Transaction Server Explorer.

class

The definition of an object, including code and data elements. Class is a template for constructing objects. A COM Component may contain several classes.

class factory

An object that implements the IClassFactory interface, which allows it to create other objects of a specific class.

class hierarchy

A group of superclasses and subclasses that are related through an inheritance tree. For example, the class Cat has logical subclasses including lions, tigers, and domestic cats. Each of these subclasses inherits certain common characteristics (such as agility), but each also has specific features and abilities of its own. In object-oriented programming, class hierarchies are used to identify common data and procedures first as a superclass and then to enable the superclass to act as a template for related object types. Subclasses of the superclass can then be defined and tailored for specific needs without the programmer having to write completely new definitions from scratch.

class identifier (CLSID)

A universally unique identifier (UUID) that identifies a COM component. Each COM component has its CLSID in the Windows Registry so that it can be loaded by other applications.

class name

Defines the type of an object. Applications that support Automation fully qualify class names using either of the following syntaxes: application.objecttype.version or objecttype.version, where application is the name of the application that supplies the object, objecttype is the object's name as defined in the object library, and version is the version number of the object or application that supplies the object, e.g., Excel.Sheet.5.

class of an object

The class or type of an **Automation** object (for example, **Application**, **WorkSheet**, **Toolbar**).

client

An application or process that requests a service from some process or component.

client batch cursor library

A library that provides client-side cursor support for ODBCDirect database applications. This library supports all four types of cursors (keyset, static, dynamic, and forward-only) and provides a number of other features including the ability to dissociate connections and perform optimistic batch updates.

client/server

A distributed application model in which client applications request services from a server application. A server can have many clients at the same time, and a client can request data from multiple servers. An application can be both a client and a server.

cluster

Two or more independent computer systems that are addressed and managed as a single system using Microsoft Cluster Server.

code component

An .exe or .dll file that provides objects created from one of the classes that the component provides. Formerly server and Automation server.

code module

A module containing public code that can be shared among all modules in a project. A code module is referred to as a standard module in later versions of Visual Basic.

collection

An object that contains a set of related objects. For example, a collection named Tax Preparation Objects might contain the names of objects such as **EndOfYear**, **RoyaltyCalc**, and **ExemptionCalc**. An object's position in the collection can change whenever a change occurs in the collection; therefore, the position of any specific object in the collection may vary.

collection list

A list of named groups of related collections. For example, Tested Components might be a list of all components that have been tested.

collection object

A grouping of exposed objects. You create collection objects when you want to address multiple occurrences of an object as a unit, such as when you want to draw a set of points.

column

The visual representation of a field in a grid. A column defines the data type, size, and other attributes of one field of a row (record) of data. All columns taken as a set define a row (record) in the database. An individual column contains data related in type and purpose throughout the table; that is, a column's definition doesn't change from row to row.

COM

See *Component Object Model.*

COM DLL

A COM component implemented as a DLL. COM DLL is sometimes referred to as an in-process component.

COM EXE

A COM component implemented as an EXE. COM EXE is sometimes referred to as an out-of-process component.**Command** object.

Contains a definition of a command that you want to run against a data source. For a data source that supports SQL, this is an SQL statement.

component

Any software that supports Automation, meaning it can be used programmatically in a custom solution. This includes ActiveX controls (.ocx files), ActiveX documents, and ActiveX code components.

component catalog

A sharable database of information that describes and manages components{bmc emdash.bmp}, generally ActiveX components (formerly called servers). A component catalog does not contain the objects themselves, but contains references to where the objects reside on a computer or network.

component object

An object that supports the component Object Model specification. Component objects can dynamically explore the capabilities of other component objects and use their services through OLE Automation. This is a breakthrough for the software industry because component objects allow independent, packaged objects to be seamlessly integrated by users and system integrators no matter what company designed the objects or which programming language was used to program them.

Component Object Model (COM)

An open architecture for cross-platform development of client/server applications based on object-oriented technology. Clients have access to an object through interfaces implemented on the object. COM is language neutral, so any language that produces ActiveX components can also produce COM applications.

compound query

A query that is composed of at least one action query (a query that copies or changes data) and at least one select query (a query that returns a **Recordset** without changing data). In DAO, a compound query is created by putting two or more SQL statements (separated by semicolons) in the **SQL** property of a **QueryDef** object.

conceptual design

Conceptual design defines the problem to be solved and frames a solution to that problem in terms that both management and end-users can understand. It embodies a process for acquiring, evaluating, creating, documenting, and then validating what the user and business envision as the solution. This process embraces a set of principles and activities that provide the basic rationale and motivation for creating (or not creating) a new system. Conceptual design captures the semantics of the business problem and resulting solution.

concurrency

The appearance of simultaneous execution of processes or transactions by interleaving the execution of multiple pieces of work.

Connection object

An open connection to a data source. You can use the **Connection** object to run commands or queries on the data source.

connection string

A string used to define the source of data for an external database. The connection string is usually assigned to the **Connect** property of a **QueryDef**, **TableDef**, **Connection**, or **Database** object or as an argument to the **OpenDatabase** method.

consistency

A state where durable data matches the state expected by the business rules that modified the data.

consistent

The state of a multiple-table **Recordset** object that allows you to only perform updates that result in a consistent view of the data. For example, in a **Recordset** that is a join of two or more tables (a one-to-many relationship), a consistent query would not allow you to set the many-side key to a value that isn't in the one-side table.

constraint definitions

Data integrity features that restrict the data values that can be inserted, or updated, into a database. SQL Server provides **Primary Key, Unique, Foreign Key, Default, Check,** and **Reference** constraints.

constructor

In C++ and Java, a special initialization function that is called automatically whenever an instance of a class is declared. This function prevents errors that result from the use of unitialized objects. The constructor has the same name as the class itself and can't return a value.

context

State that is implicitly associated with a given Microsoft Transaction Server object. Context contains information about the object's execution environment, such as the identity of the object's creator and, optionally, the transaction encompassing the work of the object. An object's context is similar in concept to the process context that an operating system maintains for an executing program. The Microsoft Transaction Server run-time environment manages a context for each object.

context object properties

Properties which can be obtained from the context object, such as Internet Information Server intrinsic objects.

control

A file in a Visual Basic project with an .OCX filename extension that is associated with a visible interface. The **Grid** and **CommonDialog** controls are examples of controls.

control array

A group of controls that share a common name, type, and event procedures. Each control in an array has a unique index number that can be used to determine which control recognizes an event.

create an instance

To create an instance of a class (instantiate); that is, to allocate and initialize an object's data structures in memory.

creator

A client that creates an object provided by a component (using **CreateObject**, **CoCreateInstance**, or the **CreateInstance** method). When a client creates an object, it is given an object reference that can be used to call the methods of that object. See also *caller*.

current record

The record in a **Recordset** object that you can use to modify or examine data. Use the **Move** method to reposition the current record in a **Recordset**. Only one record in a **Recordset** can be the current record.

cursor

Keeps track of the driver's position in the result set. The cursor is so named because it indicates the current position in the result set, just as the cursor on a CRT screen indicates current position. Cursors can scroll through and update a result set .

data access object (DAO)

An object that is defined by the Microsoft Jet database engine. You use data access objects, such as the **Database, TableDef, Recordset,** and **QueryDef** objects, to represent objects that are used to organize and manipulate data in code.

Data control

A built-in Visual Basic control used to connect a Visual Basic application with a selected data source. Bound controls require use of the **Data** control as a source of data.

Data Definition Language (DDL)

A language for modeling the structure (rather than the contents) of a database, that defines all attributes and properties of a database, especially record layouts, field definitions, key fields, file locations, and storage strategy.

data integrity

The accuracy of data and its conformity to its expected value, especially after being transmitted or processed.

data replication

The process of automatically, through software, duplicating and updating data in multiple computers on a network.

data services

Support the lowest visible level of abstraction used for the manipulation of data within an application. This support implies the ability to define, maintain, access, and update data. Data services manage and satisfy requests for data generated by business services.

data source

A named Open DataBase Connectivity (ODBC) resource that specifies the location, driver type, and other parameters needed by an ODBC driver to access an ODBC database. A data source can be any source of database information.

data source name (DSN)

The name that applications use to request a connection to an ODBC data source.

data-aware

Describes an application or control that is able to connect to a database.

data-definition query

An SQL-specific query that can create, alter, or delete a table, or create or delete an index in a database.

database

A set of data related to a particular topic or purpose. A database contains tables and can also contain queries and indexes as well as table relationships, table and field validation criteria, and linkages to external data sources.

Database object

A **Database** object is a logical representation of a physical database. A database is a set of data related to a specific topic or purpose. See also *database*.

DB-Library

Enables the database to become an integral part of an application. Transact-SQL statements can be incorporated into the application, allowing the application to retrieve and update values from a database. Through DB-Library, values from the database can be placed in program variables for manipulation by the application. Conversely, values in program variables can be inserted into the database.

deadlock

A situation in which two or more threads are permanently blocked (waiting), with each thread waiting for a resource exclusively held by one of the other threads that is blocked. For example, if thread A locks record 1 and waits to lock record 2, while thread B has locked record 2 and waits to lock record 1, the two threads are deadlocked.

declarative data integrity

Data integrity defined directly on tables and columns as part of the database definition by using the SQL **Create Table** and/or **Alter Table** statements.

declarative security

Security that is configured with the Microsoft Transaction Server Explorer. You can control access to packages, components, and interfaces by defining roles. Roles determine which users are allowed to invoke interfaces in a component. See also *programmatic security*.

dependent object

Dependent objects can only be accessed by using a method of a higher-level object. For example, the **Cells** method of the **Microsoft Excel Worksheet** object returns a **Range** object.

direct caller

The identity of the process (base client or server process) calling into the current server process.

direct creator

The identity of the process (base client or server process) that directly created the current object.

distributed COM (DCOM)

DCOM is an object protocol that enables COM components to communicate directly with each other across a network. DCOM is language neutral, so any language that produces COM components can also produce DCOM applications.

domain

In Windows NT, a collection of computers defined by the administrator of a Windows NT server network that share a common directory database. A domain provides access to the centralized user accounts and group accounts maintained by the domain administrator. Each domain has a unique name.

durability

A state that survives failures.

dynamic cursor

A cursor where committed changes made by anyone and uncommitted changes made by the cursor owner become visible the next time the user scrolls. Changes include inserts and deletes as well as changes in order and membership.

dynamic-link library (DLL)

A file that contains one or more functions that are compiled, linked, and stored separately from the processes that use them. The operating system maps the DLLs into the address space of the calling process when the process is starting or while it's running.

early bound

A form of binding where object variables are declared as variables of a specific class. Object references that use early-bound variables usually run faster than those that use late-bound variables. See also *late bound*.

encapsulation

The enclosing or hiding of the details of an abstraction or an implementation. A design practice in which the details for data structures and algorithms within a module, subroutine, or object are hidden from the clients of that module, subroutine, or object. The technique of combining data and processing logic within self-contained software objects. These objects hide their inner complexities from programmers and users. The encapsulated functionality of the object is accessed through well-defined interfaces made up of methods. OLE and the Component Object Model allow programmers to encapsulate functionality into highly reusable, binary component objects.

enterprise

When used generically, an enterprise is defined as the aggregate of all functional elements participating in a business mission regardless of the organizational structure housing those functional elements.

enterprise architecture

A framework for developing enterprise systems based on an integrated model of multiple views of the enterprise. An enterprise strategic architecture consists of a data architecture, an applications architecture, a technology architecture, and a business architecture. The integration of these four perspectives provides the underlying structure for directing the development of the enterprise's information systems and computing environment.

enterprise system

A business application consisting of reusable components that are designed to support a broad base of users across the entire enterprise.

Error Object

Contains details about data access errors pertaining to a single operation involving the provider.

Error statement

A keyword used in **Error** Function, **Error** Statement, **On Error** Statement. Error is also a Variant subtype indicating a variable is an error value.

error trapping

An action recognized by an object, such as clicking the mouse or pressing a key, and for which you can write code to respond. Events can occur as a result of a user action or program code, or they can be triggered by the system.

error-handling routine

User-written code that deals with some kinds of errors at run time.

event

An action recognized by an object, such as clicking the mouse or pressing a key, and for which you can write code to respond. Events can occur as a result of a user action or program code, or they can be triggered by the system.

event procedure

A procedure automatically invoked in response to an event initiated by the user, program code, or system. Event procedures are private by default.

event-driven

Describes an application that responds to actions initiated by the user or program code, or that are triggered by the system.

exception

An abnormal condition or error that occurs during the execution of a program and that requires the execution of software outside the normal flow of control.

exception handling

Where a service is able to inform their client in some uniform way that an exception was raised or encountered.

exclusive

Indicates whether a database or a table can be shared by other users in a multiuser environment. If the database or table is opened for exclusive use, it can't be shared by other users.

executable code

Code that Visual Basic translates into a specific action at run time, such as carrying out a command or returning a value. In contrast, nonexecutable code defines variables and constants.

executable file

A Windows-based application that can run outside the development environment. An executable file has an .EXE filename extension.

executable statement

A statement that Visual Basic translates into a specific action at run time. Most Visual Basic statements are executable. The main exceptions are declarations, constant definitions, comments, and user-defined type definitions.

explicit declaration

A declaration in which a variable is explicitly declared using **DIM**, **STATIC**, **PUBLIC**, or **PRIVATE** statements.

expose

To make available to other applications via Automation. An exposed object can be a document, a paragraph, a sentence, a graph, and so on.

failfast

A policy of Microsoft Transaction Server that facilitates fault containment. When the Transaction Server encounters an unexpected internal error condition, it immediately terminates the process and logs messages to the Windows NT event log for details about the failure.

fault isolation

Containing the effects of a fault within a component, rather than propagating the fault to other components in the system.

fault tolerance

The ability of a system to recover from an error, a failure, or a change in environmental conditions (such as loss of power). True fault tolerance provides for fully automatic recovery without disruption of user tasks or files, in contrast to manual means of recovery such as restoring data loss with backup files.

Field object

Represents a column of data with a common data type. Each **Field** object corresponds to a column in the **Recordset**. You use the **Value** property of **Field** objects to set or return data for the current record. Depending on the functionality the provider exposes, some collections, methods, or properties of a **Field** object may not be available.

foreign table

A database table used to contain foreign keys. Generally, you use a foreign table to establish or enforce referential integrity. The foreign table is usually on the many side of a one-to-many relationship. An example of a foreign table is a table of state codes or customer orders.

form code

All the procedures and declarations saved in the same file as a form and its controls.

form module

A file in a Visual Basic project with an .FRM filename extension that can contain graphical descriptions of a form; its controls and their property settings; form-level declarations of constants, variables, and external procedures; and event and general procedures.

form-level variable

A variable recognized by all procedures attached to a form.

forward-only scrolling snapshot

A snapshot-type **Recordset** object in which records can be searched only from beginning to end; the current record position can't be moved back toward the first record. Forward-scrolling snapshots are useful for quickly scanning data, such as when you're searching for a particular record.

framework

A conceptual scheme or structure for supporting a collection of distinct or independent elements to understand their interrelationships. Microsoft Solutions Framework offers a framework for the architectural and procedural aspects of building and deploying client/server applications.

function pointer

A stored memory location of a function's address.

Function procedure

A procedure that performs a specific task within a Visual Basic program and returns a value. A Function procedure begins with a Function statement and ends with an End Function statement.

global account

A normal user account in the user's home domain. Most accounts are global accounts, which is the default setting. If multiple domains are available, it's best if each user in the network has only one global account in only one domain.

group

A name that identifies a set of one or more Windows NT users accounts.

GUID

Globally unique identifier that is a unique 128-bit value used to identify objects and interfaces precisely.

handle

A unique integer value defined by the operating environment and used by a program to identify and access an object, such as a form or control.

identity

A package property that specifies the user accounts that are allowed to access the package. It can be a specific user account or a group of users within a Windows NT domain.

IID

See *interface identifier*.

implementation architecture

Refers to the logical and physical structure of a system, resulting from the design decisions made during development.

implicit declaration

Declaration that occurs when a variable is used in a procedure without previously declaring its name and type.

in-doubt transaction

A transaction that has been prepared but hasn't received a decision to commit or abort because the server coordinating the transaction is unavailable.

in-process

A COM component that shares the same memory as the container application.

in-process component

A component that runs in a client's process space. This is typically a dynamic-link library (DLL).

information technology (IT)

The architecture, structures, and processes that are the core of an information systems strategy. Traditionally, the operational responsibility for defining and supporting information technology has been a function of the information systems organization. However, in the migration to client/server, responsibility is shared increasingly with line-of-business and/or a separately chartered technology organization or group.

inner join

A join in which records from two tables are combined and added to a **Recordset** only if the values of the joined fields meet a specified condition. For instance, an equi-join is an inner join in which the values of the joined fields must be equal. See also *join*.

instance

An object of a particular component class. Each instance has its own private data elements or member variables. A component instance is synonymous with object.

instantiate

See *create an instance*.

interactive logon user

The user that is currently logged on a Windows Transaction Server computer.

interface

A set of semantically related functions (methods) used to manipulate data.

Interface Contract

Defines how a service will be exposed to the external world: how it is invoked and what rules and conditions are required for interaction. The terms by which a service performs an action are established by this definition or contract. The Interface Contract defines what is required to activate the service and establishes that expectations for using the service are known beforehand by all parties. It specifies what the consumer must provide to the supplier to satisfy the contract. The contract also identifies any dependencies that the supplier may have.

interface identifier (IID)

Unique identifier tag associated with each interface; applications use the IID to reference the interface in function calls.

interface negotiation

The process by which an object or container can query another object about a specified interface and have the object return a pointer to that interface if it is supported.

intrinsic constant

A constant provided by an application. Visual Basic constants are listed in the Visual Basic object library and can be viewed using the Object Browser.

ISAM

Indexed sequential access method.

isolation

A characteristic whereby two transactions running in parallel produce the illusion that there is no concurrency. It appears that the system runs one transaction at a time.

IUnknown

A base interface that describes the group of functions all objects must support.

join

A database operation that combines some or all records from two or more tables, such as an equi-join, outer join, or self-join. Generally, a join refers to an association between a field in one table and a field of the same data type in another table. You create a join with an SQL statement.

When you define a relationship between two tables, you create a join by specifying the primary and foreign table fields. When you add a table to a query, you need to create a join between appropriate fields in the SQL statement that defines the query.

just-in-time activation

The ability for a Microsoft Transaction Server object to be activated only as needed for executing requests from its client. Objects can be deactivated even while clients hold references to them, allowing otherwise idle server resources to be used more productively.

key

The Windows Registry stores data in a hierarchically structured tree. Each node in the tree is named a key. Each key can contain both subkeys and data entries named values.

In a database, a key is a column used as a component of an index.

keyset

The set of key values that are buffered in the client by DB-Library.

late bound

Object references are late bound if they use object variables declared as variables of the generic **Object** class. Late-bound binding is the slowest form of binding, because Visual Basic must determine at run time whether or not that object actually has the properties and methods you used in your code. See also *early bound*.

library package

A package that runs in the process of the client that creates it. Library packages do not support component tracking, role checking, or process isolation. MTS supports two types of packages: library package and server package.

load balancing

Distribution of the processing load among several servers carrying out network tasks to increase overall network performance.

local account

An account provided in a local domain for a user whose regular account isn't in a trusted domain. Local accounts cannot be used to log on interactively. Local accounts created in one domain cannot be used in trusted domains.

locked

The condition of a data page, **Recordset** object, or **Database** object that makes it read-only to all users except the one who is currently entering data in it.

locking

A system of ensuring that two processes do not try to affect the same record in a database at the same time.

logical

A view of data and processes that is independent of physical constraints and considerations.

logical design

Describes the system in terms that all participants on the project team can understand. Logical design is concerned with communicating among the team members and providing a definition of the organization, structure, and syntax of the resulting elements of a system. It embodies a process for defining, evaluating, creating, documenting, and validating what the constituent parts of the system are and how they interact. This arrangement is independent of physical implementation.

LU 6.2

LU (logical unit) 6.2 is a protocol developed by IBM that guarantees compatibility between programs communicating with one another across a network or on the same system.

main thread

A single thread used to run all objects of components marked as "single-threaded." See also *apartment thread*.

marshalling

The process of packaging and sending interface parameters across process boundaries.

member

A constituent element of a collection, object, or user-defined type.

member function

One of a group of related functions that make up an interface.

message

The invocation of an object's method and the mechanism through which objects interact (in pure object-oriented programming terms). When one object wants to call another object's functionality, it sends a message to the object. The object sending the message is sometimes named the *sender*, and the object receiving the message is sometimes named the *receiver*. In the component Object Model, collections of methods are named the *interface*.

metadata

Data about data. For example, the title, subject, author, and size of a file constitute metadata about the file.

method

A procedure (function) that acts on an object.

Microsoft Distributed Transaction Coordinator (MS DTC)

A transaction manager that coordinates transactions that span multiple resource managers. Work can be committed as an atomic transaction even if it spans multiple resource managers, potentially on separate computers.

Microsoft Transaction Server component

A COM component that executes in the Microsoft Transaction Server run-time environment. A Transaction Server component must be a dynamic-link library (DLL), implement a class factory to create objects, and describe all of the component's interfaces in a type library for standard marshalling.

Microsoft Transaction Server Explorer

An application to configure and manage Microsoft Transaction Server components within a distributed computer network.

Microsoft Transaction Server object

A COM object that executes in the Microsoft Transaction Server run-time environment and follows the Transaction Server programming and deployment model.

modal

Describes a window or dialog box that requires the user to take some action before the focus can switch to another form or dialog box.

model

A representation of a complex, real-world phenomenon; it can aid understanding and assist with answering questions about the real-world phenomenon.

modeless

Describes a window or dialog box that does not require user action before the focus can be switched to another form or dialog box.

module

A set of declarations and procedures.

module level

Describes code in the declarations section of a module. Any code outside a procedure is referred to as module-level code. Declarations must be listed first, followed by procedures. For example:

```
Dim X As Integer       'This is a module-level variable declaration
Const RO = "Readonly"  'This is a module-level constant declaration
Type MyType   'This is a module-level user-defined type declaration
  MyString As String
  MyAge As Integer
End Type
```

module variable

A variable declared outside of **Function**, **Sub**, or **Property** procedure code. Module variables must be declared outside any procedures in the module. They exist while the module is loaded, and are visible in all procedures in the module.

multiple-object application

An application that is capable of supporting more than one class of object; for example, a spreadsheet program might support charts, spreadsheets, and macros. See also *single-object application*.

named argument

An argument that has a name that is predefined in the object library. Instead of providing values for arguments in the order expected by the syntax, you can use named arguments to assign values in any order. For example, suppose a method accepts three arguments:

```
DoSomeThing namedarg1, namedarg2, namedarg3
```

By assigning values to named arguments, you can use the following statement:

```
DoSomething namedarg3:=4,namedarg2:=5,namedarg1:=20
```

Note that the arguments need not be in their normal positional order.

Null

A value that indicates missing or unknown data.

null field

A field containing no characters or values. A null field isn't the same as a zero-length string (" ") or a field with a value of 0. A field is set to null when the content of the field is unknown. For example, a Date Completed field in a task table would be left null until a task is completed.

object

A combination of code and data that can be treated as a unit, for example, a control, form, or application. Each object is defined by a class.

An object is an instance of a class that combines data with procedures.

Object Browser

A dialog box that lets you examine the contents of an object library to get information about the objects provided.

object library

A file with the .olb extension that provides information to Automation controllers (like Visual Basic) about available objects. You can use the **Object Browser** to examine the contents of an object library to get information about the objects provided.

object model

See *Component Object Model.*

object variable

A variable that contains a reference to an object.

ODBC data source

A term used to refer to a database or database server used as a source of data. ODBC data sources are referred to by their Data Source Name. Data sources can be created using the Windows control panel or the **RegisterDatabase** method.

ODBC resource dispenser

A resource dispenser that manages pools of database connections for Microsoft Transaction Server components that use the standard ODBC programming interfaces.

OLE DB

A set of interfaces used for accessing and manipulating all types of data. Examples of data types include SQL databases, file systems, e-mail, and spreadsheets.

OLE DB Provider

A software component that owns data and exposes it through an OLE DB interface. Examples of data providers include DBMSs, spreadsheets, ISAMs, and e-mail.

OLE Transactions

OLE Transactions is an object-oriented, two-phase commit protocol based on the Component Object Model (COM). Resource managers use it in order to participate in distributed transactions coordinated by Microsoft Distributed Transaction Coordinator (DTC).

Open Database Connectivity (ODBC)

A standard programming language interface used to connect to a variety of data sources.

optimistic concurrency control

Concurrency: An attempt to maximize the number of simultaneous transactions, or users.

Optimistic Concurrency control: You can use Browse Mode, or DB-Library cursors, to implement optimistic concurrency control. In this mode, no locks are held, under the assumption that no other transactions will change the data being accessed. When the transaction is committed, if another transaction has indeed changed the data, the original transaction is required to retrieve the new data and resubmit the query.

original caller

The identity of the base client that initiated the activity.

original creator

The identity of the base client that created the current object. The original caller and original creator are different only if the original creator passed the object to another base client. See also *original caller*.

out-of-process

A COM component that runs in its own memory space separate from a container application.

out-of-process component

A component that runs in a separate process space from its client. The Microsoft Transaction Server enables components implemented as DLLs to be used out-of-process from the client, by loading the components into surrogate server processes.

out of scope

When a variable loses focus or is out of scope. Scope is defined as the visibility of a variable, procedure, or object. For example, a variable declared as Public is visible to all procedures in all modules in a directly referencing project (unless Option Private Module is in effect). Variables declared in procedures are visible only within the procedure and lose their value between calls unless they are declared Static.

package

A set of components that perform related application functions. All components in a package run together in the same Microsoft Transaction Server process. A package is a trust boundary that defines when security credentials are verified, and is a deployment unit for a set of components. You can create packages with the Transaction Server Explorer. A package can be either a library package or a server package.

package file

A file that contains information about the components and roles of a package. A package file is created using the **Package Export** function of the Transaction Server Explorer. When you create a prebuilt package, the associated component files (DLLs, type libraries, and proxy-stub DLLs, if implemented) are copied to the same directory where the package file was created.

parameter query

A query that requires you to provide one or more criteria values, such as Redmond for City, before the query is run. A parameter query isn't, strictly speaking, a separate kind of query; rather, it extends the flexibility of other queries.

Parameter Object

Represents a parameter or argument associated with a **Command** object based on a parameterized query or stored procedure. **Parameter** objects represent parameters associated with parameterized queries, or the in/out arguments and the return values of stored procedures.

parent project

A project that contains one or more subprojects. A project can be both a parent project and a subproject at once, if it is in the middle of the project hierarchy.

pessimistic

A type of locking in which the page containing one or more records, including the record being edited, is unavailable to other users when you use the **Edit** method and remains unavailable until you use the **Update** method. Pessimistic locking is enabled when the **Lockedits** property of the **Recordset** object is set to **True**.

physical design

Describes the system in terms that development can understand. Physical design is concerned with communicating the necessary details of a system, including the organization, structure, and relationships of all elements. The details include constraints and considerations of location, distribution, and technology.

pointer

In programming, a variable that contains the memory location of data rather than the data itself.

polymorphism

The concept of a single interface for multiple implementations. For example, two different classes can implement a **Print** method on an interface that prints data in a format suitable for the class. One class may print squares while the other prints circles. A client using the interface will get the correct **Print** behavior regardless of the class it is using.

pooling

A performance optimization based on using collections of preallocated resources, such as objects or database connections. Pooling results in more efficient resource allocation.

prebuilt package

A package file that contains information about the components and roles of a package. A package file is created using the **Package Export** function of the Transaction Server Explorer. When you create a prebuilt package, the associated component files (DLLs, type libraries, and proxy-stub DLLs, if implemented) are copied to the same directory where the package file was created.

primary key

One or more fields whose value or values uniquely identify each record in a table. Each table can have only one primary key. An Employees table, for example, could use the social security number for the primary key.

primary table

A database table used to contain primary keys. Generally, a primary key table is used to establish or enforce referential integrity. The primary table is usually on the one side of a one-to-many relationship with a foreign table.

Private

Private variables are available only to the module in which they are declared.

procedure

A named sequence of statements executed as a unit. For example, **Function**, **Property**, and **Sub** are types of procedures.

Procedure box

A list box at the upper-right of the Code and Debug windows that displays the procedures recognized for the object displayed in the Object box.

procedure call

A statement in code that tells Visual Basic to execute a procedure.

procedural data integrity

Data integrity implemented by using stored procedures and triggers, which use the data definition language combined with the Transact-SQL language on the server.

procedure level

Describes statements located within a **Function**, **Property**, or **Sub** procedure. Declarations are usually listed first, followed by assignments and other executable code. For example:

```
Sub MySub()   ' This statement declares a sub procedure block.
  Dim A   ' This statement starts the procedure block.
  A = "My variable"   ' Procedure-level code.
  Debug.Print A   ' Procedure-level code.
End Sub   ' This statement ends a sub procedure block.
```

Note In contrast, module-level code resides outside any procedure blocks.

procedure stepping

A debugging technique that allows you to trace code execution one statement at a time. Unlike single stepping, procedure stepping does not step into procedure calls; instead, the called procedure is executed as a unit.

procedure template

The beginning and ending statements that are automatically inserted in the Code window when you specify a **Sub, Function,** or **Property** procedure in the **Insert Procedure** dialog box.

process isolation

The technique of running a server process in a separate memory space in order to isolate that process from other server processes. Process isolation protects a server process from other fatal application errors. Isolating a server process also prevents the isolated process from terminating another server process with an application fatal error. An MTS package that supports process isolation is called a Server package.

process model

The way in which activities in the systems development life cycle (SDLC) are sequenced and the time and formality committed to each life-cycle stage. It is the combination of a clearly defined life-cycle model, project team roles, delivery milestones, and solution development principles. The characteristics of the development project should determine what process model is appropriate.

programmatic identifier (progID)

A name that identifies a COM component. For example, a programmatic ID could be Bank.MoveMoney.

programmatic security

Procedural logic provided by a component to determine if a client is authorized to perform the requested operation. See also *declarative security*.

project

A group of related files, typically all the files required to develop a software component. Files can be grouped within a project to create subprojects. Projects can be defined in any way meaningful to the user(s){bmc emdash.bmp}as one project per version, or one project per language, for example. In general use, projects tend to be organized in the same way file directories are.

project file

A file with a .VBP filename extension that keeps track of the files, objects, project options, environment options, EXE options, and references associated with a project.

Project window

A window that displays a list of the form, class, and standard modules; the resource file; and references in your project. Files with .OCX and .VBX filename extensions don't appear in this window.

Properties window

A window used to display or change properties of a selected form or control at design time. Some custom controls have customized Properties windows.

property

A named attribute of an object. Properties define object characteristics such as size, color, and screen location, or the state of an object, such as enabled or disabled.

A property is a data member of an exposed object. Properties are set or returned by means of **Get** and **Let Accessor** functions. See *Property procedure*.

Property list

A two-column list in the Properties window that shows all the properties and their current settings for the selected object.

Property Object

Represents a dynamic characteristic of an ADO object that is defined by the provider. ADO objects have two types of properties: built-in and dynamic.

Property procedure

A procedure that creates and manipulates properties for a class module. A **Property** procedure begins with a **Property Let, Property Get,** or **Property Set** statement and ends with an **End Property** statement.

property setting

The value of a property.

proxy

An interface-specific object that provides the parameter marshalling and communication required for a client to call an application object that is running in a different execution environment, such as on a different thread or in another process. The proxy is located with the client and communicates with a corresponding stub that is located with the application object that is being called.

proxy stub DLLs

A COM component that contains the proxy and stub code necessary to marshal parameters for methods on one or more interfaces.

Public

Variables declared using the **Public** statement are available to all procedures in all modules in all applications unless **Option Private Module** is in effect; in which case, the variables are public only within the project in which they reside.

query

A formalized instruction to a database to either return a set of records or perform a specified action on a set of records as specified in the query. For example, the following SQL query statement returns records:

```
SELECT [Company Name] FROM Publishers WHERE State = 'NY'
```

You can create and run select, action, crosstab, parameter, and SQL-specific queries.

query parameter data types

The set of data types for a field in a parameter query. The Microsoft Jet database engine has 13 query parameter data types.

Category	Data type
Table fields	Currency, Date/Time, Memo, Automation Object, Text, and Yes/No correspond to the same data types in table fields.
Number	Byte, Single, Double, Integer, and Long Integer correspond to the five Field Size options of the Number data type in table fields.
Generic	Value is a Generic data type that doesn't accept any type of data.
Binary	You can use the Binary data type in parameter queries directed to attached tables that recognize it.

Recordset

The **Recordset** object enables your application to access data returned from an SQL query or stored procedure. Using the **Recordset** object, you can navigate through the records that have been returned, or edit their values.

reference count

The number of instances of an object loaded. This number is incremented each time an instance is loaded and decremented each time an instance is unloaded. Ensures an object is not destroyed before all references to it are released.

referential integrity

Rules that you set to establish and preserve relationships between tables when you add, change, or delete records. Enforcing referential integrity prohibits users from adding records to a related table for which there is no primary key, changing values in a primary table that would result in orphaned records in a related table, and deleting records from a primary table when there are matching related records.

If you select the Cascade Update Related Fields or Cascade Delete Related Records option for a relationship, the Microsoft Jet database engine allows changes and deletions but changes or deletes related records to ensure that the rules are still enforced.

registration

The process of adding a class, container, or object to the registration database.

registration database

A database that provides a system-wide repository of information for containers and servers that support Automation.

relational database management system

A type of database or database management system that stores information in tables — rows and columns of data — and conducts searches by using data in specified columns of one table to find additional data in another table.

remote component

A component used by a client on a different computer.

remote procedure call (RPC)

A standard that allows one process to make calls to functions that are executed in another process. The process can be on the same computer or on a different computer in the network.

replication

An operation which copies the catalog from one computer to another. Replication is used to synchronize clustered MTS servers.

resource dispenser

A service that provides the synchronization and management of nondurable resources within a process, providing for simple and efficient sharing by Microsoft Transaction Server objects. For example, the ODBC resource dispenser manages pools of database connections.

Resource Dispenser Manager

A dynamic-link library (DLL) that coordinates work among a collection of resource dispensers.

resource manager

A system service that manages durable data. Server applications use resource managers to maintain the durable state of the application, such as the record of inventory on hand, pending orders, and accounts receivable. The resource manager works in cooperation with the transaction manager to provide the application with a guarantee of atomicity and isolation (using the two-phase commit protocol). Microsoft SQL Server is an example of a resource manager.

reusable code

Software code written so that it can be used in more than one place.

role

A symbolic name that defines a class of users for a set of components. Each role defines which users are allowed to invoke interfaces on a component.

row

A set of related columns or fields used to hold data. A row is synonymous with a record in ADO. A table is composed of zero or more rows of data.

run time

The time when code is running. During run time, you interact with the code as a user would.

run-time error

An error that occurs when code is running. A run-time error results when a statement attempts an invalid operation.

safe reference

A reference to the current object that is safe to pass outside the current object's context.

scope

Defines the visibility of a variable, procedure, or object. For example, a variable declared as Public is visible to all procedures in all modules in a directly referencing project (unless Option Private Module is in effect). Variables declared in procedures are visible only within the procedure and lose their value between calls unless they are declared Static.

security ID (SID)

A unique name that identifies a logged-on user to the security system. SIDs can identify one user or a group of users.

select query

A query that asks a question about the data stored in your tables and returns a **Recordset** object without changing the data. Once the **Recordset** data is retrieved, you can examine and make changes to the data in the underlying tables. In contrast, action queries can make changes to your data, but they don't return data records.

semaphore

A locking mechanism used inside resource managers or resource dispensers. Semaphores have no symbolic names, only shared and exclusive mode access, no deadlock detection, and no automatic release or commit.

sequential access

A type of file access that allows you to access records in text files and variable-length record files sequentially; that is, one after another.

server

An application or DLL that provides its objects to other applications. You can use any of these objects in your Visual Basic application.

server package

A package that runs isolated in its own process on the local computer. Server packages support role-based security, resource sharing, process isolation, and process management (such as package tracking). MTS supports two types of packages: library and server package.

server process

A process that hosts Microsoft Transaction Server components.

A Microsoft Transaction Server component can be loaded into a surrogate server process, either on the client's computer or into a client application process.

service

(Noun) The occupation or function of serving; a set of articles for a particular use. (Verb) To perform services for.

services model

A way of viewing applications as a set of features or services that are used to fulfill consumer requests. By encouraging the developer to model an application as a collection of discrete services, features and functionality can be packaged for reuse, sharing, and distribution across functional boundaries.

services-based architecture

An application model in which the feature set of the business application is expressed conceptually as a collection of services. These services can be grouped based on common characteristics, for example, semantics, behavior, analysis, and design techniques. The Microsoft Solutions Framework identifies three such groupings of services: user services, business services, and data services.

set

To assign a value to a property.

shared property

A variable that is available to all objects in the same server process via the Shared Property Manager. The value of the property can be any type that can be represented by a variant.

shared state

Multiple Microsoft Transaction Server objects that hold state accumulated from the execution of one or more client calls running in the same process.

signature

For a COM interface, the order of the methods, method names, parameter types, and return types. These define the signature of the interface. Once defined, the signature of an interface can never change.

single-object application

A server that exposes only one class of object.

SNA gateway

A computer that provides a transfer point and protocol conversion between a LAN or WAN, and a mainframe or AS/400 server.

snap-in

An administrative program hosted by the Microsoft Management Console (MMC). The MTS Explorer on Windows NT is a snap-in.

SQL database

A database that can be accessed through use of Open Database Connectivity (ODBC) data sources.

SQL Server

A relational database engine running on a network-accessible server. SQL Servers are responsible for comprehensive management of one or more relational databases residing on the server. They are controlled by and information is passed to and from these servers by way of Structured Query Language (SQL) statements. There are two types of SQL Server: Microsoft SQL Server and Sybase SQL Server.

SQL statement/string

1. An expression that defines a Structured Query Language (SQL) command, such as SELECT, UPDATE, or DELETE, and includes clauses such as WHERE and ORDER BY. SQL strings and statements are typically used in queries, **Recordset** objects, and aggregate functions but can also be used to create or modify a database structure.

2. A set of commands written using a dialect of Structured Query Language used to retrieve or pass information to a relational database. SQL statement syntax is determined by the SQL Server or other relational database engine on which it is intended to execute.

stack

A fixed amount of memory used by Visual Basic to preserve local variables and arguments during procedure calls.

stateful object

An object that holds private state accumulated from the execution of one or more client calls.

stateless object

An object that doesn't hold private state accumulated from the execution of one or more client calls.

Static

A Visual Basic keyword you can use to preserve the value of a local variable.

static cursor

Neither the cursor owner nor any other user can change the results set while the cursor is open. Values, membership, and order remain fixed until the cursor is closed. You can either take a 'snapshot' (temporary table) of the results set, or you can lock the entire results set to prevent updates. When you take a snapshot of the results set, the results set diverges increasingly from the snapshot as updates are made.

stored procedures

Pre-compiled software functions that are managed and that run within a remote database management system (RDBMS).

string expression

Any expression that evaluates to a sequence of contiguous characters.

Structured Query Language (SQL)

A language used in querying, updating, and managing relational databases. SQL can be used to retrieve, sort and filter specific data to be extracted from the database.

You can use SQL SELECT statements anywhere a table name, query name, or field name is accepted. For example, you can use an SQL statement in place of a table name in the OpenRecordset method.

stub

An interface-specific object that provides the parameter marshalling and communication required for an application object to receive calls from a client that is running in a different execution environment, such as on a different thread or in another process. The stub is located with the application object and communicates with a corresponding proxy that is located with the client that calls it.

Sub procedure

A procedure that performs a specific task within a program, but returns no explicit value. A Sub procedure begins with a **Sub** statement and ends with an **End Sub** statement.

subroutine

A section of code that can be invoked (executed) within a program.

symmetric multiprocessing

A computer architecture in which multiple processors share the same memory, which contains one copy of the operating system, one copy of any applications that are in use, and one copy of the data. Because the operating system divides the workload into tasks and assigns those tasks to whatever processors are free, SMP speeds transaction time.

synchronous call

A function call in which the caller waits for the reply before continuing. Most interface methods are synchronous calls. An operation that completes synchronously performs all of its processing in the function call made by the application. The function returns different values depending on its success or failure.

synchronous processing

When the data interface blocks until an operation is complete or at least until the first row of the results is ready. Opposite of asynchronous processing.

syntax

The rules regarding the structure and arrangement of words, elements, or symbols. The way in which elements are put together. The graphic, textual, or other structural conventions used in constructing a design or model. They govern the shape and configuration of a system, model, or design. Refers to the form of a design or model, rather than its content.

table

The basic unit of data storage in a relational database. A table stores data in records (rows) and fields (columns) and is usually about a particular category of things, such as employees or parts. Also called a base table.

team model

Promotes the concept of a team of peers working in interdependent and cooperating roles. Each team member has a well-defined role on the project and is focused on a specific mission.

thread

The basic entity to which the operating system allocates CPU time. A thread can execute any part of the application's code, including a part currently being executed by another thread. All threads of a process share the virtual address space, global variables, and operating-system resources of the process.

three-tier architecture

An application model in which the feature set of the business application is expressed conceptually as three layers, each of which supplies services to the adjacent layers: user presentation, core business, and data management. Note that this is a conceptual architecture; while all business applications can be expressed conceptually in terms of these three layers, the implementation architecture may not be three layers.

trace message

A message that includes the current status of various Microsoft Transaction Server activities, such as startup and shutdown.

transaction

A unit of work that is done as an atomic operation — that is, the operation succeeds or fails as a whole.

transaction context

An object used to allow a client to dynamically include one or more objects in one transaction.

transaction manager

A system service responsible for coordinating the outcome of transactions in order to achieve atomicity. The transaction manager ensures that the resource managers reach a consistent decision on whether the transaction should commit or abort.

transaction timeout

The maximum period of time that a transaction can remain active before it's automatically aborted by the transaction manager.

translation bridging

A gateway needed to translate the addressing information from the source format into the destination format to ensure validity across messaging domains.

trigger

Record-level event code that runs after an insert, update, or delete. Different actions can be attached to the different events. Triggers run last, after rules, and don't run during buffered updates. They are most often used for cross-table integrity.

two-phase commit

A protocol that ensures that transactions that apply to more than one server are completed on all servers or none at all. Two-phase commit is coordinated by the transaction manager and supported by resource managers.

type description

The information used to build the type information for one or more aspects of an application's interface. Type descriptions are written in Object Description Language (ODL) and include both programmable and nonprogrammable interfaces. The component of an Automation controller used to write programming tools that create type libraries. The type description interfaces provide a way to read and bind to the descriptions of objects in a type library. The descriptions are used by Automation controllers when they browse, create, and manipulate **Automation** objects.

type information

1. Information that describes the interfaces of an application. Type information is created from type descriptions by using Automation tools, such as the **MkTypLib** or **CreateDispTypeInfo** function. Type information can be accessed through the **ITypeInfo** interface.

2. Type information is the Automation standard for describing exposed objects, properties, and methods to an application or programming tool that accesses an exposed object. You provide type information in one of two ways: As a type library written in Microsoft Object Description Language (ODL) and compiled by **MkTypLib**, or as a data structure exported at run time.

type library

A file containing standard descriptions of data types, modules, and interfaces that can be used to fully expose objects with ActiveX technology.

union query

An SQL-specific select query that creates a snapshot-type **Recordset** object containing data from all specified records in two or more tables with any duplicate records removed. To include the duplicates, add the keyword **ALL**.

For instance, a union query of the Customers table and the Suppliers table results in a snapshot-type **Recordset** that contains all suppliers that are also customers.

unmarshalling

The processing of unpackaging parameters that have been sent across process boundaries. In a given call, the method arguments are marshalled and unmarshalled in one direction, while the return values are marshalled and unmarshalled in the other direction.

update query

An action query that changes a set of records according to criteria you specify. An update query doesn't return any records.

user name

The name that identifies a Windows NT user account.

user service

User services for an application support the activities users perform. These services also bind together a collection of business services to deliver the business capabilities of the application. User services present information and gather data from the user.

validation

The process of checking whether entered data meets certain conditions or limitations.

VBSQL

Visual Basic Library for SQL Server.

views

An alternate way of looking at data from one or more tables in the database, a view is a "virtual table." A view is usually created as a subset of columns from one or more tables. The tables from which views are derived are called base tables. A view can also be derived from another view. The definition of a view (the base tables from which it is derived) is stored in the database. The data that you view is stored in only one place, the base tables. No separate copies of data are associated with this stored definition. A view looks almost exactly like any other database table. You can display it and operate on it almost as you can on any other table.

Windows API

The Windows API (Application Programming Interface) consists of the functions, messages, data structures, data types, and statements you can use in creating applications that run under Microsoft Windows. The parts of the API you use most are code elements included for calling API functions from Windows. These include procedure declarations (for the **Windows** functions), user-defined type definitions (for data structures passed to those functions), and constant declarations (for values passed to and returned from those functions).

XA protocol

The two-phase commit protocol defined by the X/Open DTP group. XA is natively supported by many Unix databases, including Informix, Oracle, and DB2.

zero-defect

A deliverable has the zero-defect characteristic if no outstanding bugs or issues against the deliverable prevent it from meeting the goals in the Functional Specification and no outstanding bugs or issues against the deliverable prevent *another* deliverable from meeting its goals as identified in the Functional Specification.

Index

A

Component Object Model (COM) (continued)
   components. *See* COM DLLs
   implementing, 11
   implementing with VB, 257
   interfaces, 52
COM Transaction Integrator for CICS and IMS
(COMTI), 309
COM DLLs 39
   activating, 60
   class modules and COM, 51
   class modules, using, 42
   creating, 40
   creating methods for classes, 45
   creating Visual Basic projects, 42
   error handling, 46
   implementing business services, 40
   in-process vs. out-of-process, 41
   Initialize event, 44
   MTS constraints, 41
   registering, 56–58
   removing, 57
   setting class module properties, 49
   setting project properties, 47
   Terminate event, 44
   testing, 55
   version compatibility, 53
   working with, 47
Command object stored procedures
   executing, 170
   populating **Parameters** collection, 171
   return codes in, 173
   using, 170
commands
   creating from connections, 149
   executing, 149
compatibility, version, 53
Component Object Model. *See* COM
components. *See also* Component Object
   Model (COM)
   building, 101
   calling **CreateInstance** method, 102

components (continued)
   calling **EnableCommit, DisableCommit**
      methods, 106
   calling **SetComplete, SetAbort** methods, 104
   debugging, 128
   determining transaction outcome, 107
   developing, 99
   getting context objects, 101
   setting security, 229
   sharing in Microsoft Repository, 34
consumers, 143. *See also* Universal Data
   Access (UDA)
COMTI
   advanced client/server technologies, 310
concurrency model, MTS, 70
conditional execution, 204. *See also* flow-control
   statements
   stored procedures, SQL Server, 203
configuring
   clients, MTS, 88
   ODBC drivers for connection pooling, 123
conflicts, resolving, disconnected recordsets, 166
connection pooling, 123
connections, ADO. *See* ADO connections
Consistency property, 97
context objects
   getting, 101, 102
   transactions, 98
contracts, interface definition, 259
CreateInstance method, calling, 102, 103
creating
   ADO connections, 147, 149, 151, 154, 156
   class instances, 42, 43
   COM DLLs, 40
   commands, 149, 150
   connections, 191
   disconnected recordsets, 165
   interfaces, 261
   logins, 246
   methods for classes, 45
   objects, 43, 60, 102
   packages, 79
   properties, 119

SetAbort method, 105
SetComplete method, 104
setting
    breakpoints, 55
    class module properties, 49
    class properties, 83
    package identity, 231
    package properties, 80
    permissions, 242, 246
    project properties, 47
    transaction attributes, 99
shared properties, creating, 118
Shared Property Manager (SPM), 118
    creating properties in, 118
    storing object states in, 116
Shared Property Managers, MTS, working with, 74
SharedProperty object, 118
sharing components in Microsoft Repository, 32
SPM. See Shared Property Manager (SPM)
SQL Enterprise Manager, 190
SQL Security Manager, 245
SQL Server
    connection pooling, 123
SQL Server security, 237. See also security
    integrated, 244–246
    logins and permissions, 242
    modes of, 237
SQL Server stored procedures, 187
    adding parameters to, 199
    business logic, 188
    creating, 197, 199, 200
    creating in Data View, 197
    and data integrity, 193, 194
    debugging in, 201
    declaring variables in, 202
    and enterprise solutions, 189
    and flow-control statements, 203, 204
    managing databases in, 190
    transactions, 205
    variables, 202, 203
stand-alone command objects, 150
standard security, 238. See also SQL Server security
static cursors, 159. See also cursors

stored procedures, ADO
    executing, 170
    populating Parameters collection, 171
    return codes, 173
    using, 170
stored procedures, SQL Server. See SQL Server Stored
    Procedures
storing object state, 116
support services, MTS, 74
Symmetric Multiprocessing (SMP), 305. See also
    server clustering
synchronous communication, 291. See also message
    queuing
T-SQL Debugger, debugging stored procedures,
    SQL Server, 201

T

Terminate event, 44, 116
testing COM DLLs, 55
threading models, choosing, 49
three-tier applications and disconnected
    recordsets, 163
three-tier client/server architecture, 2. See also client/
server architecture
    Internet as, 7
    Merrill Lynch case study, 8
three-tier security, 221. See also security
tiers, 2. See also client/server architecture
tools, Microsoft Visual Studio, Enterprise Edition, 32
Transaction Processing (TP)
    advanced client/server technologies, 310
Trace Messages window, 131
tracing source code, 56
Transact-SQL. See SQL Server, stored procedures
Transaction List window, 131
Transaction Statistics window, 131
transactions, 96
    attributes of, 99
    best practices, 132
    building components in, 101, 102, 104, 106, 107
    calling CreateInstance method, 102
    calling EnableCommit, DisableCommit methods, 106

MICROSOFT LICENSE AGREEMENT
Book Companion CD

IMPORTANT—READ CAREFULLY: This Microsoft End-User License Agreement ("EULA") is a legal agreement between you (either an individual or an entity) and Microsoft Corporation for the Microsoft product identified above, which includes computer software and may include associated media, printed materials, and "online" or electronic documentation ("SOFTWARE PRODUCT"). Any component included within the SOFTWARE PRODUCT that is accompanied by a separate End-User License Agreement shall be governed by such agreement and not the terms set forth below. By installing, copying, or otherwise using the SOFTWARE PRODUCT, you agree to be bound by the terms of this EULA. If you do not agree to the terms of this EULA, you are not authorized to install, copy, or otherwise use the SOFTWARE PRODUCT; you may, however, return the SOFTWARE PRODUCT, along with all printed materials and other items that form a part of the Microsoft product that includes the SOFTWARE PRODUCT, to the place you obtained them for a full refund.

SOFTWARE PRODUCT LICENSE

The SOFTWARE PRODUCT is protected by United States copyright laws and international copyright treaties, as well as other intellectual property laws and treaties. The SOFTWARE PRODUCT is licensed, not sold.

1. **GRANT OF LICENSE.** This EULA grants you the following rights:

    a. **Software Product.** You may install and use one copy of the SOFTWARE PRODUCT on a single computer. The primary user of the computer on which the SOFTWARE PRODUCT is installed may make a second copy for his or her exclusive use on a portable computer.

    b. **Storage/Network Use.** You may also store or install a copy of the SOFTWARE PRODUCT on a storage device, such as a network server, used only to install or run the SOFTWARE PRODUCT on your other computers over an internal network; however, you must acquire and dedicate a license for each separate computer on which the SOFTWARE PRODUCT is installed or run from the storage device. A license for the SOFTWARE PRODUCT may not be shared or used concurrently on different computers.

    c. **License Pak.** If you have acquired this EULA in a Microsoft License Pak, you may make the number of additional copies of the computer software portion of the SOFTWARE PRODUCT authorized on the printed copy of this EULA, and you may use each copy in the manner specified above. You are also entitled to make a corresponding number of secondary copies for portable computer use as specified above.

    d. **Sample Code.** Solely with respect to portions, if any, of the SOFTWARE PRODUCT that are identified within the SOFTWARE PRODUCT as sample code (the "SAMPLE CODE"):

    i. **Use and Modification.** Microsoft grants you the right to use and modify the source code version of the SAMPLE CODE, *provided* you comply with subsection (d)(iii) below. You may not distribute the SAMPLE CODE, or any modified version of the SAMPLE CODE, in source code form.

    ii. **Redistributable Files.** Provided you comply with subsection (d)(iii) below, Microsoft grants you a nonexclusive, royalty-free right to reproduce and distribute the object code version of the SAMPLE CODE and of any modified SAMPLE CODE, other than SAMPLE CODE, or any modified version thereof, designated as not redistributable in the Readme file that forms a part of the SOFTWARE PRODUCT (the "Non-Redistributable Sample Code"). All SAMPLE CODE other than the Non-Redistributable Sample Code is collectively referred to as the "REDISTRIBUTABLES."

    iii. **Redistribution Requirements.** If you redistribute the REDISTRIBUTABLES, you agree to: (i) distribute the REDISTRIBUTABLES in object code form only in conjunction with and as a part of your software application product; (ii) not use Microsoft's name, logo, or trademarks to market your software application product; (iii) include a valid copyright notice on your software application product; (iv) indemnify, hold harmless, and defend Microsoft from and against any claims or lawsuits, including attorney's fees, that arise or result from the use or distribution of your software application product; and (v) not permit further distribution of the REDISTRIBUTABLES by your end user. Contact Microsoft for the applicable royalties due and other licensing terms for all other uses and/or distribution of the REDISTRIBUTABLES.

2. **DESCRIPTION OF OTHER RIGHTS AND LIMITATIONS.**

    - **Limitations on Reverse Engineering, Decompilation, and Disassembly.** You may not reverse engineer, decompile, or disassemble the SOFTWARE PRODUCT, except and only to the extent that such activity is expressly permitted by applicable law notwithstanding this limitation.

    - **Separation of Components.** The SOFTWARE PRODUCT is licensed as a single product. Its component parts may not be separated for use on more than one computer.

    - **Rental.** You may not rent, lease, or lend the SOFTWARE PRODUCT.

    - **Support Services.** Microsoft may, but is not obligated to, provide you with support services related to the SOFTWARE PRODUCT ("Support Services"). Use of Support Services is governed by the Microsoft policies and programs described in the user manual, in "online" documentation, and/or in other Microsoft-provided materials. Any supplemental software code provided to you as part of the Support Services shall be considered part of the SOFTWARE PRODUCT and subject to the terms and conditions of this EULA. With respect to technical information you provide to Microsoft as part of the Support Services, Microsoft may use such information for its business purposes, including for product support and development. Microsoft will not utilize such technical information in a form that personally identifies you.

- **Software Transfer.** You may permanently transfer all of your rights under this EULA, provided you retain no copies, you transfer all of the SOFTWARE PRODUCT (including all component parts, the media and printed materials, any upgrades, this EULA, and, if applicable, the Certificate of Authenticity), **and** the recipient agrees to the terms of this EULA.

- **Termination.** Without prejudice to any other rights, Microsoft may terminate this EULA if you fail to comply with the terms and conditions of this EULA. In such event, you must destroy all copies of the SOFTWARE PRODUCT and all of its component parts.

3. **COPYRIGHT.** All title and copyrights in and to the SOFTWARE PRODUCT (including but not limited to any images, photographs, animations, video, audio, music, text, SAMPLE CODE, REDISTRIBUTABLES, and "applets" incorporated into the SOFTWARE PRODUCT) and any copies of the SOFTWARE PRODUCT are owned by Microsoft or its suppliers. The SOFTWARE PRODUCT is protected by copyright laws and international treaty provisions. Therefore, you must treat the SOFTWARE PRODUCT like any other copyrighted material **except** that you may install the SOFTWARE PRODUCT on a single computer provided you keep the original solely for backup or archival purposes. You may not copy the printed materials accompanying the SOFTWARE PRODUCT.

4. **U.S. GOVERNMENT RESTRICTED RIGHTS.** The SOFTWARE PRODUCT and documentation are provided with RESTRICTED RIGHTS. Use, duplication, or disclosure by the Government is subject to restrictions as set forth in subparagraph (c)(1)(ii) of the Rights in Technical Data and Computer Software clause at DFARS 252.227-7013 or subparagraphs (c)(1) and (2) of the Commercial Computer Software—Restricted Rights at 48 CFR 52.227-19, as applicable. Manufacturer is Microsoft Corporation/One Microsoft Way/Redmond, WA 98052-6399.

5. **EXPORT RESTRICTIONS.** You agree that you will not export or re-export the SOFTWARE PRODUCT, any part thereof, or any process or service that is the direct product of the SOFTWARE PRODUCT (the foregoing collectively referred to as the "Restricted Components"), to any country, person, entity, or end user subject to U.S. export restrictions. You specifically agree not to export or re-export any of the Restricted Components (i) to any country to which the U.S. has embargoed or restricted the export of goods or services, which currently include, but are not necessarily limited to, Cuba, Iran, Iraq, Libya, North Korea, Sudan, and Syria, or to any national of any such country, wherever located, who intends to transmit or transport the Restricted Components back to such country; (ii) to any end user who you know or have reason to know will utilize the Restricted Components in the design, development, or production of nuclear, chemical, or biological weapons; or (iii) to any end user who has been prohibited from participating in U.S. export transactions by any federal agency of the U.S. government. You warrant and represent that neither the BXA nor any other U.S. federal agency has suspended, revoked, or denied your export privileges.

DISCLAIMER OF WARRANTY

NO WARRANTIES OR CONDITIONS. MICROSOFT EXPRESSLY DISCLAIMS ANY WARRANTY OR CONDITION FOR THE SOFTWARE PRODUCT. THE SOFTWARE PRODUCT AND ANY RELATED DOCUMENTATION ARE PROVIDED "AS IS" WITHOUT WARRANTY OR CONDITION OF ANY KIND, EITHER EXPRESS OR IMPLIED, INCLUDING, WITHOUT LIMITATION, THE IMPLIED WARRANTIES OF MERCHANTABILITY, FITNESS FOR A PARTICULAR PURPOSE, OR NONINFRINGEMENT. THE ENTIRE RISK ARISING OUT OF USE OR PERFORMANCE OF THE SOFTWARE PRODUCT REMAINS WITH YOU.

LIMITATION OF LIABILITY. TO THE MAXIMUM EXTENT PERMITTED BY APPLICABLE LAW, IN NO EVENT SHALL MICROSOFT OR ITS SUPPLIERS BE LIABLE FOR ANY SPECIAL, INCIDENTAL, INDIRECT, OR CONSEQUENTIAL DAMAGES WHATSOEVER (INCLUDING, WITHOUT LIMITATION, DAMAGES FOR LOSS OF BUSINESS PROFITS, BUSINESS INTERRUPTION, LOSS OF BUSINESS INFORMATION, OR ANY OTHER PECUNIARY LOSS) ARISING OUT OF THE USE OF OR INABILITY TO USE THE SOFTWARE PRODUCT OR THE PROVISION OF OR FAILURE TO PROVIDE SUPPORT SERVICES, EVEN IF MICROSOFT HAS BEEN ADVISED OF THE POSSIBILITY OF SUCH DAMAGES. IN ANY CASE, MICROSOFT'S ENTIRE LIABILITY UNDER ANY PROVISION OF THIS EULA SHALL BE LIMITED TO THE GREATER OF THE AMOUNT ACTUALLY PAID BY YOU FOR THE SOFTWARE PRODUCT OR US$5.00; PROVIDED, HOWEVER, IF YOU HAVE ENTERED INTO A MICROSOFT SUPPORT SERVICES AGREEMENT, MICROSOFT'S ENTIRE LIABILITY REGARDING SUPPORT SERVICES SHALL BE GOVERNED BY THE TERMS OF THAT AGREEMENT. BECAUSE SOME STATES AND JURISDICTIONS DO NOT ALLOW THE EXCLUSION OR LIMITATION OF LIABILITY, THE ABOVE LIMITATION MAY NOT APPLY TO YOU.

MISCELLANEOUS

This EULA is governed by the laws of the State of Washington USA, except and only to the extent that applicable law mandates governing law of a different jurisdiction.

Should you have any questions concerning this EULA, or if you desire to contact Microsoft for any reason, please contact the Microsoft subsidiary serving your country, or write: Microsoft Sales Information Center/One Microsoft Way/Redmond, WA 98052-6399.